ΟΙΔΙΠΟΥΣ ΤΥΡΑΝΝΟΣ.

ἄνδρα δ᾽ ὠφελεῖν ἀφ᾽ ὧν
ἔχοι τε καὶ δύναιτο κάλλιστος πόνων.

THE

ŒDIPUS TYRANNUS

OF

SOPHOCLES.

EDITED,

FOR THE USE OF SCHOOLS, WITH ENGLISH NOTES AND AN INTRODUCTION,

BY

JOHN WILLIAMS WHITE, A. M.

REVISED EDITION.

Nulla Sophocleo veniet jactura cothurno.
OVID.

BOSTON:
GINN BROTHERS, PUBLISHERS,
1875.

University Press: Welch, Bigelow, & Co.,
Cambridge.

TO

MY FATHER,

THE REV. JOHN W. WHITE,

This Work

Is Affectionately Inscribed.

PREFACE.

THIS edition of the Œdipus Tyrannus has been made for the class-room. The wants of a student, who in taking up the present tragedy makes his first acquaintance with the Greek drama, have been kept steadily in view. The book is for learners.

It is certainly true that by the time the student reaches the present play, he should be master of the main principles of Greek grammar and be able to apply them; but it is also true that this is often not the fact. To meet this case, and to avoid the necessity of settling grammatical questions in the class-room at that point in his course when the time should be spent otherwise, much help has been given in the way of grammatical references. These references are for those who need them.

The Text is that of Campbell. The places where other readings than his have been adopted are specified in the list that immediately follows the Notes. I wish here to express my high estimate of Dr. Campbell's edition of Sophocles, and to say that I have found it a constant help. Much aid has been received also from other editors. I have endeavored at all points to acknowledge my obligations. It is the fact, however, not only in the case of Sophocles, but in that of every Greek author as well, who has been frequently edited, that there is much matter in the way of annotation that has become common property.

The play has been illustrated only from itself, the grammars, and by means of such examples in classic English as I found apposite.

Following the Preface will be found a list of such editions of this tragedy as would prove valuable to the student. It is not at all exhaustive, and presents in the main only the more recent school editions of the drama. Some others, however, on various grounds, have been added. The Introduction is an adaptation of the first three parts of Schneidewin's celebrated Einleitung. Mr. Browne's translation, in T. K. Arnold's edition of Sophocles, has been used, subjected, however, to a revision.

There follows the Notes in the present volume a Rhythmical Scheme of the Lyrical Parts of the Text. It was at first a part of my general plan to add to the book an Appendix on Greek Rhythmic and Metric, which should be a brief statement of the subject, on the theory of Dr. J. Heinrich Schmidt. This, however, has not been done. What would have been given there will appear in a separate volume, which has already been announced by the publishers. Just how soon this will be ready is uncertain. The work will be done with all reasonable expedition.

I desire to acknowledge my obligations to Dr. Goodwin of Harvard University for valuable suggestions; and also to Dr. William G. Williams of the Ohio Wesleyan University, at whose suggestion this work was undertaken, and whose kindly sympathy and aid have greatly assisted in its prosecution.

Whoever will inform me of errors detected, or suggest how the book might be improved, will receive my hearty thanks.

JOHN W. WHITE.

BALDWIN UNIVERSITY,
November 17, 1873.

PREFACE TO THE REVISED EDITION.

In this revised edition typographical errors have been corrected, a few of the notes somewhat changed or rewritten, the rhythmical scheme rearranged, and a commentary added with references to the "Introduction to the Study of the Rhythmic and Metric of the Classical Languages." An appendix also has been added on the differentiation of choreic and logaoedic, and of dactylic and Doric rhythms.

In January of the present year, I associated with myself in the translation of Dr. Schmidt's "Leitfaden in der Rhythmik und Metrik der Classischen Sprachen," my good friend Dr. Carl Riemenschneider, Professor of Ancient Languages in German Wallace College. This translation has been completed, and when revised by the author, to whom it has already been sent, will go to the printer. The commentary in the present volume containing references to this translation has been made very full, and yet it must not be supposed that this fulness renders a preceding systematic study of the "Introduction" unnecessary. The student will not be able to get a satisfactory insight into the poetical structure and the rhythm of the present drama unless such a study has been made of at least the more important parts of the "Introduction." I am indebted to the personal kindness of Dr. Schmidt for the Appendix.

Let me add a grateful acknowledgment of the general favor with which this book has been received. While conscious that it must be more or less defective in details, I am at the same time glad to know that the general plan on which it was written, one of avowed *simplicity*, is generally approved. The day for putting a bare text and a Greek-Latin lexicon into the hands of a student, and telling him to elicit the beauties of his author, is happily past. The method of instruction that inducts the learner thoroughly into the spirit of what he reads, and makes him for the time a living, feeling actor in its scenes, *must* be the better.

My thanks are due to Dr. B. L. Gildersleeve of the University of Virginia for valuable suggestions. Correspondence is solicited.

JOHN WILLIAMS WHITE.

HARVARD COLLEGE,
Cambridge, Mass., Oct. 6, 1874.

A PARTIAL LIST OF THE EDITIONS OF THE ŒDIPUS TYRANNUS.

SOPHOCLES, with English Notes. By the Rev. F. H. M. Blaydes, M. A. Vol. I. 8vo. pp. lvi & 634. 18*s.* London: Whittaker. 1859. (This is a volume in the Bibliotheca Classica, and contains, besides the Œd. Tyr., the Œd. Col. and the Ant. The second volume has never appeared.)

THE ŒDIPUS REX OF SOPHOCLES, with Critical, Philological, and Explanatory Notes. By the Rev. John Brasse, D. D. Post 8vo. pp. xi & 94. 5*s.* London: Longman. 1838.

SOPHOCLES, THE PLAYS AND FRAGMENTS. Edited, with English Notes and Introductions, by Lewis Campbell, M. A., LL. D., Professor of Greek in the University of St. Andrews. Vol. I. 8vo. pp. viii & 495. 14*s.* Oxford: Clarendon Press. 1871. (This volume contains the Œd. Tyr., Œd. Col., and Ant., together with a valuable Introductory Essay on the Language of Sophocles. The second volume has not yet appeared.)

THE ŒDIPUS TYRANNUS OF SOPHOCLES, with English Notes. By Howard Crosby, D. D. Ninth Ed. 12mo. pp. 138. New York: Appleton. 1866.

SOPHOCLIS ŒDIPUS REX ex Recensione et cum Commentariis G. Dindorfii. Third Ed. 12mo. pp. 130. 2*s.* 6*d.* Oxford: Parker. 1860. (Usually bound in one thick volume with the Œd. Col., Ant., and Ajax, with a preface, pp. xxi. This with the companion volume at 21*s.*)

SOPHOCLIS ŒDIPUS TYRANNUS ex Recensione Petri Elmsley, A. M., qui et Annotationes Suas Adjecit. 8vo. pp. xlv & 90. 5*s.* Oxford: Parker. 1825. (To this are added (pp. 40) — Scholia Antiqua in Sophoclis Œdipum Tyrannum. Ex Codice Laurentiano Plut. xxxii. 9.)

SOPHOCLIS ŒDIPUS REX. Emendavit, Varietatem Lectionis, Scholia Notasque tum Aliorum tum Suas Adjecit Car. Gtlo. Aug. Erfurdt. 8vo. pp. xiv & 483. 3 Thal. Leipsic: Gerhard Fleischer. 1809.

FREUND'S SCHÜLER-BIBLIOTHEK. Präparation zu Sophocles' Werken. IV. König Oedipus. Pp. 246. 5 Sgr. Leipsic: Wilhelm Violet. 1869.

SOPHOCLES' KÖNIG OEDIPUS. Griechisch mit metrischer Uebersetzung und prüfenden und erklärenden Anmerkungen, von J. H. Hartung. Large 12mo. pp. 249. 21 Sgr. Leipsic: W. Engelmann. 1851.

THE ŒDIPUS REX OF SOPHOCLES, with Notes. By William Basil Jones, M. A. 16mo. pp. 60 & 73. 1*s.* 6*d.* Oxford: Clarendon Press. 1867.

ŒDIPUS TYRANNUS OF SOPHOCLES, with Notes, Critical and Explanatory. By T. Mitchell, A. M. 8vo. pp. viii & 203. 5*s.* Oxford: Parker. 1840.

THE ŒDIPUS TYRANNUS OF SOPHOCLES, with short English Notes. 18mo. pp. 55 & 34. 1*s.* Oxford: Parker. 1853. (Oxford Pocket Classics.)

SOPHOKLES' KÖNIG OIDIPUS. Nach der ältesten Handschrift und den Zeugnissen der alten Grammatiker berichtigt, übersetzt, durch einen exegetisch-kritischen Commentar erklärt von Franz Ritter. Large 8vo. pp. viii & 252. 1 Thal. 20 Sgr. Leipsic: Teubner. 1870.

SOPHOKLES ERKLÄRT von F. W. Schneidewin. Œdipus Tyrannus. Fünfte Auflage besorgt von Aug. Nauck. 8vo. pp. 174. 10 Sgr. Berlin: Weidmansche Buchhandlung. 1866. (There is an English translation of the first edition of this in Arnold's School Classics, made by Henry Browne. 4*s.* London: Rivington. 1852.)

THE ŒDIPUS TYRANNUS OF SOPHOCLES, with Notes and a Critique on the Subject of the Play. By J. W. Stuart, Professor of Greek and Roman Literature in the College of South Carolina. Pp. vi & 222. New York: Gould and Newman. 1837.

LES TRAGÉDIES DE SOPHOCLE. Texte grec, publié d'après les travaux les plus récents de la philologie, avec un commentaire critique et explicatif, une introduction et une notice, par Éd. Tournier. Ouvrage couronné par l'Association pour l'encouragement des études grecques. 8vo. pp. xxxii & 781. 12 *fr.* Paris : Hachette et Cie. 1867. (There is also a 16mo. edition of this work. Each tragedy of this smaller edition may be had separately at 1 *fr.*)

SOPHOCLIS ŒDIPUS REX. Edidit et adnotavit Henricus Van Herwerden. Editio Major. Trajecti ad Rhenum, apud L. E. Bosch et Fil. Large 8vo. pp. viii & 216. 1 Thal. 20 Sgr. 1866.

SOPHOKLES KÖNIG OIDIPUS. Für den Schulgebrauch erklärt von Gustav Wolff. Large 8vo. pp. vi & 159. 10 Sgr. Leipsic: Teubner. 1870.

SOPHOCLIS TRAGŒDIÆ. Recensuit et explanavit Ed. Wunderus. Vol. I., Sect. II., continens Œdipum Regem. Fourth Ed. large 8vo. pp. 167. 12 Sgr. Leipsic: Teubner. 1859. (There is an English translation of this. 3*s.* London. 1851.)

SOPHOCLES ŒDIPUS TYRANNUS, with Notes. By Henry Young. 12mo. pp. viii & 84. 1*s.* London: Lockwood. 1871. (Weale's Classical Series.)

LEXICA.

LEXICON SOPHOCLEUM. Edidit Guilelmus Dindorfius. Lex. 8vo. pp. viii & 534. 3 Thal. 20 Sgr. Leipsic: Teubner. 1870. (This lexicon was seized by the police soon after its publication as an infringement on Ellendt's, and is now, consequently, hard to obtain.)

LEXICON SOPHOCLEUM. Composuit Fridericus Ellendt, A. M. Editio Altera Emendata. Curavit Hermannus Genthe. Lex. 8vo. pp. xvi & 812. 8 Thal. Berlin: Bornträger Bros. 1872. (The first edition of this celebrated work appeared in 1835. An English translation and abridgment was published in 1841. 8vo. pp. 275. Now quoted at 3*s.* Oxford: Talboys.)

INTRODUCTION.

ADAPTED FROM SCHNEIDEWIN.

LAÏUS, son of Labdacus, king of Thebes, had been warned by an oracle of Apollo that he was destined to die by the hand of a son whom he should beget from his wife Jocasta, daughter of Menœceus. By what offence he had incurred this doom, Sophocles leaves untold; not so the pretended oracle: —

> Λάϊε Λαβδακίδη, παίδων γένος ὄλβιον αἰτεῖς.
> δώσω τοι φίλον υἱόν· ἀτὰρ πεπρωμένον ἐστὶν
> σοῦ παιδὸς χείρεσσι λιπεῖν φάος· ὣς γὰρ ἔνευσεν
> Ζεὺς Κρονίδης Πέλοπος στυγεραῖς ἀραῖσι πιθήσας,
> οὗ φίλον ἥρπασας υἱόν· ὁ δ' ηὔξατό σοι τάδε πάντα.

Accordingly, a son being born to him, Laïus binds his ankles together, and in this condition gives him into the hands of a slave, with orders to expose him upon the mountain. So Jocasta herself tells the story, 711 sqq., but suppresses some of the particulars. One of the omissions the old slave himself supplies, to the effect that he received the child, with command to make away with it, the rather from the mother's own hands, 1173, its feet being bound with a thong through holes cruelly bored in its ankles, which treatment was intended, without killing it outright, to insure its perishing, and to prevent its being taken up by others. Jocasta also keeps back the fact that it was on the subject of posterity that Laïus consulted Apollo, who warned him against begetting a son. Cf. 1184, ἀφ' ὧν οὐ χρῆν. The slave, however, takes compassion on the babe, and gives it, on Mount Cithæron, to a herdsman from Corinth, 1142 sq. But he, instead of rearing it for himself, gives it to his childless master, King Polybus, and his wife Merope. With kindly affection the pair bring up the foundling, which, from its swelled feet, they name **Οἰδίπους** (1036). He is generally accounted the first of the citizens of Corinth, until an apparently insignificant occurrence disturbs him in his youthful felicity. At a banquet, — as he himself, 779 sqq., relates, — one of his drunken companions assails him with the reproach that he is only the supposititious son of Polybus. Being stung by the affront, he with difficulty restrains himself for that day. On the morrow he presents himself before father and mother, tells them what has happened, and wishes to learn the truth. They are incensed against the author of the taunt, but fail to satisfy his doubts. The reproach still rankles in his breast, and will not let him rest. At length, without the knowledge of his parents, he sets off for Delphi, to obtain satisfaction from Apollo; but the god, instead of answering his question, announces to him as his destiny, that *he shall wed his own mother, beget a race hideous to mankind, and be the slayer of his own father.* Cf. 788 sqq., 994 sqq. Having received this oracle, he resolves, hard as it may be to him, never again to see his parents (999), but to turn his back forever upon his Corinthian home, in order to escape from the doom predicted by Apollo; for that he is truly the son of the affectionate fosterers of his infancy, he thinks he can no longer doubt. Alone he wanders, unknowing whither, through Phocis. At this same time (114 sqq.) it chanced that Laïus was on his way from Thebes to Apollo's oracle at Delphi, we know not upon what errand. At the point where the highroads from Delphi and from Daulia (733 sq.) meet in a narrow pass (*στενωπός*), the wanderer is met by an old man riding in a chariot, the driver at the time leading the horses. Cf. the note on 804. Both with violence attempt to force him out of the way. Being enraged, he deals the driver a blow, and then essays to pursue his way quietly. The old man, however, watches his opportunity, and at the moment when Œdipus is in the act of passing the chariot, with his double goad deals him a blow right on the middle of his head. Upon this Œdipus instantly strikes him a fatal blow with his walking-staff; he falls backward from the chariot and dies. In the heat of his rage, Œdipus slays the other attendants also. So at least he believes: but one of them escapes, and to save himself from the reproach of a cowardly flight, on his arrival in Thebes relates that a band of robbers had fallen upon the party, 122 sq. This falsehood was indispensable for the poet, in order that Œdipus might not be allowed to come too soon upon the right track; so likewise was the representation that only one escaped, whose account of the matter could not be contradicted by other witnesses.

Proceeding on his way, Œdipus arrives in the neighborhood of Thebes a short time after the escaped attendant has brought the intelligence of the violent death of Laïus. Here, at that precise time, the Sphinx had her lair, a monster who, seizing on all that passed that way, propounded her enigma, and if they could not solve it, hurled them headlong from the rock, thereby decimating the city. Her enigma is couched by an unknown poet in the following verses: —

> *Ἔστι δίπουν ἐπὶ γῆς καὶ τετράπον, οὗ μία φωνή,*
> *καὶ τρίπον· ἀλλάσσει δὲ φυὴν μόνον ὅσσ' ἐπὶ γαῖαν*
> *ἑρπετὰ κινεῖται ἀνά τ' αἰθέρα καὶ κατὰ πόντον.*
> *ἀλλ' ὁπόταν πλείστοισιν ἐρειδόμενον ποσὶ βαίνῃ,*
> *ἔνθα τάχος γυίοισιν ἀφαυρότατον πέλει αὐτοῦ.*

Œdipus also passes by the mountain of the Sphinx, a stranger, and not as yet apprised by the Thebans concerning her proceedings; yet he intrepidly tries his fortune, and solves the Enigma of Man, whereupon the monster throws herself from the rock. This **λύσις** also has been put in verse: —

> *Κλῦθι καὶ οὐκ ἐθέλουσα, κακόπτερε Μοῦσα θανόντων,*
> *φωνῆς ἡμετέρης σὸν τέλος ἀμπλακίης·*

ἄνθρωπον κατέλεξας, ὃς ἡνίκα γαῖαν ἐφέρπει,
πρῶτον ἔφυ τετράπους νήπιος ἐκ λαγόνων.
γηραλέος δὲ πέλων τρίτατον πόδα βάκτρον ἐρείδει,
αὐχένα φορτίζων, γήραϊ καμπτόμενος.

He is recognized as the savior of the state, and receives, together with the throne left vacant by the death of Laïus, the widow of the king as his wife, and now as king in Thebes passes many years in undisturbed prosperity. Jocasta bears him four children; the city honors him as the greatest and best of men, who, not without the special favor of the gods, overcame the Sphinx, 33 sqq. But suddenly, after long years (561), the happiness which the gods awarded him is disturbed by a blight upon the fruits of the earth, and a pestilence on man and beast, — the punishment sent by Apollo because of the neglected expiation of the old murder. In his vigilant care for the city, Œdipus has sent the man who stands next to himself and to the throne, his wife's brother Creon, with whom he has ever lived in undisturbed friendship (590 sqq.), to Delphi, for the purpose of invoking, in this trying emergency likewise, the aid of the Pythian god. At this point begins the action of the tragedy.

Prologos, 1 – 150. The distress having risen to the highest point, the whole population, not as yet acquainted with the measures taken by the king, has formed suppliant processions to the sanctuaries of the gods. Those who are the most in need of help, gray-headed old priests, young children, and chosen youths, repair to the palace of their sovereign on the Cadmeia. Œdipus, as a father, comes forth among his children, to inform himself of the purpose of this assembly, and to express his readiness to aid them to the utmost of his power. The priest of Zeus, whose age and dignity call him to be spokesman, depicts the general distress as the cause of their thus betaking themselves to him, the approved deliverer, who owes it to himself to be still the savior of the state. Deeply moved, Œdipus replies to this confiding and honorable address, that without waiting for any exhortation from others, he has of his own accord taken thought for all that can be done for the deliverance of his people from a calamity which indeed presses upon him above all others. Creon has been sent to Delphi, and whatever the god may order for the deliverance of the city, that will he do willingly.

To the joy of all, Creon appears. At the express wish of Œdipus, he announces, in the presence of the whole assembly, that Apollo peremptorily demands from the citizens that *the slayer of Laïus, who is living in the land, be either banished or put to death,* seeing this polluted person has brought upon Thebes the present calamity. Hereupon, while the points of moment for the connection of the fable are brought out by a series of questions and answers, Œdipus learns that Laïus upon a time having left Thebes upon a *θεωρία*, — with what object, and to what oracle, is purposely not specified, — never returned; it was only known that he had been slain by a band of robbers. That no search was made at the time for the doer of this deed was caused by the Sphinx, who obliged them to confine their thoughts to their own immediate concerns. Œdipus, all unsuspecting, is prompt with his resolve to lose not a moment in executing the divine injunction. Needs must he himself apprehend that so daring a murderer, who, he fancies, must have been set on by political opponents in Thebes, may lay hands on him likewise! He then bids the assembled suppliants withdraw, and appoints one of his attendants to summon the principal citizens of Thebes, as he will leave nothing unattempted that may lead to the desired end.

Œdipus and Creon go within the palace. Creon advises him to send a messenger for Tiresias, which he does, and after a time, impatient at his not arriving, he despatches a second. The citizens, whom the king has summoned, appear before the palace. As the age, sex, and position of the choreutæ are for the most part chosen to match the protagonistes, so here the χώρας ἄνακτες form the Chorus, as in the Œd. Col. old men, in the Electra maidens, in the Ajax comrades in war, in the Philoctetes mariners. The deficiency in mental acumen and insight into the bearings of the events which appears in our choreutæ was necessary for the poet in the management of the action; they must needs be men of limited minds and slow perception, that they may not, any more than their king, be able to see through the true connection and dependence of the incidents, and may still enter into and echo their master's tone of feeling. At the same time, their quietude makes them well adapted for thoughtful appreciation of the stormy passions which rave before them. As they take their place in the orchestra around the thymele, they strike up the PARODOS, 151–215. Aware of Creon's return, but as yet unacquainted with the purport of the oracle brought by him, with their expectation wrought up to the highest pitch, they invoke, in solemn rhythm, the chiefest of Thebes' tutelary deities, and depict in vivid colors the tribulations of their city; and then once more supplicate the succor of the gods, severally invoking them in long detail. By thus separating the Chorus from the ἱκέται, Sophocles gets a natural occasion for letting Œdipus, by his announcement of the oracle, and of the measures which he has taken accordingly, exhibit himself in all his security and consciousness of innocence; while, at the same time, his address shows how heinous he considers the crime to be, and how earnestly he takes the injunction of the god.

FIRST EPEISODION, 216–462. Œdipus, who, shortly before the close of the choral song, again appears, takes up the concluding thought, and bids the Chorus depend upon his active zeal, to which the command of the god has appointed its course of proceeding. But in his haste to obey the god, he neglects to acquaint the Chorus, in the first place, with that which they so ardently desired to know, — the purport of the oracle. This they learn only by way of corollary, 242, in quite general terms. For Œdipus, hurried on unawares by a supernatural excitement, begins with emphatically protesting his own utter ignorance, until now, of that which he is about to communicate, thereby explaining how it comes that he, hitherto the wise counsellor in time of need, is obliged, for this time, to have recourse to the help of the citizens. Upon these he solemnly enjoins it as a duty in every way to aid in the discovery of the slayer of Laïus, upon whom he imprecates the heaviest curse, should he remain secret, while he commends the innocent population to the abiding protection of the gods. Upon the spectator, apprised from the outset of the real bearings of the events, the impassioned address of Œdipus must have had a thrilling effect. His speech, now quiet and gentle, now vehement and impetuous, becomes most impassioned at the very point where he imprecates upon the perpetrator and the abettor the evil that falls back upon himself.

The Chorus protests its innocence and ignorance, but counsels to send for Tiresias. For this Œdipus has already taken care. In his disquietude, he marvels that the seer, though two messengers have been sent, has not yet made his appearance. The chorágus then meditatively remarks that the story once current in the mouths of the people leads to nothing. Œdipus, not despising any, even the slightest trace, bids him tell what this was; but he learns nothing more than what Creon had already communicated as the report of the escaped attendant, that Laïus was slain by robbers, or, as it is here said with a nearer approximation to the truth, by travellers.

Then comes the blind seer Tiresias, whose mental eye has long clearly seen through all, and from whom the Chorus, with confidence, hopes that he will bring the doer of the deed to light; as in fact does come to pass, though in a manner wholly unexpected. Œdipus also expects speedy deliverance through Tiresias; and so it comes about that the very man on whom the entire population had built all its hope looks for help to the blind seer, who yet in the times of the Sphinx had held his peace!

The king welcomes the prophet with most honorable expressions of entire confidence, lays before him the purport of the oracle, and calls upon him to put forth all the resources of his art for the deliverance of the city. Tiresias, embarrassed, and repenting of his coming, adjures him to desist: his knowledge profits him not! It has been out of forbearance to the well-deserving ruler that he has so long shut up the secret in his own breast, and even now only upon provocation does he make the disclosures which follow. The king importunes, the seer persists in his refusal: let him be wroth if he will, — it will all come to light without a word from him! By degrees the already excited king is wrought up into a towering passion. Conscious that he himself is doing everything to carry out the injunction of the god, it exasperates him that Tiresias, having the power to help, refuses his aid. In bitter altercation he gives vent to the accusation that Tiresias himself was the instigator of the murder. Upon this, the seer, himself by this time angered, declares that Œdipus is the murderer. But the king, his suspicions once having been roused, listens no longer to the child of night. Tiresias adds yet further — and in this Œdipus, in a calmer state of mind, could not have failed to perceive an echo of his own old oracle — that he is cohabiting with his nearest kindred in horrible intimacy. But no sooner has the seer appealed to Apollo, who will presently bring the matter to an issue, than a new suspicion adds to the infatuation which already possesses the blinded king. At the very hearing of Apollo, it flashes upon him that Creon — the bearer of the oracle from Delphi — is at the bottom of the matter, and that the seer, for love of base gain, has been acting upon his suggestions. This thought, rendered in some measure plausible by the fact that it was Creon who had advised the sending for the seer, in the impetuous Œdipus becomes at once a certainty; and the rather as, on the very first hearing of the matter, it had occurred to him that the murderer must have been set on by political motives. Following it up, he indignantly accuses Creon (who in company with Œdipus had left the stage at 146, and is not now present) as a conspirator with whom Tiresias is leagued to compass his overthrow. Now he scoffs at that which he has just before so highly extolled, — the prophetic skill of Tiresias, — a man who, for all his pretensions, had no power to help in the time of the Sphinx! His confidence shaken in all whom he had revered and loved, Œdipus, once so discreet, now sets up his γνώμη against the τέχνη of the professed seer, with all its infallibility, and menaces both the conspirators with the punishment they deserve.

Tiresias now, for the second time, reveals in connected detail (412–428) the calamities which await Œdipus, living, as he does, in most disastrous unconsciousness of the horrors by which he is surrounded. In a burst of wrath, he bids the seer be gone. The latter, in replying to the taunt of his having uttered nothing but follies, with the answer, "Thy parents thought me wise," has launched at the king a new shaft, so that from this time the painful recollection of the old unexplained mystery of his extraction mixes itself up with his present solicitude. With his demand for enlightenment Tiresias declines to comply, but darkly hints that this day, ere it close, will explain all. Then, before he withdraws, he for the third time expresses himself concerning the murderer in terms awfully enigmatical, but still clearly calculated to remind Œdipus of the old oracle; not now, however, as before, addressing the king himself, and expressly mentioning him by name, but speaking as if concerning a third person. He concludes with the words, "If these sayings be not made good, then Œdipus shall say that Tiresias knows nothing of the art which he professes." The king, also, for whom each fancied access of insight but deepens his blindness, retires into the palace. The spectator has now before him, in all its completeness, the prodigious contrast between the outward semblance and the reality. The truth which Œdipus desires to have he thrusts from him, and falls at variance, moreover, with the seer, until now his well-wisher, and with his most faithful friend. It sets this contrast in a sharper light that the Chorus is involved in the same delusions with its lord. This short-sightedness of the Chorus appears immediately in bold relief in the FIRST STASIMON, 463 – 512.

SECOND EPEISODION, 513 – 862, with a KOMMOS, 649 – 697, with interposed trimeters. With great art the following scene is brought on by the dialogue with Tiresias. Creon, informed of the accusation raised against him by Œdipus, indignantly appears and endeavors to learn from the Chorus whether that harsh charge had indeed been made by a sane mind. But while the Chorus, in its loyal attachment to its lord, considerately shrinks from satisfying the inquiry, the king himself appears, and so the full explanation is reserved for the dialogue between the parties concerned. He gives his wife's brother a rough reception. To have the audacity to come into his presence, — him, his detected murderer and the robber of his throne! Creon must needs regard him a coward or fool, if he thinks to delude him, or supposes that his plottings will not be promptly met! Creon, on the other hand, advises Œdipus first to look calmly into the facts of the case. And now the king, to make his grounds sure, commences an examination, point by point. He asks whether it was not Creon's suggestion that he should send for the seer. This being answered in the affirmative, he asks whether Tiresias had ever, in former times, pointed at him as the guilty person. If he, who now all on the sudden thinks fit to mark him as the murderer, has before this held his peace, it is to him a demonstrated fact that he was prompted by Creon, who coveted the throne. The more conclusive Œdipus deems this inference, the more firmly does he here once more fix himself in his error.

Hereupon Creon, having first shown how near he stands to Œdipus and his queen, goes into a long train of argument, wishing to demonstrate, by a rational discussion of all the circumstances, how utterly absurd it would be in him to entertain the ambitious design upon the throne of which he is accused. If Œdipus can convict him of having a crafty understanding with Tiresias, he protests himself ready to die a shameful death. Without listening to this oath, or taking heed to the pacific admonitions of the Chorus, the king insists that Creon must die as a traitor.

At this point the choragus, 631 sqq., announces the approach of Jocasta, whom the altercation has called from the palace. She bids them for shame desist, in the midst of the general distress, from stirring up private quarrels. Upon this, Œdipus lays before her his impeachment of Creon, and the latter by the most solemn oath again asseverates his innocence. It is only upon the most urgent entreaties of his wife and of the choreutæ, that the king lets Creon go, — not in the least convinced that he has wronged his wife's brother, — but with the express declaration that he will never cease to hate him. Creon withdraws, protesting that his sovereign has misjudged him, whereas the whole city knows that he is still what he always was; and he ominously predicts that Œdipus will be pained by the thought of his injustice, when once his passion is allayed.

Upon Creon's departure, at Jocasta's desire, her husband relates the occasion of the quarrel, the Chorus having vainly besought him to let the matter rest. Creon, he says, would fain make him out to be the murderer; so little is he able to free himself from his preconceived opinion that Tiresias was suborned by him to accuse him of the deed! With shrewd womanly art, Jocasta now sets herself to convince her husband, already more than enough entangled in a web of self-deception, that the vaunted science of the seers is not worth heeding. There was an old oracle given to Laïus which was so far from receiving its fulfilment, that foreign robbers, as the story goes, — this then she trusts implicitly, without much questioning its grounds or want of grounds, — slew him on the common highway: as for her child, it was exposed immediately after its birth. Thus was the response of the ministers of the Delphian temple put to shame!

But here the punishment follows close on the heels of the blasphemy. This very story, which was meant to set her husband's mind quite at rest as regarded one oracle, by the instance of another oracle which was falsified by the event, produces just the opposite result. The words of the seer, so plain and pointed, remained an enigma for Œdipus: now one casual harmless word arrests his attention and staggers him in the confidence he has thus far felt. Now begins the wonderfully contrived περιπέτεια; a faint presentiment of the truth arises in the hero's mind, but the poet has the skill yet for a long time to retard the full discovery. Not only now but again and again hereafter this same tragical effect attends the process of the discovery, that the gradual uplifting of the veil is effected by the very persons who are endeavoring to relieve the hero's mind of its growing anxieties.

When, namely, Jocasta mentions that Laïus was slain πρὸς τριπλαῖς ἁμαξιτοῖς, — a spot where there would naturally be frequent encounters of people coming from different directions, — Œdipus eagerly catches at this description of the locality, and inquires whither the pass led, how long ago this occurrence befell, how old Laïus was, and of what appearance. When all tallies with his own old adventure, an indescribable anxiety takes possession of his mind, lest after all Tiresias be found to see but too truly. For even the number of the attendants accords; and now he desires Jocasta to send with all speed for the slave who had then returned, that he may gain the satisfaction he needs from him. The slave had recognized in the highly praised deliverer of the city, and husband of the queen, the slayer of his lord. As the sight of him must ever remind him of his falsehood about the band of robbers, he had withdrawn from Thebes. Of the fact that the new king was the son of Laïus, he had no knowledge. It was a necessary contrivance of the poet's that the slave, whom Œdipus had omitted to summon in the first instance (118), should not be present, yet not too remote; and the mention by Jocasta, just at this point, where the elucidation of the mystery lies so close at hand, of the reason why he wished to be dismissed into the country, is ominously significant.

Jocasta, having as yet no foreboding of the ground of her husband's anxiety, wishes to learn what it is; whereupon Œdipus, who in Thebes was universally held to be the son of Polybus, frankly relates his juvenile history, and the adventure in the σχιστὴ ὁδός. If the old man whom he slew was Laïus, he must bewail himself as of all mortal men the most hated of the gods, since upon him must then light all the heavy curses which he has openly denounced upon the murderer. In his contemplation of this contingency, he is still so blind that he bewails the hard fate which makes it impossible for him, if the case be so, ever to return to his old home and his beloved parents at Corinth, if he would not incur the yet worse misery of fulfilling the old oracle by slaying Polybus and wedding Merope. At every step which the hero takes toward the truth, the poet has the art to excite afresh, and with more intensity, the ἔλεος and φόβος of the spectator. The way in which, step by step, the truth comes out, is managed with inimitable art. As yet the hero's misgiving is limited to the milder half of his disastrous condition, the apprehension that he may have been the slayer of the royal husband of his wife; his parents he innocently assumes to be living in Corinth, and dreads the possible fulfilment of that which lies long years behind him in the past! Even for that milder object of his apprehension, dreadful as the contemplation of it is to the high-souled king, he has still a ray of hope.

If, namely, the herdsman shall persist in his story that *robbers* were the slayers of the old king, he, a solitary individual, cannot be the culprit. Jocasta goes yet further; even if the herdsman

2

should vary in his tale, this need not trouble him. Loxias plainly declared that her husband should fall by the hand of his own son; but this son perished long before his father. Consequently she will never believe in prophecy and divination. Meanwhile she will send forthwith for the herdsman; until then let Œdipus with her enter their palace.

Second Stasimon, 863 – 910. The pious old men, deeply offended by the daring levity shown by Jocasta in her avowed disregard of the utterances of the gods, and by the godless way in which she has spoken of her past life, especially the icy coldness of heart which she betrayed in her account of the exposure of her infant, pray to Zeus that he will confirm the truth of the oracle given to Laïus. Armed with the holy primeval laws of religion and morality, they contend for their inviolable sanctity, unchecked by any misgiving that the object they would obtain by their prayer is indeed none other than the speedy overthrow of the king to whom they still adhere with the same devoted loyalty as ever.

Third Epeisodion, 911 – 1085. Suddenly Jocasta comes forth, and explains that a fancy has taken her to offer to the gods. Need teaches prayer. Within doors she cannot breathe freely; while Œdipus, a prey to boundless dejection, persists in rejecting all that she can suggest for the quieting of his disturbed mind, and lends an ear only to the most alarming representations. Jocasta draws near to the altar of the very god whose utterances she has but now again treated with contempt, and whose wisdom she will presently, on the first seeming lull of the storm, once more, with her usual levity, turn into derision. The impression made by the language of the profane queen — irreligious even in her devotions — tells with the greater effect by contrast with the loftiness and purity of the sentiments to which the magnificent ode, whose last accents have but just died away, has attuned the minds of the spectators.

Apparently, the god instantly grants the prayer, that the reality, when it comes, may be all the more crushing. A messenger appears from Corinth, who, in the belief that he is the bringer of joyful tidings, shows a cheerful bearing. Polybus is dead; and he, in hope of rich reward, has immediately set off on his journey hither to be the first bearer of the tidings to Œdipus, whom, as he says he has heard, the Corinthians intend to make their king. On hearing this, Jocasta triumphantly calls out her husband. There now are the oracles again falsified! And now even the pious king, with this new fact before him, cannot forbear to chime in with her exultation, and emboldens himself to speak disparagingly of oracle and flight of birds. True, upon recollecting the studied ambiguity and equivocal character of the language of oracles, it occurs to him — always ready-minded, and always at fault in the direction of his reflections — that Polybus' death may have been caused by grief for the loss of him, in which case the god will yet be true, and he, in a sense, the slayer of his father. So difficult does he find it to accord with Jocasta's tone of feeling, and so much does his pious mind revolt from her profane levity, that rather than doubt the truth of the divine words, he chooses to take refuge in casuistical refinements. And then forthwith the other part of the old oracle falls heavily on his soul, — that he should become the husband of his mother. Jocasta, indeed, is prompt with her woman's counsel; one must drive such crotchets out of one's head; that is the only way to live comfortably, 977 sqq. But the messenger from Corinth, to whom Œdipus makes known the cause of his fear, hastes, with the best intentions, to relieve him of his distress. Polybus was of no kin to Œdipus; from his own hands the pair received the boy. Laïus' herdsman, who handed the child over to him upon a time when they were together in Cithæron, would be able to throw further light upon the subject. The Chorus recognizes in this herdsman the very man who has been summoned to explain the circumstances of the old king's death. For he it was that had accompanied Laïus and escaped with the tidings of his death to Thebes. Jocasta, the scales now at once falling from her eyes, adjures Œdipus to desist from further investigation; but this he peremptorily declines. Upon this Jocasta hurries off from the scene, with words which portend some frightful resolve on her part. Œdipus, again misapprehending the true bearings of the case, imagines that Jocasta's vanity is wounded; that she fears he may be found to be of ignoble extraction. For his part, he will not rest until he gets at the whole truth of his parentage; come what will, he regards himself as a son of Tyche, who has made him small and great. Nothing daunts the strong hero; before all things he will learn the full truth.

A Hyporchema, 1086–1109, of cheerful character serves, just before the catastrophe, to shed a last gleam of light upon the gathering gloom, while the Chorus, wholly entering into the tone of the protagonist, pictures to itself that Œdipus may perchance be the child of a god by some mountain-nymph of Cithæron.

Fourth Epeisodion, 1110–1185. The herdsman for whose coming Œdipus has longed appears, and is recognized by the Corinthian as the person from whose hands he received the child. Of the attack made upon Laïus by a number of robbers, which was the point on which the king desired satisfaction when he was urgent to have this man summoned, we hear no more, now that matters have taken a new turn, in consequence of which all is cleared up at once so soon as the hero's origin is brought to light. The other recalls to the recollection of the Theban herdsman the days they spent together on the mountains, and thinks to give him a joyful surprise with the discovery that the boy whom the other handed over to him is none other than the king before whom they stand. The horrified Theban is forced by violent menaces to confess that Jocasta herself consigned the child to his hands for destruction, moved to this by fear of an oracle which foretold that the child would one day slay his father. That he would also wed his mother was no part of the oracle given to Laïus; this was only prophesied to Œdipus. Now first the whole hideous reality, in all its parts, is laid bare before the eyes of the king. Having, with a bitter cry, bid farewell to the light of day, and summed up with pregnant brevity the chain of horrors through which Tiresias so well saw, he rushes into the house.

THIRD STASIMON, 1186–1222. The Chorus having contemplated *the sudden vicissitudes of all earthly things*, then follows,

The EXODOS, 1223 to the end. Inserted in this is a second KOMMOS, 1313–1368, intermixed with trimeters by the Chorus.

An exangelus gives a relation of the portentous horrors which have befallen in the palace. Jocasta has strangled herself in the thalamus; Œdipus, like a maniac, with loud yell, has burst in, and with Jocasta's golden clasps bored out both his eyes, to escape the sight of his misery and misdeeds. So, says the messenger, has measureless wretchedness entered in, where once dwelt high prosperity.

Then, to show to the Thebans in his horribly mutilated condition — for which the description given by the messenger has prepared them — the unhappy sufferer, whose noble spirit, as it never knew concealment, so now will have no disguises, the palace-doors fly open, and Œdipus totters forth. He now bewails alternately with the Chorus, without reproaching any other than himself, his self-inflicted blindness, and his disastrous destiny. Anon, collecting himself, he speaks (from 1369) of the fearful punishment he has inflicted upon himself; he weighs the circumstances which made it impossible for him any longer to behold the light. He concludes with the prayer that the Chorus will thrust him out of the land, or make away with him. So little is he content with the punishment which, in his frenzy, he has inflicted upon himself, until the oracle of the Pythian god concerning the slayer of Laïus be also satisfied to the uttermost.

The Chorus refers him to Creon, whom it sees approaching.

During the minority of the sons, Creon is the natural successor to the throne, as Sophocles makes the hero forthwith abdicate the sovereignty. So, after the lapse of a few hours, Creon, without doing anything toward it himself, has through Œdipus' own proceedings attained to the very dignity which he was previously accused of unrighteously affecting! The unhappy king, who has now seen how greatly he was deceived in the suspicion he was led to entertain of his old friend, is alarmed at the announcement of Creon's approach. But, as in the Ajax, Ulysses, after the death of his enemy, comes forward as the noble vindicator of his merits, and in the Philoctetes the position of Neoptolemus relative to Philoctetes in the course of the action undergoes a complete revolution, so the relation of Creon to Œdipus takes an unexpected turn; for Creon, entirely vindicated by the events, comes forward as a sympathizing friend and helper in time of need, and makes it plain that he has retained no recollection of the offence. In the first place he desires them immediately to withdraw from the light of day the shocking spectacle of the unhappy sufferer; but when Œdipus addresses to him also the request that, agreeably with the dictate of Apollo, he may be banished, he bids him wait patiently for the decision of the god, which he holds himself bound to seek once more before taking any further measures. Submitting to this arrangement, and having commended to Creon's pious care the obsequies of his wretched sister, on his own behalf he has nothing more to ask but that he may be thrust out to Cithæron, the place once appointed by his parents for his grave; only the thought of his two poor daughters weighs heavily upon his fatherly heart; as for the sons, they are already able to help themselves. The latter he does not ask to see, — their character as godless men is fixed in the myth, — but the maidens, whom he dearly loves, he would fain embrace once more. Even for this, Creon, who knows the heartfelt love which their unhappy father has ever borne them, has taken thought. Cordially thanking him for this kindness, Œdipus pathetically surveys all the painful circumstances which may await the orphaned maidens, who, in the innocence of their hearts, incapable of comprehending the horrors of the situation, stand mutely by. With warm affection he commends them to the faithful guardianship of Creon, who must supply to them the place of a father. So the poet manages to give to the horrors of the drama a milder close, and to afford the spectator a consolatory glance into the future.

Upon this Creon bids him go in: if such be the will of the god, he will surely obtain his desire of quitting the land.

In the concluding trochees, the Chorus points out how in the man who but now was extolled as wisest and greatest of men, the maxim of Solon is verified, that *no mortal must be accounted happy until one has learned by experience whether his good fortune will be faithful to him unto the end of his days.* Undoubtedly this is the most evident idea that suggests itself to us in our contemplation of the Drama of the Fall of Œdipus: as accordingly it is carried out at greater length in the last stasimon, and is also brought forward by the exangelus, 1282 sqq. Here also that reflection of Ulysses in the Ajax is in place, *ὁρῶ γὰρ ἡμᾶς οὐδὲν ὄντας ἄλλο πλὴν εἴδωλ', ὅσοιπερ ζῶμεν, ἢ κούφη σκιά.* But it would be a great mistake to imagine that Sophocles intended in this gnome to put at once into our hands the idea which his drama was meant to enforce, and in which all should find its central unity. The world unfolded in this drama exhibits a portraiture much too individually marked for any such conception; its relations, bearings, characters, are far too special to admit of our spanning with this formula the poetical conception of the drama considered in its essence. The vicissitude exhibited is but the external consequence of inward contradictions; it lights upon Œdipus, who seems to have been singled out by fate as the ball of its caprice. His entire life is one continued oscillation between unmitigated opposites; his endeavor and will stand to the actual result in the most crying contradiction; where he strives after the best, he works misery; where he thinks to go right cleverly to work, his sagacity is ever at fault, while, if he does hit the truth, it is but by accident, unconsciously and unavailingly. The language of the oracles he misinterprets throughout: the Sphinx's riddle he solves while yet his own being is, and continues to be, to him an enigma. Personally conscious of no guilt, he becomes entangled in the most disastrous destinies: circumstances, seemingly the most unfavorable, lend him a hand to unlooked-for success. As these contrasts are seen in that part of his life which is external to the action of our drama, so in the drama itself they lie before us in all their asperity. The deep tragedy of the play lies in the very circumstance that a terrible utterance of the god receives its fulfilment at the very point where Œdipus has not had a remote conception of it; that where he most zealously and with keen eye explores the traces of another's guilt, he accelerates the downfall of his own prosperity, and puts a sharper edge to his unhappy destiny by blind precipitancy in consequence of his seeming wisdom; that he attains the object to which he has bent his mind day and night, the salvation of the state, but that the new deliverance of the city he has once happily delivered is his own destruction. The pestilence which gave occasion to the discovery of the truth ceases; the sorely visited and yet innocent city breathes freely again, and the perdition falls upon the very man who at the opening of the play, alone together with those belonging to him, seemed exempt from the general destruction, of which, nevertheless, he was the cause.

The higher Œdipus seems to stand in outward felicity, in endowments of understanding and heart, the vaster the separation, as the drama develops it, between truth and semblance. He was worthy of a better fate: but even before he was begotten he was chosen to be the unnatural instrument of the divine vengeance upon his father and his mother: their transgression should thereby undergo the severest retribution. He takes the life of him who gave him life; she, the mother who would put her child out of the way, conceives children by this her child. It is she who undergoes the most hideous fate, because it was she who seduced Laïus to slight the prohibition of Apollo, and because she thereafter stifled the natural voice of a mother's love.

If now we trace more closely the contrasts in the hero's life and destinies, as Sophocles has carried them out in minutest detail, we are met by the wide chasm between the outward welfare of the son of Tyche (1080 sqq.) and the misery once for all doomed to him by the gods from his very birth. Scarce three days old is he, when by the hands of the parents — who nevertheless longed for heirs — he is ruthlessly maimed, and consigned to destruction. Given over to a foreign shepherd to be brought up as his child, he is presented as a gift to a childless pair in ἀφνειὸς Κόρινθος, and by their consentient love is reared — he, the foreign-born, the maimed foundling, the child of unknown parents — as own offspring of royal parents, as heir of an illustrious throne. A mere chance, in a party met for pleasure, shatters the juvenile happiness of the youth who in the eyes of every man ranked as first of the Corinthian citizens. Thirsting for the clearing up of his doubts, he thinks to betake him to the surest source; but concerning the past, which he wishes to know, Apollo is silent, and intimates all that is most horrible concerning the future, for which he was not questioned. He would fain secure himself against the fulfilment of the oracle. What it is in the power of man to do, he does. But while the homeless pilgrim wanders lonely and without an aim into the country where he may be farthest removed from his Corinthian parents, he slays his true father in an encounter wherein he was justified in using violence in self-defence. For that father purposes at the cross-roads also to slay him, unknown, whom as a child he had wittingly sought to put out of the way; but this time also his attempt miscarries, that the will of the gods may be done. Chance leads the young man to Thebes: he solves the enigma at which all before him had labored in vain; and this very fortune hurls him into the deepest abyss of ruin. The community of his native city rewards him with the vacant throne and the hand of his mother. Then, long undisturbed domestic and public felicity. But the gods leave no sin unpunished, be it early or late; and blood once shed, above all the blood of a father shed by the hand of a child, may not remain unavenged, be the culprit accountable or not. Apollo sends blight and pestilence upon the city which harbors the blood-guilty one. Again Œdipus betakes him to the same god who has once prophesied to him, and whom he must needs regard as the author of his prosperity, seeing that his oracle, by warning him against returning to Corinth, has been the means of his present exaltation. At last, when he has wandered through many a maze of error, his eyes — and this is the matter of our play — are opened. Ere this, he who solved the Enigma of Humanity is left, concerning his own human relations, to grope his way, even to the hideous catastrophe, in utter darkness. It is a point of deep significance — and this formed from the first a marked trait of the popular fiction — that he takes revenge upon the bodily eye for the blindness of his mind; that the darkened mind in the midst of light may have its counterpart in the seeing mind and darkened body.

The character of the Sophoclean Œdipus is spotless, as in fact he stands there in the popular fiction, — the innocent victim of ruthless destiny. From his youth up he has confidingly surrendered himself to the guidance of the bright god of Delphi, and with him will he stand or fall (145). Passionate he is, no doubt, else were he no subject for tragedy. But the poet is ever anxious to let it be seen that even his excesses spring from noble impulses. To him, as the prologue and many other passages of the play declare, the public weal is supreme above all other considerations. Conscious of the purest aims, and convinced that he is serving the god, he becomes harsh and suspicious toward those whose proceedings seem not to be directed to the same end: he loses his steadfastness of self-command and self-consistency, thereby aggravating the miserable lot, which cannot be, nor is meant to be, referred to this as its cause. Without these darker shades in the portraiture of the hero, otherwise sagacious in insight and mild in disposition, yet ever putting himself palpably in the wrong, the dramatic action would lose in inner truthfulness and consistency. As it is, the sentiment in the Antigone, 622 – 624, becomes applicable to him, *τὸ κακὸν δοκεῖν ποτ' ἐσθλὸν τῷδ' ἔμμεν ὅτῳ φρένας θεὸς ἄγει πρὸς ἄταν.* So, likewise, and only so, the way in which the poet has contrived, with wonderful skill, to retard the catastrophe acquires its ground of psychological truth. The passion, too, is quite natural; it is, as Œdipus says (334), enough to provoke a stone to see Tiresias so reluctant to serve his god. And, as if it were not enough that he has in this way thrown the king off his self-possession, the seer must needs also awaken the old uncomfortable feelings about his parentage, and moreover gives him occasion to impute a criminal design to Creon, though Creon has not the slightest notion of the true state of the case. And then, when all at once the seer turns round and impeaches him as the murderer, is it not enough to set him ablaze with indignation? For he could not possibly see that Tiresias had all these years kept silence only out of respect for his noble qualities as a man, and for the wisdom with which as king he was guiding the state. And Tiresias, likewise, himself loses his temper, and is forced out of the dignified repose of his sacred character. In all else Œdipus is throughout a grand, heroic figure; not, indeed, to be scanned by the rule of later times, but one of the forms of the gigantesque olden time, and of that hard, granite-like generation with which old Nestor conversed in his younger days. In particular, the princely stock of the Cadmeiones is characterized by a lofty sternness and stubbornness which in fact makes the traditions of that race stand in such marked contrast to those of the Achaian houses. If to others Œdipus is harsh, his greatest harshness is to himself; the utmost severity of punishment that could of right be visited upon him, he outdoes by the measureless vengeance he takes upon his innocent eyes. For such is the length to which the tragic illusion is carried, that in the state into which his feelings are wrought up, he does not pause to examine the facts of his case in their proper characters, but holds himself alone responsible for all that through him has come to pass.

Œdipus, then, the hated of the gods, is a standing example of that article of the popular creed according to which a man, in spite of the purest intentions, may fail utterly, only because he is an object of aversion to the gods; a faith which took its rise from observation of the enormous disparity which is so often seen between men's merits and their fate. Let it not be thought that this conception of the Œdipus is not that which in a moral point of view would commend itself to the religious mind of a Sophocles. It should be remembered that for the basis of this surpassingly wonderful creation of his genius, he found the story ready-made to his hand. To settle the odds of guilt and punishment could never be the task he set himself, unless he would mar the whole sense of the fable. Further, it should be considered that Œdipus, however pure in his own person, bore with him an inherited sin; for as, in the faith of the ancients, the misdeeds of the parents were often left unpunished in them, to be visited on children and children's children, so likewise the parents' sin imparts itself to the children, and weighs upon them; nay, even in the common intercourse of life, the sin of the impure passes by contagion to the pure, and draws them together into the same destruction.

All things considered, the fundamental idea of the drama can be no other than this: *For mortal man, be he ever so good, not all the watchfulness he can use in pondering his steps will suffice to guard him against misgoings; not all the penetration he can exercise in the discovery of the right will avail for his good, if once the love of the gods be withheld. Be the outward semblance ever so dazzling, the longer the respite the deeper the perdition into which the gods, by inexorable necessity, will at last hurl the* *ἐχθροδαίμων*. In Œdipus we have the impersonation of the utter impotence of man when put upon his own resources. What has it availed him that the gods, by fore-announcement of his destiny, have given him a look into the future which lies before him? Destiny has spread her toils for him, and he falls into them at the very point where he thinks right cleverly to evade them, and to secure his safety. That it is the duty of man humbly to submit himself to a higher guidance, was the general popular faith; this lowly resignation expresses itself in the fact of their praying to the gods that they would grant the power to do that which was right. Of the too harsh destiny which lights upon Œdipus, a righteous compensation is afforded in his end: this is the idea presented in the counterpart of our play, the Œdipus at Colonus, which at the same time affords the fullest proof that the conception of the Œdipus as here stated was, and must have been, that which Sophocles from the first intended.

The parts assigned to all the other persons of the drama seem intended, from first to last, to furnish motives to the procedure of the protagonist, and to draw out his character in a stronger light. In particular, Jocasta stands there beside her noble husband, with a mind how differently constituted! It is her maxim to live for the day. Should anything occur to disturb the god-forgetting tenor of her course, she seeks only to thrust it aside as soon as possible. The earnestness of Œdipus in learning the truth, regardless of what may follow, is to her alien. For truth and right she cares less than for present comfort. To her first husband, reckless of the divine warning he has received, she, having by her arts infatuated him, bears a child, and then, fearing the consequences, without more ado, puts it out of her sight: whether it was really destroyed, of this she had no certainty. Set at rest for the moment, she asks no further questions: gods and oracles give her no concern, save at the actual pinch of need; at other times, her daring levity carries her even to the length of reckless blasphemy. Her marriage with the young Corinthian prince makes her oblivious of the sacred duty of bringing to light her husband's murderers. The old slave she willingly dismisses, because his presence must continually remind her of her child, and of her former husband. She meets with nothing beyond her demerits, when in the full view of the horrors of which her wickedness has been the guilty cause, with her own hands she strangles herself. It is wisely done that the poet dismisses her from the scene before the final disclosure, that the sympathy of the spectators may not be frittered away and diverted from the more worthy Œdipus.

TEXT.

ΤΑ ΤΟΥ ΔΡΑΜΑΤΟΣ ΠΡΟΣΩΠΑ.

ΟΙΔΙΠΟΥΣ.

ΙΕΡΕΥΣ.	ΙΟΚΑΣΤΗ.
ΚΡΕΩΝ.	ΑΓΓΕΛΟΣ.
ΧΟΡΟΣ *γερόντων Θηβαίων.*	ΘΕΡΑΠΩΝ *Λαΐου.*
ΤΕΙΡΕΣΙΑΣ.	ΕΞΑΓΓΕΛΟΣ.

ΟΙΔΙΠΟΥΣ ΤΥΡΑΝΝΟΣ.

DRAMATIS PERSONÆ.

ŒD′ I-PUS, *King of Thebes.*
JO-CAS′ TA, *his wife.*
CRE′ ON, *her brother.*
TI-RE′ SI-AS, *a blind seer.*
PRIEST *of Zeus.*
CHORUS *of Theban old men.*
MESSENGER *from Corinth.*
MESSENGER *from within the palace.*
SERVANT *of* LA′ I-US.

MUTÆ PERSONÆ.

AN-TIG′ O-NE, } *Youthful daughters*
IS-ME′ NE, } *of* ŒDIPUS.
SUPPLIANTS; BOY, *attendant on* TIRESIAS; ATTENDANTS *on* ŒDIPUS, JOCASTA, *and* CREON, *two to each.*

SCENE, *before the royal palace in Bœotian Thebes. Along its front stand altars and images of the gods. The priest of Jupiter and certain aged companions, a few chosen youths and several children, all with woollen fillets upon olive branches, slowly enter from the city. They ascend the stage and place their suppliant boughs on the altars and statues of the gods, and then seat themselves on the steps of the former, looking expectantly toward the palace, from which, through its central door, Œdipus comes forth and addresses them.*

ΟΙΔΙΠΟΥΣ.

Ω ΤΕΚΝΑ, Κάδμου τοῦ πάλαι νέα τροφή, [*Introit.*
τίνας ποθ᾽ ἕδρας τάσδε μοι θοάζετε
ἱκτηρίοις κλάδοισιν ἐξεστεμμένοι;
πόλις δ᾽ ὁμοῦ μὲν θυμιαμάτων γέμει,
ὁμοῦ δὲ παιάνων τε καὶ στεναγμάτων·
ἁγὼ δικαιῶν μὴ παρ᾽ ἀγγέλων, τέκνα,
ἄλλων ἀκούειν αὐτὸς ὧδ᾽ ἐλήλυθα,
ὁ πᾶσι κλεινὸς Οἰδίπους καλούμενος.
ἀλλ᾽, ὦ γεραιέ, φράζ᾽, ἐπεὶ πρέπων ἔφυς
πρὸ τῶνδε φωνεῖν, τίνι τρόπῳ καθέστατε,
δείσαντες ἢ στέρξαντες; ὡς θέλοντος ἂν

ἐμοῦ προσαρκεῖν πᾶν· δυσάλγητος γὰρ ἂν
εἴην τοιάνδε μὴ οὐ κατοικτείρων ἕδραν.

ΙΕΡΕΥΣ.

ἀλλ', ὦ κρατύνων Οἰδίπους χώρας ἐμῆς,
ὁρᾷς μὲν ἡμᾶς ἡλίκοι προσήμεθα
βωμοῖσι τοῖς σοῖς, οἱ μὲν οὐδέπω μακρὰν
πτέσθαι σθένοντες, οἱ δὲ σὺν γήρᾳ βαρεῖς,
ἱερῆς, ἐγὼ μὲν Ζηνός, οἱ δ' ἐπ' ᾐθέων
λεκτοί· τὸ δ' ἄλλο φῦλον ἐξεστεμμένον
ἀγοραῖσι θακεῖ, πρός τε Παλλάδος διπλοῖς
ναοῖς, ἐπ' Ἰσμηνοῦ τε μαντείᾳ σποδῷ.
πόλις γάρ, ὥσπερ καὐτὸς εἰσορᾷς, ἄγαν
ἤδη σαλεύει κἀνακουφίσαι κάρα
βυθῶν ἔτ' οὐχ οἵα τε φοινίου σάλου,
φθίνουσα μὲν κάλυξιν ἐγκάρποις χθονός,
φθίνουσα δ' ἀγέλαις βουνόμοις, τόκοισί τε
ἀγόνοις γυναικῶν· ἐν δ' ὁ πυρφόρος θεὸς
σκήψας ἐλαύνει, λοιμὸς ἔχθιστος, πόλιν,
ὑφ' οὗ κενοῦται δῶμα Καδμεῖον· μέλας δ'
Ἅιδης στεναγμοῖς καὶ γόοις πλουτίζεται.
θεοῖσι μέν νυν οὐκ ἰσούμενόν σ' ἐγὼ
οὐδ' οἵδε παῖδες ἑζόμεσθ' ἐφέστιοι,
ἀνδρῶν δὲ πρῶτον ἔν τε συμφοραῖς βίου
κρίνοντες ἔν τε δαιμόνων συναλλαγαῖς·
ὅς τ' ἐξέλυσας, ἄστυ Καδμεῖον μολών,
σκληρᾶς ἀοιδοῦ δασμὸν ὃν παρείχομεν·
καὶ ταῦθ' ὑφ' ἡμῶν οὐδὲν ἐξειδὼς πλέον

οὐδ᾽ ἐκδιδαχθείς, ἀλλὰ προσθήκῃ θεοῦ
λέγει νομίζει θ᾽ ἡμὶν ὀρθῶσαι βίον·
νῦν τ᾽, ὦ κράτιστον πᾶσιν Οἰδίπου κάρα,
ἱκετεύομέν σε πάντες οἵδε πρόστροποι
ἀλκήν τιν᾽ εὑρεῖν ἡμίν, εἴτε του θεῶν
φήμην ἀκούσας εἴτ᾽ ἀπ᾽ ἀνδρὸς οἶσθά που·
ὡς τοῖσιν ἐμπείροισι καὶ τὰς ξυμφορὰς
ζώσας ὁρῶ μάλιστα τῶν βουλευμάτων.
ἴθ᾽, ὦ βροτῶν ἄριστ᾽, ἀνόρθωσον πόλιν·
ἴθ᾽, εὐλαβήθηθ᾽· ὡς σὲ νῦν μὲν ἥδε γῆ
σωτῆρα κλῄζει τῆς πάρος προθυμίας·
ἀρχῆς δὲ τῆς σῆς μηδαμῶς μεμνώμεθα
στάντες τ᾽ ἐς ὀρθὸν καὶ πεσόντες ὕστερον,
ἀλλ᾽ ἀσφαλείᾳ τήνδ᾽ ἀνόρθωσον πόλιν.
ὄρνιθι γὰρ καὶ τὴν τότ᾽ αἰσίῳ τύχην
παρέσχες ἡμῖν, καὶ τανῦν ἴσος γενοῦ.
ὡς εἴπερ ἄρξεις τῆσδε γῆς, ὥσπερ κρατεῖς,
ξὺν ἀνδράσιν κάλλιον ἢ κενῆς κρατεῖν·
ὡς οὐδέν ἐστιν οὔτε πύργος οὔτε ναῦς
ἔρημος ἀνδρῶν μὴ ξυνοικούντων ἔσω.

ΟΙΔΙΠΟΥΣ.

ὦ παῖδες οἰκτροί, γνωτὰ κοὐκ ἄγνωτά μοι
προσήλθεθ᾽ ἱμείροντες. εὖ γὰρ οἶδ᾽ ὅτι
νοσεῖτε πάντες, καὶ νοσοῦντες, ὡς ἐγὼ
οὐκ ἔστιν ὑμῶν ὅστις ἐξ ἴσου νοσεῖ.
τὸ μὲν γὰρ ὑμῶν ἄλγος εἰς ἕν᾽ ἔρχεται
μόνον καθ᾽ αὑτόν, κοὐδέν᾽ ἄλλον, ἡ δ᾽ ἐμὴ

ψυχὴ πόλιν τε κἀμὲ καὶ σ' ὁμοῦ στένει.
ὥστ' οὐχ ὕπνῳ γ' εὕδοντά μ' ἐξεγείρετε,
ἀλλ' ἴστε πολλὰ μέν με δακρύσαντα δή,
πολλὰς δ' ὁδοὺς ἐλθόντα φροντίδος πλάνοις.
ἣν δ' εὖ σκοπῶν εὕρισκον ἴασιν μόνην,
ταύτην ἔπραξα· παῖδα γὰρ Μενοικέως
Κρέοντ', ἐμαυτοῦ γαμβρόν, ἐς τὰ Πυθικὰ
ἔπεμψα Φοίβου δώμαθ', ὡς πύθοιθ' ὅ τι
δρῶν ἢ τί φωνῶν τήνδε ῥυσαίμην πόλιν.
καί μ' ἦμαρ ἤδη ξυμμετρούμενον χρόνῳ
λυπεῖ τί πράσσει· τοῦ γὰρ εἰκότος πέρα
ἄπεστι πλείω τοῦ καθήκοντος χρόνου.
ὅταν δ' ἵκηται, τηνικαῦτ' ἐγὼ κακὸς
μὴ δρῶν ἂν εἴην πάνθ' ὅσ' ἂν δηλοῖ θεός.

ΙΕΡΕΥΣ.

ἀλλ' εἰς καλὸν σύ τ' εἶπας οἵδε τ' ἀρτίως
Κρέοντα προσστείχοντα σημαίνουσί μοι.

ΟΙΔΙΠΟΥΣ.

ὦναξ Ἄπολλον, εἰ γὰρ ἐν τύχῃ γέ τῳ
σωτῆρι βαίη λαμπρὸς ὥσπερ ὄμματι.

ΙΕΡΕΥΣ.

ἀλλ' εἰκάσαι μέν, ἡδύς· οὐ γὰρ ἂν κάρα
πολυστεφὴς ὧδ' εἷρπε παγκάρπου δάφνης.

ΟΙΔΙΠΟΥΣ.

τάχ' εἰσόμεσθα· ξύμμετρος γὰρ ὡς κλύειν.
ἄναξ, ἐμὸν κήδευμα, παῖ Μενοικέως,
τίν' ἡμὶν ἥκεις τοῦ θεοῦ φήμην φέρων;

ΚΡΕΩΝ.

ἐσθλήν· λέγω γὰρ καὶ τὰ δύσφορ', εἰ τύχοι [Introit.
κατ' ὀρθὸν ἐξελθόντα, πάντ' ἂν εὐτυχεῖν.

ΟΙΔΙΠΟΥΣ.

ἔστιν δὲ ποῖον τοὔπος; οὔτε γὰρ θρασὺς
οὔτ' οὖν προδείσας εἰμὶ τῷ γε νῦν λόγῳ.

ΚΡΕΩΝ.

εἰ τῶνδε χρῄζεις πλησιαζόντων κλύειν,
ἕτοιμος εἰπεῖν, εἴτε καὶ στείχειν ἔσω.

ΟΙΔΙΠΟΥΣ.

ἐς πάντας αὔδα. τῶνδε γὰρ πλέον φέρω
τὸ πένθος ἢ καὶ τῆς ἐμῆς ψυχῆς πέρι.

ΚΡΕΩΝ.

λέγοιμ' ἂν οἷ' ἤκουσα τοῦ θεοῦ πάρα.
ἄνωγεν ἡμᾶς Φοῖβος ἐμφανῶς ἄναξ
μίασμα χώρας, ὡς τεθραμμένον χθονὶ
ἐν τῇδ', ἐλαύνειν, μηδ' ἀνήκεστον τρέφειν.

ΟΙΔΙΠΟΥΣ.

ποίῳ καθαρμῷ; τίς ὁ τρόπος τῆς ξυμφορᾶς;

ΚΡΕΩΝ.

ἀνδρηλατοῦντας, ἢ φόνῳ φόνον πάλιν
λύοντας, ὡς τόδ' αἷμα χειμάζον πόλιν.

ΟΙΔΙΠΟΥΣ.

ποίου γὰρ ἀνδρὸς τήνδε μηνύει τύχην;

ΚΡΕΩΝ.

ἦν ἡμὶν, ὦναξ, Λάϊός ποθ᾽ ἡγεμὼν
γῆς τῆσδε, πρὶν σὲ τήνδ᾽ ἀπευθύνειν πόλιν.

ΟΙΔΙΠΟΥΣ.

ἔξοιδ᾽ ἀκούων· οὐ γὰρ εἰσεῖδόν γέ πω.

ΚΡΕΩΝ.

τούτου θανόντος νῦν ἐπιστέλλει σαφῶς
τοὺς αὐτοέντας χειρὶ τιμωρεῖν τινας.

ΟΙΔΙΠΟΥΣ.

οἱ δ᾽ εἰσὶ ποῦ γῆς; ποῦ τόδ᾽ εὑρεθήσεται
ἴχνος παλαιᾶς δυστέκμαρτον αἰτίας;

ΚΡΕΩΝ.

ἐν τῇδ᾽ ἔφασκε γῇ. τὸ δὲ ζητούμενον
ἁλωτόν, ἐκφεύγει δὲ τἀμελούμενον.

ΟΙΔΙΠΟΥΣ.

πότερα δ᾽ ἐν οἴκοις, ἢ ᾽ν ἀγροῖς ὁ Λάϊος,
ἢ γῆς ἐπ᾽ ἄλλης τῷδε συμπίπτει φόνῳ;

ΚΡΕΩΝ.

θεωρός, ὡς ἔφασκεν, ἐκδημῶν, πάλιν
πρὸς οἶκον οὐκέθ᾽ ἵκεθ᾽, ὡς ἀπεστάλη.

ΟΙΔΙΠΟΥΣ.

οὐδ᾽ ἄγγελός τις οὐδὲ συμπράκτωρ ὁδοῦ
κατεῖδεν, οὗ τις ἐκμαθὼν ἐχρήσατ᾽ ἄν;

ΚΡΕΩΝ.

θνήσκουσι γάρ, πλὴν εἷς τις, ὃς φόβῳ φυγὼν
ὧν εἶδε πλὴν ἓν οὐδὲν εἶχ' εἰδὼς φράσαι.

ΟΙΔΙΠΟΥΣ.

τὸ ποῖον ; ἓν γὰρ πόλλ' ἂν ἐξεύροι μαθεῖν,
ἀρχὴν βραχεῖαν εἰ λάβοιμεν ἐλπίδος.

ΚΡΕΩΝ.

λῃστὰς ἔφασκε συντυχόντας οὐ μιᾷ
ῥώμῃ κτανεῖν νιν, ἀλλὰ σὺν πλήθει χερῶν.

ΟΙΔΙΠΟΥΣ.

πῶς οὖν ὁ λῃστής, εἴ τι μὴ ξὺν ἀργύρῳ
ἐπράσσετ' ἐνθένδ', ἐς τόδ' ἂν τόλμης ἔβη ;

ΚΡΕΩΝ.

δοκοῦντα ταῦτ' ἦν· Λαΐου δ' ὀλωλότος
οὐδεὶς ἀρωγὸς ἐν κακοῖς ἐγίγνετο.

ΟΙΔΙΠΟΥΣ.

κακὸν δὲ ποῖον ἐμποδὼν τυραννίδος
οὕτω πεσούσης εἶργε τοῦτ' ἐξειδέναι ;

ΚΡΕΩΝ.

ἡ ποικιλῳδὸς Σφὶγξ τὸ πρὸς ποσὶ σκοπεῖν
μεθέντας ἡμᾶς τἀφανῆ προσήγετο.

ΟΙΔΙΠΟΥΣ.

ἀλλ' ἐξ ὑπαρχῆς αὖθις αὔτ' ἐγὼ φανῶ.
ἐπαξίως γὰρ Φοῖβος, ἀξίως δὲ σὺ
πρὸς τοῦ θανόντος τήνδ' ἔθεσθ' ἐπιστροφήν·

ὥστ' ἐνδίκως ὄψεσθε κἀμὲ σύμμαχον,
γῇ τῇδε τιμωροῦντα τῷ θεῷ θ' ἅμα.
ὑπὲρ γὰρ οὐχὶ τῶν ἀπωτέρω φίλων,
ἀλλ' αὐτὸς αὑτοῦ, τοῦτ' ἀποσκεδῶ μύσος.
ὅστις γὰρ ἦν ἐκεῖνον ὁ κτανὼν τάχ' ἂν
κἄμ' ἂν τοιαύτῃ χειρὶ τιμωρεῖν θέλοι.
κείνῳ προσαρκῶν οὖν ἐμαυτὸν ὠφελῶ.
ἀλλ' ὡς τάχιστα, παῖδες, ὑμεῖς μὲν βάθρων
ἵστασθε, τούσδ' ἄραντες ἱκτῆρας κλάδους,
ἄλλος δὲ Κάδμου λαὸν ὧδ' ἀθροιζέτω,
ὡς πᾶν ἐμοῦ δράσοντος. ἢ γὰρ εὐτυχεῖς
σὺν τῷ θεῷ φανούμεθ', ἢ πεπτωκότες.

[*Exeunt* Œdipus *et* Creon.

ΙΕΡΕΥΣ.

ὦ παῖδες, ἱστώμεσθα. τῶνδε γὰρ χάριν
καὶ δεῦρ' ἔβημεν ὧν ὅδ' ἐξαγγέλλεται.
Φοῖβος δ' ὁ πέμψας τάσδε μαντείας ἅμα
σωτήρ θ' ἵκοιτο καὶ νόσου παυστήριος.

[*Exeunt supplices.*

ΧΟΡΟΣ.

στρ. ά.

ὦ Διὸς ἁδυεπὲς Φάτι, τίς ποτε τᾶς πολυχρύσου [*Introit.*
Πυθῶνος ἀγλαὰς ἔβας
Θήβας; ἐκτέταμαι, φοβερὰν φρένα δείματι πάλλων,
ἰήϊε Δάλιε Παιάν,
ἀμφὶ σοὶ ἁζόμενος, τί μοι ἢ νέον ἢ περιτελλομέναις
ὥραις πάλιν
ἐξανύσεις χρέος· εἰπέ μοι, ὦ χρυσέας τέκνον Ἐλπίδος, ἄμβροτε Φάμα.

ἀντ. ά.

πρῶτά σε κεκλόμενος, θύγατερ Διός, ἄμβροτ' Ἀθάνα,
γαιάοχόν τ' ἀδελφεὰν
Ἄρτεμιν, ἃ κυκλόεντ' ἀγορᾶς θρόνον εὐκλέα θάσσει,
καὶ Φοῖβον ἑκαβόλον, ἰώ,
τρισσοὶ ἀλεξίμοροι προφάνητέ μοι, εἴ ποτε καὶ προτέρας ἄτας ὕπερ
ὀρνυμένας πόλει ἠνύσατ' ἐκτοπίαν φλόγα πήματος, ἔλθετε καὶ νῦν.

στρ. β'.

ὦ πόποι, ἀνάριθμα γὰρ φέρω
πήματα· νοσεῖ δέ μοι πρόπας
στόλος, οὐδ' ἔνι φροντίδος ἔγχος
ᾧ τις ἀλέξεται· οὔτε γὰρ ἔκγονα
κλυτᾶς χθονὸς αὔξεται, οὔτε τόκοισιν
ἰηΐων καμάτων ἀνέχουσι γυναῖκες·
ἄλλον δ' ἂν ἄλλῳ προσίδοις, ἅπερ εὔπτερον ὄρνιν
κρεῖσσον ἀμαιμακέτου πυρὸς ὄρμενον
ἀκτὰν πρὸς ἑσπέρου θεοῦ·

ἀντ. β'.

ὧν πόλις ἀνάριθμος ὄλλυται·
νηλέα δὲ γένεθλα πρὸς πέδῳ
θαναταφόρα κεῖται ἀνοίκτως·
ἐν δ' ἄλοχοι πολιαί τ' ἐπὶ ματέρες
ἀκτὰν παρὰ βώμιον ἄλλοθεν ἄλλαι
λυγρῶν πόνων ἱκτῆρες ἐπιστενάχουσιν.
παιὰν δὲ λάμπει στονόεσσά τε γῆρυς ὅμαυλος·
ὧν ὕπερ, ὦ χρυσέα θύγατερ Διός,
εὐῶπα πέμψον ἀλκάν·

στρ. γ΄.

Ἀρεά τε τὸν μαλερόν, ὃς νῦν ἄχαλκος ἀσπίδων
φλέγει με περιβόατος ἀντιάζων,
παλίσσυτον δράμημα νωτίσαι πάτρας
ἄπουρον, εἴτ᾽ ἐς μέγαν θάλαμον Ἀμφιτρίτας,
εἴτ᾽ ἐς τὸν ἀπόξενον ὅρμον Θρῄκιον κλύδωνα·
τέλει γὰρ εἴ τι νὺξ ἀφῇ, τοῦτ᾽ ἐπ᾽ ἦμαρ ἔρχεται·
τόν, ὦ τᾶν πυρφόρων ἀστραπᾶν κράτη νέμων,
ὦ Ζεῦ πάτερ, ὑπὸ σῷ φθίσον κεραυνῷ.

ἀντ. γ΄.

Λύκει᾽ ἄναξ, τά τε σὰ χρυσοστρόφων ἀπ᾽ ἀγκυλᾶν
βέλεα θέλοιμ᾽ ἂν ἀδάματ᾽ ἐνδατεῖσθαι
ἀρωγὰ προσταχθέντα, τάς τε πυρφόρους
Ἀρτέμιδος αἴγλας, ξὺν αἷς Λύκι᾽ ὄρη διᾴσσει· [*Introit* Œd.
τὸν χρυσομίτραν τε κικλήσκω τᾶσδ᾽ ἐπώνυμον γᾶς,
οἰνῶπα Βάκχον εὔιον, Μαινάδων ὁμόστολον
πελασθῆναι φλέγοντ᾽ ἀγλαῶπι σύμμαχον
πεύκᾳ ᾽πὶ τὸν ἀπότιμον ἐν θεοῖς θεόν.

ΟΙΔΙΠΟΥΣ.

αἰτεῖς· ἃ δ᾽ αἰτεῖς, τἄμ᾽ ἐὰν θέλῃς ἔπη
κλύων δέχεσθαι τῇ νόσῳ θ᾽ ὑπηρετεῖν,
ἀλκὴν λάβοις ἂν κἀνακούφισιν κακῶν·
ἁγὼ ξένος μὲν τοῦ λόγου τοῦδ᾽ ἐξερῶ,
ξένος δὲ τοῦ πραχθέντος. οὐ γὰρ ἂν μακρὰν
ἴχνευον αὐτός, οὐκ ἔχων τι σύμβολον.
νῦν δ᾽, ὕστερος γὰρ ἀστὸς εἰς ἀστοὺς τελῶ,
ὑμῖν προφωνῶ πᾶσι Καδμείοις τάδε·
ὅστις ποθ᾽ ὑμῶν Λάϊον τὸν Λαβδάκου

κάτοιδεν ἀνδρὸς ἐκ τίνος διώλετο,
τοῦτον κελεύω πάντα σημαίνειν ἐμοί·
κεἰ μὲν φοβεῖται, τοὐπίκλημ' ὑπεξελὼν
αὐτὸς καθ' αὑτοῦ. πείσεται γὰρ ἄλλο μὲν
ἀστεργὲς οὐδέν, γῆς δ' ἄπεισιν ἀσφαλής·
εἰ δ' αὖ τις ἄλλον οἶδεν ἐξ ἄλλης χθονὸς
τὸν αὐτόχειρα, μὴ σιωπάτω· τὸ γὰρ
κέρδος τελῶ 'γὼ χἠ χάρις προσκείσεται.
εἰ δ' αὖ σιωπήσεσθε, καί τις ἢ φίλου
δείσας ἀπώσει τοὔπος ἢ χαὐτοῦ τόδε,
ἁκ τῶνδε δράσω, ταῦτα χρὴ κλύειν ἐμοῦ.
τὸν ἄνδρ' ἀπαυδῶ τοῦτον, ὅστις ἐστί, γῆς
τῆσδ', ἧς ἐγὼ κράτη τε καὶ θρόνους νέμω,
μήτ' ἐσδέχεσθαι μήτε προσφωνεῖν τινα,
μήτ' ἐν θεῶν εὐχαῖσι μήτε θύμασιν
κοινὸν ποιεῖσθαι, μήτε χέρνιβος νέμειν·
ὠθεῖν δ' ἀπ' οἴκων πάντας, ὡς μιάσματος
τοῦδ' ἡμὶν ὄντος, ὡς τὸ Πυθικὸν θεοῦ
μαντεῖον ἐξέφηνεν ἀρτίως ἐμοί.
ἐγὼ μὲν οὖν τοιόσδε τῷ τε δαίμονι
τῷ τ' ἀνδρὶ τῷ θανόντι σύμμαχος πέλω·
κατεύχομαι δὲ τὸν δεδρακότ', εἴτε τις
εἷς ὢν λέληθεν εἴτε πλειόνων μέτα,
κακὸν κακῶς νιν ἄμορον ἐκτρῖψαι βίον.
ἐπεύχομαι δ', οἴκοισιν εἰ ξυνέστιος
ἐν τοῖς ἐμοῖς γένοιτ' ἐμοῦ συνειδότος,
παθεῖν ἅπερ τοῖσδ' ἀρτίως ἠρασάμην.
ὑμῖν δὲ ταῦτα πάντ' ἐπισκήπτω τελεῖν,

ὑπέρ τ' ἐμαυτοῦ, τοῦ θεοῦ τε, τῆσδέ τε
γῆς ὧδ' ἀκάρπως κἀθέως ἐφθαρμένης.
οὐδ' εἰ γὰρ ἦν τὸ πρᾶγμα μὴ θεήλατον,
ἀκάθαρτον ὑμᾶς εἰκὸς ἦν οὕτως ἐᾶν,
ἀνδρός γ' ἀρίστου βασιλέως τ' ὀλωλότος,
ἀλλ' ἐξερευνᾶν· νῦν δ' ἐπεὶ κυρῶ γ' ἐγὼ
ἔχων μὲν ἀρχάς, ἃς ἐκεῖνος εἶχε πρίν,
ἔχων δὲ λέκτρα καὶ γυναῖχ' ὁμόσπορον,
κοινῶν τε παίδων κοίν' ἄν, εἰ κείνῳ γένος
μὴ 'δυστύχησεν, ἦν ἂν ἐκπεφυκότα,
νῦν δ' ἐς τὸ κείνου κρᾶτ' ἐνήλαθ' ἡ τύχη·
ἀνθ' ὧν ἐγὼ τάδ', ὡσπερεὶ τοὐμοῦ πατρός,
ὑπερμαχοῦμαι κἀπὶ πάντ' ἀφίξομαι,
ζητῶν τὸν αὐτόχειρα τοῦ φόνου λαβεῖν
τῷ Λαβδακείῳ παιδὶ Πολυδώρου τε καὶ
τοῦ πρόσθε Κάδμου τοῦ πάλαι τ' Ἀγήνορος·
καὶ ταῦτα τοῖς μὴ δρῶσιν εὔχομαι θεοὺς
μήτ' ἄροτον αὐτοῖς γῆς ἀνιέναι τινὰ
μήτ' οὖν γυναικῶν παῖδας, ἀλλὰ τῷ πότμῳ
τῷ νῦν φθερεῖσθαι κἄτι τοῦδ' ἐχθίονι·
ὑμῖν δὲ τοῖς ἄλλοισι Καδμείοις, ὅσοις
τάδ' ἔστ' ἀρέσκονθ', ἥ τε σύμμαχος Δίκη
χοἰ πάντες εὖ ξυνεῖεν εἰσαεὶ θεοί.

ΧΟΡΟΣ.

ὥσπερ μ' ἀραῖον ἔλαβες, ὧδ', ἄναξ, ἐρῶ.
οὔτ' ἔκτανον γὰρ οὔτε τὸν κτανόντ' ἔχω
δεῖξαι. τὸ δὲ ζήτημα τοῦ πέμψαντος ἦν
Φοίβου τόδ' εἰπεῖν, ὅστις εἴργασταί ποτε.

ΟΙΔΙΠΟΥΣ.

δίκαι' ἔλεξας· ἀλλ' ἀναγκάσαι θεοὺς
ἂν μὴ θέλωσιν οὐδ' ἂν εἷς δύναιτ' ἀνήρ.

ΧΟΡΟΣ.

τὰ δεύτερ' ἐκ τῶνδ' ἂν λέγοιμ' ἁμοὶ δοκεῖ.

ΟΙΔΙΠΟΥΣ.

εἰ καὶ τρίτ' ἐστι, μὴ παρῇς τὸ μὴ οὐ φράσαι.

ΧΟΡΟΣ.

ἄνακτ' ἄνακτι ταὔθ' ὁρῶντ' ἐπίσταμαι
μάλιστα Φοίβῳ Τειρεσίαν, παρ' οὗ τις ἂν
σκοπῶν τάδ', ὦναξ, ἐκμάθοι σαφέστατα.

ΟΙΔΙΠΟΥΣ.

ἀλλ' οὐκ ἐν ἀργοῖς οὐδὲ τοῦτ' ἐπραξάμην.
ἔπεμψα γὰρ Κρέοντος εἰπόντος διπλοῦς
πομπούς· πάλαι δὲ μὴ παρὼν θαυμάζεται.

ΧΟΡΟΣ.

καὶ μὴν τά γ' ἄλλα κωφὰ καὶ παλαί' ἔπη.

ΟΙΔΙΠΟΥΣ.

τὰ ποῖα ταῦτα; πάντα γὰρ σκοπῶ λόγον.

ΧΟΡΟΣ.

θανεῖν ἐλέχθη πρός τινων ὁδοιπόρων.

ΟΙΔΙΠΟΥΣ.

ἤκουσα κἀγώ· τὸν δ' ἰδόντ' οὐδεὶς ὁρᾷ.

ΧΟΡΟΣ.

ἀλλ' εἴ τι μὲν δὴ δειμάτων ἔχει μέρος,
τὰς σὰς ἀκούων οὐ μενεῖ τοιάσδ' ἀράς.

ΟΙΔΙΠΟΥΣ.

ᾧ μή 'στι δρῶντι τάρβος, οὐδ' ἔπος φοβεῖ.

ΧΟΡΟΣ.

ἀλλ' οὑξελέγχων αὐτὸν ἔστιν· οἵδε γὰρ
τὸν θεῖον ἤδη μάντιν ὧδ' ἄγουσιν, ᾧ
τἀληθὲς ἐμπέφυκεν ἀνθρώπων μόνῳ.

ΟΙΔΙΠΟΥΣ.

ὦ πάντα νωμῶν Τειρεσία, διδακτά τε
ἄρρητά τ', οὐράνιά τε καὶ χθονοστιβῆ, [*Introit* TIRESIAS.
πόλιν μέν, εἰ καὶ μὴ βλέπεις, φρονεῖς δ' ὅμως
οἵᾳ νόσῳ σύνεστιν· ἧς σὲ προστάτην
σωτῆρά τ', ὦναξ, μοῦνον ἐξευρίσκομεν.
Φοῖβος γάρ, εἰ καὶ μὴ κλύεις τῶν ἀγγέλων,
πέμψασιν ἡμῖν ἀντέπεμψεν, ἔκλυσιν
μόνην ἂν ἐλθεῖν τοῦδε τοῦ νοσήματος,
εἰ τοὺς κτανόντας Λάϊον μαθόντες εὖ
κτείναιμεν, ἢ γῆς φυγάδας ἐκπεμψαίμεθα.
σὺ δ' οὖν φθονήσας μήτ' ἀπ' οἰωνῶν φάτιν
μήτ' εἴ τιν' ἄλλην μαντικῆς ἔχεις ὁδόν,
ῥῦσαι σεαυτὸν καὶ πόλιν, ῥῦσαι δ' ἐμέ,
ῥῦσαι δὲ πᾶν μίασμα τοῦ τεθνηκότος.
ἐν σοὶ γὰρ ἐσμέν· ἄνδρα δ' ὠφελεῖν ἀφ' ὧν
ἔχοι τε καὶ δύναιτο κάλλιστος πόνων.

ΤΕΙΡΕΣΙΑΣ.

φεῦ φεῦ, φρονεῖν ὡς δεινὸν ἔνθα μὴ τέλη
λύῃ φρονοῦντι. ταῦτα γὰρ καλῶς ἐγὼ
εἰδὼς διώλεσ᾽· οὐ γὰρ ἂν δεῦρ᾽ ἱκόμην.

ΟΙΔΙΠΟΥΣ.

τί δ᾽ ἔστιν; ὡς ἄθυμος εἰσελήλυθας.

ΤΕΙΡΕΣΙΑΣ.

ἄφες μ᾽ ἐς οἴκους· ῥᾷστα γὰρ τὸ σόν τε σὺ
κἀγὼ διοίσω τοὐμόν, ἢν ἐμοὶ πίθῃ.

ΟΙΔΙΠΟΥΣ.

οὔτ᾽ ἔννομ᾽ εἶπας οὔτε προσφιλῆ πόλει
τῇδ᾽, ἥ σ᾽ ἔθρεψε, τήνδ᾽ ἀποστερῶν φάτιν.

ΤΕΙΡΕΣΙΑΣ.

ὁρῶ γὰρ οὐδὲ σοὶ τὸ σὸν φώνημ᾽ ἰὸν
πρὸς καιρόν· ὡς οὖν μηδ᾽ ἐγὼ ταὐτὸν πάθω —

ΟΙΔΙΠΟΥΣ.

μὴ πρὸς θεῶν φρονῶν γ᾽ ἀποστραφῇς, ἐπεὶ
πάντες σε προσκυνοῦμεν οἵδ᾽ ἱκτήριοι.

ΤΕΙΡΕΣΙΑΣ.

πάντες γὰρ οὐ φρονεῖτ᾽. ἐγὼ δ᾽ οὐ μή ποτε
τἄμ᾽ ὡς ἂν εἴπω μὴ τὰ σ᾽ ἐκφήνω κακά.

ΟΙΔΙΠΟΥΣ.

τί φῄς; ξυνειδὼς οὐ φράσεις, ἀλλ᾽ ἐννοεῖς
ἡμᾶς προδοῦναι καὶ καταφθεῖραι πόλιν;

ΤΕΙΡΕΣΙΑΣ.

ἐγὼ οὔτ' ἐμαυτὸν οὔτε σ' ἀλγυνῶ. τί ταῦτ'
ἄλλως ἐλέγχεις; οὐ γὰρ ἂν πύθοιό μου.

ΟΙΔΙΠΟΥΣ.

οὐκ, ὦ κακῶν κάκιστε, καὶ γὰρ ἂν πέτρου
φύσιν σύ γ' ὀργάνειας, ἐξερεῖς ποτε,
ἀλλ' ὧδ' ἄτεγκτος κἀτελεύτητος φανεῖ;

ΤΕΙΡΕΣΙΑΣ.

ὀργὴν ἐμέμψω τὴν ἐμήν, τὴν σὴν δ' ὁμοῦ
ναίουσαν οὐ κατεῖδες, ἀλλ' ἐμὲ ψέγεις.

ΟΙΔΙΠΟΥΣ.

τίς γὰρ τοιαῦτ' ἂν οὐκ ἂν ὀργίζοιτ' ἔπη
κλύων, ἃ νῦν σὺ τήνδ' ἀτιμάζεις πόλιν;

ΤΕΙΡΕΣΙΑΣ.

ἥξει γὰρ αὐτά, κἂν ἐγὼ σιγῇ στέγω.

ΟΙΔΙΠΟΥΣ.

οὐκοῦν ἅ γ' ἥξει καὶ σὲ χρὴ λέγειν ἐμοί.

ΤΕΙΡΕΣΙΑΣ.

οὐκ ἂν πέρα φράσαιμι. πρὸς τάδ', εἰ θέλεις,
θυμοῦ δι' ὀργῆς ἥτις ἀγριωτάτη.

ΟΙΔΙΠΟΥΣ.

καὶ μὴν παρήσω γ' οὐδέν, ὡς ὀργῆς ἔχω,
ἅπερ ξυνίημ'. ἴσθι γὰρ δοκῶν ἐμοὶ
καὶ ξυμφυτεῦσαι τοὔργον, εἰργάσθαι θ', ὅσον
μὴ χερσὶ καίνων· εἰ δ' ἐτύγχανες βλέπων,
καὶ τοὔργον ἂν σοῦ τοῦτ' ἔφην εἶναι μόνου.

ΤΕΙΡΕΣΙΑΣ.

ἄληθες ; ἐννέπω δὲ τῷ κηρύγματι
ᾧπερ προεῖπας ἐμμένειν, κἀφ' ἡμέρας
τῆς νῦν προσαυδᾶν μήτε τούσδε μήτ' ἐμέ,
ὡς ὄντι γῆς τῆσδ' ἀνοσίῳ μιάστορι.

ΟΙΔΙΠΟΥΣ.

οὕτως ἀναιδῶς ἐξεκίνησας τόδε
τὸ ῥῆμα ; καὶ ποῦ τοῦτο φεύξεσθαι δοκεῖς ;

ΤΕΙΡΕΣΙΑΣ.

πέφευγα· τἀληθὲς γὰρ ἰσχῦον τρέφω.

ΟΙΔΙΠΟΥΣ.

πρὸς τοῦ διδαχθείς ; οὐ γὰρ ἔκ γε τῆς τέχνης.

ΤΕΙΡΕΣΙΑΣ.

πρὸς σοῦ· σὺ γάρ μ' ἄκοντα προὐτρέψω λέγειν.

ΟΙΔΙΠΟΥΣ.

ποῖον λόγον ; λέγ' αὖθις, ὡς μᾶλλον μάθω.

ΤΕΙΡΕΣΙΑΣ.

οὐχὶ ξυνῆκας πρόσθεν ; ἢ 'κπειρᾷ λόγῳ ;

ΟΙΔΙΠΟΥΣ.

οὐχ ὥστε γ' εἰπεῖν γνωστόν· ἀλλ' αὖθις φράσον.

ΤΕΙΡΕΣΙΑΣ.

φονέα σέ φημι τἀνδρὸς οὗ ζητεῖς κυρεῖν.

ΟΙΔΙΠΟΥΣ.

ἀλλ' οὔ τι χαίρων δίς γε πημονὰς ἐρεῖς.

ΤΕΙΡΕΣΙΑΣ.

εἴπω τι δῆτα κἄλλ', ἵν' ὀργίζῃ πλέον;

ΟΙΔΙΠΟΥΣ.

ὅσον γε χρῄζεις· ὡς μάτην εἰρήσεται.

ΤΕΙΡΕΣΙΑΣ.

λεληθέναι σέ φημι σὺν τοῖς φιλτάτοις
αἴσχισθ' ὁμιλοῦντ', οὐδ' ὁρᾶν ἵν' εἶ κακοῦ.

ΟΙΔΙΠΟΥΣ.

ἦ καὶ γεγηθὼς ταῦτ' ἀεὶ λέξειν δοκεῖς;

ΤΕΙΡΕΣΙΑΣ.

εἴπερ τί γ' ἔστι τῆς ἀληθείας σθένος.

ΟΙΔΙΠΟΥΣ.

ἀλλ' ἔστι, πλὴν σοί· σοὶ δὲ τοῦτ' οὐκ ἔστ', ἐπεὶ
τυφλὸς τά τ' ὦτα τόν τε νοῦν τά τ' ὄμματ' εἶ.

ΤΕΙΡΕΣΙΑΣ.

σὺ δ' ἄθλιός γε ταῦτ' ὀνειδίζων, ἃ σοὶ
οὐδεὶς ὃς οὐχὶ τῶνδ' ὀνειδιεῖ τάχα.

ΟΙΔΙΠΟΥΣ.

μιᾶς τρέφει πρὸς νυκτός, ὥστε μήτ' ἐμὲ
μήτ' ἄλλον, ὅστις φῶς ὁρᾷ, βλάψαι ποτ' ἄν.

ΤΕΙΡΕΣΙΑΣ.

οὐ γάρ σε μοῖρα πρός γ' ἐμοῦ πεσεῖν, ἐπεὶ
ἱκανὸς Ἀπόλλων, ᾧ τάδ' ἐκπρᾶξαι μέλει.

ΟΙΔΙΠΟΥΣ.

Κρέοντος, ἢ σοῦ ταῦτα τἀξευρήματα;

ΤΕΙΡΕΣΙΑΣ.

Κρέων δέ σοι πῆμ' οὐδέν, ἀλλ' αὐτὸς σὺ σοί.

ΟΙΔΙΠΟΤΣ.

ὦ πλοῦτε καὶ τυραννὶ καὶ τέχνη τέχνης
ὑπερφέρουσα τῷ πολυζήλῳ βίῳ,
ὅσος παρ' ὑμῖν ὁ φθόνος φυλάσσεται,
εἰ τῆσδέ γ' ἀρχῆς οὕνεχ', ἣν ἐμοὶ πόλις
δωρητόν, οὐκ αἰτητόν, εἰσεχείρισεν,
ταύτης Κρέων ὁ πιστός, οὑξ ἀρχῆς φίλος,
λάθρα μ' ὑπελθὼν ἐκβαλεῖν ἱμείρεται,
ὑφεὶς μάγον τοιόνδε μηχανορράφον,
δόλιον ἀγύρτην, ὅστις ἐν τοῖς κέρδεσιν
μόνον δέδορκε, τὴν τέχνην δ' ἔφυ τυφλός.
ἐπεί, φέρ' εἰπέ, ποῦ σὺ μάντις εἶ σαφής;
πῶς οὐχ, ὅθ' ἡ ῥαψῳδὸς ἐνθάδ' ἦν κύων,
ηὔδας τι τοῖσδ' ἀστοῖσιν ἐκλυτήριον;
καίτοι τό γ' αἴνιγμ' οὐχὶ τοὐπιόντος ἦν
ἀνδρὸς διειπεῖν, ἀλλὰ μαντείας ἔδει·
ἣν οὔτ' ἀπ' οἰωνῶν σὺ προυφάνης ἔχων
οὔτ' ἐκ θεῶν του γνωτόν· ἀλλ' ἐγὼ μολών,
ὁ μηδὲν εἰδὼς Οἰδίπους, ἔπαυσά νιν,
γνώμῃ κυρήσας οὐδ' ἀπ' οἰωνῶν μαθών·
ὃν δὴ σὺ πειρᾷς ἐκβαλεῖν, δοκῶν θρόνοις
παραστατήσειν τοῖς Κρεοντείοις πέλας.
κλαίων δοκεῖς μοι καὶ σὺ χὠ συνθεὶς τάδε
ἀγηλατήσειν· εἰ δὲ μὴ 'δόκεις γέρων
εἶναι, παθὼν ἔγνως ἂν οἷά περ φρονεῖς.

ΧΟΡΟΣ.

ἡμῖν μὲν εἰκάζουσι καὶ τὰ τοῦδ' ἔπη
ὀργῇ λελέχθαι καὶ τὰ σ', Οἰδίπου, δοκεῖ.
δεῖ δ' οὐ τοιούτων, ἀλλ' ὅπως τὰ τοῦ θεοῦ
μαντεῖ' ἄριστα λύσομεν, τόδε σκοπεῖν.

ΤΕΙΡΕΣΙΑΣ.

εἰ καὶ τυραννεῖς, ἐξισωτέον τὸ γοῦν
ἴσ' ἀντιλέξαι· τοῦδε γὰρ κἀγὼ κρατῶ.
οὐ γάρ τι σοὶ ζῶ δοῦλος, ἀλλὰ Λοξίᾳ·
ὥστ' οὐ Κρέοντος προστάτου γεγράψομαι.
λέγω δ', ἐπειδὴ καὶ τυφλόν μ' ὠνείδισας,
σὺ καὶ δέδορκας κοὐ βλέπεις ἵν' εἶ κακοῦ,
οὐδ' ἔνθα ναίεις, οὐδ' ὅτων οἰκεῖς μέτα,
—ἆρ' οἶσθ' ἀφ' ὧν εἶ;—καὶ λέληθας ἐχθρὸς ὢν
τοῖς σοῖσιν αὐτοῦ νέρθε κἀπὶ γῆς ἄνω,
καί σ' ἀμφιπλὴξ μητρός τε καὶ τοῦ σοῦ πατρὸς
ἐλᾷ ποτ' ἐκ γῆς τῆσδε δεινόπους ἀρά,
βλέποντα νῦν μὲν ὄρθ', ἔπειτα δὲ σκότον.
βοῆς δὲ τῆς σῆς ποῖος οὐκ ἔσται λιμήν,
ποῖος Κιθαιρὼν οὐχὶ σύμφωνος τάχα,
ὅταν καταίσθῃ τὸν ὑμέναιον, ὃν δόμοις
ἄνορμον εἰσέπλευσας, εὐπλοίας τυχών;
ἄλλων δὲ πλῆθος οὐκ ἐπαισθάνει κακῶν,
ἅ σ' ἐξισώσει σοί τε καὶ τοῖς σοῖς τέκνοις.
πρὸς ταῦτα καὶ Κρέοντα καὶ τοὐμὸν στόμα
προπηλάκιζε. σοῦ γὰρ οὐκ ἔστιν βροτῶν
κάκιον ὅστις ἐκτριβήσεταί ποτε.

ΟΙΔΙΠΟΥΣ.

ἦ ταῦτα δῆτ᾽ ἀνεκτὰ πρὸς τούτου κλύειν;
οὐκ εἰς ὄλεθρον; οὐχὶ θᾶσσον; οὐ πάλιν
ἄψορρος οἴκων τῶνδ᾽ ἀποστραφεὶς ἄπει;

ΤΕΙΡΕΣΙΑΣ.

οὐδ᾽ ἱκόμην ἔγωγ᾽ ἄν, εἰ σὺ μὴ ᾽κάλεις.

ΟΙΔΙΠΟΥΣ.

οὐ γάρ τί σ᾽ ᾔδη μῶρα φωνήσοντ᾽, ἐπεὶ
σχολῇ σ᾽ ἂν οἴκους τοὺς ἐμοὺς ἐστειλάμην.

ΤΕΙΡΕΣΙΑΣ.

ἡμεῖς τοιοίδ᾽ ἔφυμεν, ὡς μὲν σοὶ δοκεῖ,
μῶροι, γονεῦσι δ᾽, οἵ σ᾽ ἔφυσαν, ἔμφρονες.

ΟΙΔΙΠΟΥΣ.

ποίοισι; μεῖνον. τίς δέ μ᾽ ἐκφύει βροτῶν;

ΤΕΙΡΕΣΙΑΣ.

ἥδ᾽ ἡμέρα φύσει σε καὶ διαφθερεῖ.

ΟΙΔΙΠΟΥΣ.

ὡς πάντ᾽ ἄγαν αἰνικτὰ κἀσαφῆ λέγεις.

ΤΕΙΡΕΣΙΑΣ.

οὔκουν σὺ ταῦτ᾽ ἄριστος εὑρίσκειν ἔφυς;

ΟΙΔΙΠΟΥΣ.

τοιαῦτ᾽ ὀνείδιζ᾽, οἷς ἔμ᾽ εὑρήσεις μέγαν.

ΤΕΙΡΕΣΙΑΣ.

αὕτη γε μέντοι σ᾽ ἡ τύχη διώλεσεν.

ΟΙΔΙΠΟΥΣ.

ἀλλ' εἰ πόλιν τήνδ' ἐξέσωσ', οὔ μοι μέλει.

ΤΕΙΡΕΣΙΑΣ.

ἄπειμι τοίνυν· καὶ σύ, παῖ, κόμιζέ με.

ΟΙΔΙΠΟΥΣ.

κομιζέτω δῆθ'· ὡς παρὼν σύ γ' ἐμποδὼν
ὀχλεῖς, συθείς τ' ἂν οὐκ ἂν ἀλγύναις πλέον.

ΤΕΙΡΕΣΙΑΣ.

εἰπὼν ἄπειμ' ὧν οὕνεκ' ἦλθον, οὐ τὸ σὸν
δείσας πρόσωπον· οὐ γὰρ ἔσθ' ὅπου μ' ὀλεῖς.
λέγω δέ σοι, τὸν ἄνδρα τοῦτον, ὃν πάλαι
ζητεῖς ἀπειλῶν κἀνακηρύσσων φόνον
τὸν Λαΐειον, οὗτός ἐστιν ἐνθάδε,
ξένος λόγῳ μέτοικος, εἶτα δ' ἐγγενὴς
φανήσεται Θηβαῖος, οὐδ' ἡσθήσεται
τῇ ξυμφορᾷ· τυφλὸς γὰρ ἐκ δεδορκότος
καὶ πτωχὸς ἀντὶ πλουσίου ξένην ἔπι
σκήπτρῳ προδεικνὺς γαῖαν ἐμπορεύσεται.
φανήσεται δὲ παισὶ τοῖς αὑτοῦ ξυνὼν
ἀδελφὸς αὑτὸς καὶ πατήρ, κἀξ ἧς ἔφυ
γυναικὸς υἱὸς καὶ πόσις, καὶ τοῦ πατρὸς
ὁμόσπορός τε καὶ φονεύς. καὶ ταῦτ' ἰὼν
εἴσω λογίζου· κἂν λάβῃς ἐψευσμένον,
φάσκειν ἔμ' ἤδη μαντικῇ μηδὲν φρονεῖν. [*Exeunt.*

ΧΟΡΟΣ.

στρ. ά.

τίς ὅντιν' ἁ θεσπιέπεια Δελφὶς εἶπε πέτρα
ἄρρητ' ἀρρήτων τελέσαντα φοινίαισι χερσίν;

ὥρα νιν ἀελλάδων
ἵππων σθεναρώτερον
φυγᾷ πόδα νωμᾶν.
ἔνοπλος γὰρ ἐπ' αὐτὸν ἐπενθρώσκει
πυρὶ καὶ στεροπαῖς ὁ Διὸς γενέτας·
δειναὶ δ' ἅμ' ἕπονται Κῆρες ἀναπλάκητοι.

ἀντ. α'.

ἔλαμψε γὰρ τοῦ νιφόεντος ἀρτίως φανεῖσα
φάμα Παρνασοῦ τὸν ἄδηλον ἄνδρα πάντ' ἰχνεύειν.
φοιτᾷ γὰρ ὑπ' ἀγρίαν
ὕλαν ἀνά τ' ἄντρα καὶ
πετραῖος ὁ ταῦρος,
μέλεος μελέῳ ποδὶ χηρεύων,
τὰ μεσόμφαλα γᾶς ἀπονοσφίζων
μαντεῖα· τὰ δ' ἀεὶ ζῶντα περιποτᾶται.

στρ. β'.

δεινὰ μὲν οὖν, δεινὰ ταράσσει σοφὸς οἰωνοθέτας
οὔτε δοκοῦντ' οὔτ' ἀποφάσκονθ'· ὅ τι λέξω δ' ἀπορῶ.
πέτομαι δ' ἐλπίσιν οὔτ' ἐνθάδ' ὁρῶν οὔτ' ὀπίσω.
τί γὰρ ἢ Λαβδακίδαις
ἢ τῷ Πολύβου νεῖκος ἔκειτ' οὔτε πάροιθέν ποτ' ἔγωγ' οὔτε τανῦν πω
ἔμαθον, πρὸς ὅτου χρησάμενος δὴ βασάνῳ
ἐπὶ τὰν ἐπίδαμον
φάτιν εἶμ' Οἰδιπόδα Λαβδακίδαις ἐπίκουρος ἀδήλων θανάτων.

ἀντ. β'.

ἀλλ' ὁ μὲν οὖν Ζεὺς ὅ τ' Ἀπόλλων ξυνετοὶ καὶ τὰ βροτῶν

εἰδότες· ἀνδρῶν δ' ὅτι μάντις πλέον ἢ 'γὼ φέρεται,
κρίσις οὐκ ἔστιν ἀληθής· σοφίᾳ δ' ἂν σοφίαν
παραμείψειεν ἀνήρ.
ἀλλ' οὔποτ' ἔγωγ' ἄν, πρὶν ἴδοιμ' ὀρθὸν ἔπος, μεμφομένων
ἂν καταφαίην.
φανερὰ γὰρ ἐπ' αὐτῷ πτερόεσσ' ἦλθε κόρα
ποτέ, καὶ σοφὸς ὤφθη
βασάνῳ θ' ἁδύπολις· τῷ ἀπ' ἐμᾶς φρενὸς οὔποτ' ὀφλήσει
κακίαν.

ΚΡΕΩΝ.

ἄνδρες πολῖται, δείν' ἔπη πεπυσμένος [*Introit.*
κατηγορεῖν μου τὸν τύραννον Οἰδίπουν
πάρειμ' ἀτλητῶν. εἰ γὰρ ἐν ταῖς ξυμφοραῖς
ταῖς νῦν νομίζει πρός γ' ἐμοῦ πεπονθέναι
λόγοισιν εἴτ' ἔργοισιν εἰς βλάβην φέρον,
οὔτοι βίου μοι τοῦ μακραίωνος πόθος,
φέροντι τήνδε βάξιν. οὐ γὰρ εἰς ἁπλοῦν
ἡ ζημία μοι τοῦ λόγου τούτου φέρει,
ἀλλ' ἐς μέγιστον, εἰ κακὸς μὲν ἐν πόλει,
κακὸς δὲ πρὸς σοῦ καὶ φίλων κεκλήσομαι.

ΧΟΡΟΣ.

ἀλλ' ἦλθε μὲν δὴ τοῦτο τοὔνειδος τάχ' ἂν
ὀργῇ βιασθὲν μᾶλλον ἢ γνώμῃ φρενῶν.

ΚΡΕΩΝ.

τοῦ πρὸς δ' ἐφάνθη ταῖς ἐμαῖς γνώμαις ὅτι
πεισθεὶς ὁ μάντις τοὺς λόγους ψευδεῖς λέγοι;

ΧΟΡΟΣ.

ηὐδᾶτο μὲν τάδ', οἶδα δ' οὐ γνώμῃ τίνι.

ΚΡΕΩΝ.

ἐξ ὀμμάτων δ' ὀρθῶν τε κἀξ ὀρθῆς φρενὸς
κατηγορεῖτο τοὐπίκλημα τοῦτό μου;

ΧΟΡΟΣ.

οὐκ οἶδ'· ἃ γὰρ δρῶσ' οἱ κρατοῦντες οὐχ ὁρῶ.
αὐτὸς δ' ὅδ' ἤδη δωμάτων ἔξω περᾷ.

ΟΙΔΙΠΟΥΣ.

οὗτος σύ, πῶς δεῦρ' ἦλθες; ἦ τοσόνδ' ἔχεις [Introit.
τόλμης πρόσωπον ὥστε τὰς ἐμὰς στέγας
ἵκου, φονεὺς ὢν τοῦδε τἀνδρὸς ἐμφανῶς
λῃστής τ' ἐναργὴς τῆς ἐμῆς τυραννίδος;
φέρ' εἰπὲ πρὸς θεῶν, δειλίαν ἢ μωρίαν
ἰδών τιν' ἐν ἐμοὶ ταῦτ' ἐβουλεύσω ποιεῖν;
ἢ τοὔργον ὡς οὐ γνωρίσοιμί σου τόδε
δόλῳ προσέρπον κοὐκ ἀλεξοίμην μαθών;
ἆρ' οὐχὶ μῶρόν ἐστι τοὐγχείρημά σου,
ἄνευ τε πλήθους καὶ φίλων τυραννίδα
θηρᾶν, ὃ πλήθει χρήμασίν θ' ἁλίσκεται;

ΚΡΕΩΝ.

οἶσθ' ὡς ποίησον; ἀντὶ τῶν εἰρημένων
ἴσ' ἀντάκουσον, κᾆτα κρῖν' αὐτὸς μαθών.

ΟΙΔΙΠΟΥΣ.

λέγειν σὺ δεινός, μανθάνειν δ' ἐγὼ κακὸς
σοῦ· δυσμενῆ γὰρ καὶ βαρύν σ' εὕρηκ' ἐμοί.

ΚΡΕΩΝ.

τοῦτ' αὐτὸ νῦν μου πρῶτ' ἄκουσον ὡς ἐρῶ.

ΟΙΔΙΠΟΥΣ.

τοῦτ' αὐτὸ μή μοι φράζ', ὅπως οὐκ εἶ κακός.

ΚΡΕΩΝ.

εἴ τοι νομίζεις κτῆμα τὴν αὐθαδίαν
εἶναί τι τοῦ νοῦ χωρίς, οὐκ ὀρθῶς φρονεῖς.

ΟΙΔΙΠΟΥΣ.

εἴ τοι νομίζεις ἄνδρα συγγενῆ κακῶς
δρῶν οὐχ ὑφέξειν τὴν δίκην, οὐκ εὖ φρονεῖς.

ΚΡΕΩΝ.

ξύμφημί σοι ταῦτ' ἔνδικ' εἰρῆσθαι· τὸ δὲ
πάθημ' ὁποῖον φῂς παθεῖν δίδασκέ με.

ΟΙΔΙΠΟΥΣ.

ἔπειθες, ἢ οὐκ ἔπειθες, ὡς χρείη μ' ἐπὶ
τὸν σεμνόμαντιν ἄνδρα πέμψασθαί τινα;

ΚΡΕΩΝ.

καὶ νῦν ἔθ' αὐτός εἰμι τῷ βουλεύματι.

ΟΙΔΙΠΟΥΣ.

πόσον τιν' ἤδη δῆθ' ὁ Λάϊος χρόνον —

ΚΡΕΩΝ.

δέδρακε ποῖον ἔργον; οὐ γὰρ ἐννοῶ.

ΟΙΔΙΠΟΥΣ.

ἄφαντος ἔρρει θανασίμῳ χειρώματι;

ΚΡΕΩΝ.

μακροὶ παλαιοί τ' ἂν μετρηθεῖεν χρόνοι.

ΟΙΔΙΠΟΥΣ.

τότ' οὖν ὁ μάντις οὗτος ἦν ἐν τῇ τέχνῃ;

ΚΡΕΩΝ.

σοφός γ' ὁμοίως κἀξ ἴσου τιμώμενος.

ΟΙΔΙΠΟΥΣ.

ἐμνήσατ' οὖν ἐμοῦ τι τῷ τότ' ἐν χρόνῳ;

ΚΡΕΩΝ.

οὔκουν ἐμοῦ γ' ἑστῶτος οὐδαμοῦ πέλας.

ΟΙΔΙΠΟΥΣ.

ἀλλ' οὐκ ἔρευναν τοῦ θανόντος ἔσχετε;

ΚΡΕΩΝ.

παρέσχομεν, πῶς δ' οὐχί; κοὐκ ἠκούσαμεν.

ΟΙΔΙΠΟΥΣ.

πῶς οὖν τόθ' οὗτος ὁ σοφὸς οὐκ ηὔδα τάδε;

ΚΡΕΩΝ.

οὐκ οἶδ'· ἐφ' οἷς γὰρ μὴ φρονῶ σιγᾶν φιλῶ.

ΟΙΔΙΠΟΥΣ.

τοσόνδε γ' οἶσθα καὶ λέγοις ἂν εὖ φρονῶν.

ΚΡΕΩΝ.

ποῖον τόδ'; εἰ γὰρ οἶδά γ', οὐκ ἀρνήσομαι.

ΟΙΔΙΠΟΥΣ.

ὁθούνεκ', εἰ μὴ σοὶ ξυνῆλθε, τὰς ἐμὰς
οὐκ ἄν ποτ' εἶπε Λαΐου διαφθοράς.

ΚΡΕΩΝ.

εἰ μὲν λέγει τάδ᾽, αὐτὸς οἶσθ᾽· ἐγὼ δέ σου
μαθεῖν δικαιῶ ταὔθ᾽ ἅπερ κἀμοῦ σὺ νῦν.

ΟΙΔΙΠΟΥΣ.

ἐκμάνθαν᾽· οὐ γὰρ δὴ φονεὺς ἁλώσομαι.

ΚΡΕΩΝ.

τί δῆτ᾽; ἀδελφὴν τὴν ἐμὴν γήμας ἔχεις;

ΟΙΔΙΠΟΥΣ.

ἄρνησις οὐκ ἔνεστιν ὧν ἀνιστορεῖς.

ΚΡΕΩΝ.

ἄρχεις δ᾽ ἐκείνῃ ταὐτὰ γῆς ἴσον νέμων;

ΟΙΔΙΠΟΥΣ.

ἂν ᾖ θέλουσα πάντ᾽ ἐμοῦ κομίζεται.

ΚΡΕΩΝ.

οὔκουν ἰσοῦμαι σφῷν ἐγὼ δυοῖν τρίτος;

ΟΙΔΙΠΟΥΣ.

ἐνταῦθα γὰρ δὴ καὶ κακὸς φαίνει φίλος.

ΚΡΕΩΝ.

οὔκ, εἰ διδοίης γ᾽ ὡς ἐγὼ σαυτῷ λόγον.
σκέψαι δὲ τοῦτο πρῶτον, εἴ τιν᾽ ἂν δοκεῖς
ἄρχειν ἑλέσθαι ξὺν φόβοισι μᾶλλον ἢ
ἄτρεστον εὕδοντ᾽, εἰ τά γ᾽ αὔθ᾽ ἕξει κράτη.
ἐγὼ μὲν οὖν οὔτ᾽ αὐτὸς ἱμείρων ἔφυν

τύραννος εἶναι μᾶλλον ἢ τύραννα δρᾶν,
οὔτ' ἄλλος ὅστις σωφρονεῖν ἐπίσταται.
νῦν μὲν γὰρ ἐκ σοῦ πάντ' ἄνευ φόβου φέρω,
εἰ δ' αὐτὸς ἦρχον, πολλὰ κἂν ἄκων ἔδρων.
πῶς δῆτ' ἐμοὶ τυραννὶς ἡδίων ἔχειν
ἀρχῆς ἀλύπου καὶ δυναστείας ἔφυ;
οὔπω τοσοῦτον ἠπατημένος κυρῶ
ὥστ' ἄλλα χρῄζειν ἢ τὰ σὺν κέρδει καλά.
νῦν πᾶσι χαίρω, νῦν με πᾶς ἀσπάζεται,
νῦν οἱ σέθεν χρῄζοντες ἐκκαλοῦσί με·
τὸ γὰρ τυχεῖν αὐτοῖσι πᾶν ἐνταῦθ' ἔνι.
πῶς δῆτ' ἐγὼ κεῖν' ἂν λάβοιμ' ἀφεὶς τάδε;
οὐκ ἂν γένοιτο νοῦς κακὸς καλῶς φρονῶν.
ἀλλ' οὔτ' ἐραστὴς τῆσδε τῆς γνώμης ἔφυν
οὔτ' ἂν μετ' ἄλλου δρῶντος ἂν τλαίην ποτέ.
καὶ τῶνδ' ἔλεγχον τοῦτο μὲν Πυθώδ' ἰὼν
πεύθου τὰ χρησθέντ', εἰ σαφῶς ἤγγειλά σοι·
τοῦτ' ἄλλ', ἐάν με τῷ τερασκόπῳ λάβῃς
κοινῇ τι βουλεύσαντα, μή μ' ἁπλῇ κτάνῃς
ψήφῳ, διπλῇ δέ, τῇ τ' ἐμῇ καὶ σῇ, λαβών.
γνώμῃ δ' ἀδήλῳ μή με χωρὶς αἰτιῶ.
οὐ γὰρ δίκαιον οὔτε τοὺς κακοὺς μάτην
χρηστοὺς νομίζειν οὔτε τοὺς χρηστοὺς κακούς.
φίλον γὰρ ἐσθλὸν ἐκβαλεῖν ἴσον λέγω
καὶ τὸν παρ' αὑτῷ βίοτον, ὃν πλεῖστον φιλεῖ.
ἀλλ' ἐν χρόνῳ γνώσει τάδ' ἀσφαλῶς, ἐπεὶ
χρόνος δίκαιον ἄνδρα δείκνυσιν μόνος,
κακὸν δὲ κἂν ἐν ἡμέρᾳ γνοίης μιᾷ.

ΧΟΡΟΣ.

καλῶς ἔλεξεν εὐλαβουμένῳ πεσεῖν,
ἄναξ· φρονεῖν γὰρ οἱ ταχεῖς οὐκ ἀσφαλεῖς.

ΟΙΔΙΠΟΥΣ.

ὅταν ταχύς τις οὑπιβουλεύων λάθρα
χωρῇ, ταχὺν δεῖ κἀμὲ βουλεύειν πάλιν.
εἰ δ' ἡσυχάζων προσμενῶ, τὰ τοῦδε μὲν
πεπραγμέν' ἔσται, τἀμὰ δ' ἡμαρτημένα.

ΚΡΕΩΝ.

τί δῆτα χρῄζεις; ἦ με γῆς ἔξω βαλεῖν;

ΟΙΔΙΠΟΥΣ.

ἥκιστα· θνήσκειν, οὐ φυγεῖν σε βούλομαι.

ΚΡΕΩΝ.

ὅταν προδείξῃς οἷόν ἐστι τὸ φθονεῖν.

ΟΙΔΙΠΟΥΣ.

ὡς οὐχ ὑπείξων οὐδὲ πιστεύσων λέγεις;

ΚΡΕΩΝ.

οὐ γὰρ φρονοῦντά σ' εὖ βλέπω.

ΟΙΔΙΠΟΥΣ.

τὸ γοῦν ἐμόν.

ΚΡΕΩΝ.

ἀλλ' ἐξ ἴσου δεῖ κἀμόν.

ΟΙΔΙΠΟΥΣ.

ἀλλ' ἔφυς κακός.

ΚΡΕΩΝ.

εἰ δὲ ξυνίης μηδέν;

ΟΙΔΙΠΟΥΣ.

ἀρκτέον γ' ὅμως.

ΚΡΕΩΝ.

οὔτοι κακῶς γ' ἄρχοντος.

ΟΙΔΙΠΟΥΣ.

ὦ πόλις πόλις.

ΚΡΕΩΝ.

κἀμοὶ πόλεως μέτεστιν, οὐχὶ σοὶ μόνῳ.

ΧΟΡΟΣ.

παύσασθ', ἄνακτες· καιρίαν δ' ὑμῖν ὁρῶ
τήνδ' ἐκ δόμων στείχουσαν Ἰοκάστην, μεθ' ἧς
τὸ νῦν παρεστὸς νεῖκος εὖ θέσθαι χρεών.

ΙΟΚΑΣΤΗ.

τί τὴν ἄβουλον, ὦ ταλαίπωροι, στάσιν [*Introit.*
γλώσσης ἐπήρασθ'; οὐδ' ἐπαισχύνεσθε, γῆς
οὕτω νοσούσης, ἴδια κινοῦντες κακά;
οὐκ εἶ σύ τ' οἴκους σύ τε, Κρέον, κατὰ στέγας,
καὶ μὴ τὸ μηδὲν ἄλγος εἰς μέγ' οἴσετε;

ΚΡΕΩΝ.

ὅμαιμε, δεινά μ' Οἰδίπους ὁ σὸς πόσις
δρᾶσαι δικαιοῖ, δυοῖν ἀποκρίνας κακοῖν,
ἢ γῆς ἀπῶσαι πατρίδος, ἢ κτεῖναι λαβών—

ΟΙΔΙΠΟΥΣ.

ξύμφημι· δρῶντα γάρ νιν, ὦ γύναι, κακῶς
εἴληφα τοὐμὸν σῶμα σὺν τέχνῃ κακῇ.

ΚΡΕΩΝ.

μή νυν ὀναίμην, ἀλλ' ἀραῖος, εἴ σέ τι
δέδρακ', ὀλοίμην, ὧν ἐπαιτιᾷ με δρᾶν.

ΙΟΚΑΣΤΗ.

ὦ πρὸς θεῶν πίστευσον, Οἰδίπους, τάδε,
μάλιστα μὲν τόνδ' ὅρκον αἰδεσθεὶς θεῶν,
ἔπειτα κἀμὲ τούσδε θ' οἳ πάρεισί σοι.

ΧΟΡΟΣ.

στρ.

πιθοῦ θελήσας φρονήσας τ', ἄναξ, λίσσομαι.

ΟΙΔΙΠΟΥΣ.

τί σοι θέλεις δῆτ' εἰκάθω;

ΧΟΡΟΣ.

τὸν οὔτε πρὶν νήπιον νῦν τ' ἐν ὅρκῳ μέγαν καταίδεσαι.

ΟΙΔΙΠΟΥΣ.

οἶσθ' οὖν ἃ χρῄζεις;

ΧΟΡΟΣ.

οἶδα.

ΟΙΔΙΠΟΥΣ.

φράζε δή· τί φῄς;

ΧΟΡΟΣ.

τὸν ἐναγῆ φίλον μήποτ' ἐν αἰτίᾳ
σὺν ἀφανεῖ λόγῳ σ' ἄτιμον βαλεῖν.

ΟΙΔΙΠΟΥΣ.

εὖ νυν ἐπίστω, ταῦθ' ὅταν ζητῇς, ἐμοὶ
ζητῶν ὄλεθρον ἢ φυγὴν ἐκ τῆσδε γῆς.

ΧΟΡΟΣ.

οὐ τὸν πάντων θεῶν θεὸν πρόμον
Ἅλιον· ἐπεὶ ἄθεος ἄφιλος ὅ τι πύματον
ὀλοίμαν, φρόνησιν εἰ τάνδ' ἔχω.
ἀλλά μοι δυσμόρῳ γᾶ φθινὰς
τρύχει ψυχάν, τάδ' εἰ κακοῖς κακὰ
προσάψει τοῖς πάλαι τὰ πρὸς σφῷν.

ΟΙΔΙΠΟΥΣ.

ὁ δ' οὖν ἴτω, κεἰ χρή με παντελῶς θανεῖν,
ἢ γῆς ἄτιμον τῆσδ' ἀπωσθῆναι βίᾳ.
τὸ γὰρ σόν, οὐ τὸ τοῦδ', ἐποικτείρω στόμα
ἐλεινόν· οὗτος δ', ἔνθ' ἂν ᾖ, στυγήσεται.

ΚΡΕΩΝ.

στυγνὸς μὲν εἴκων δῆλος εἶ, βαρὺς δ', ὅταν
θυμοῦ περάσῃς. αἱ δὲ τοιαῦται φύσεις
αὑταῖς δικαίως εἰσὶν ἄλγισται φέρειν.

ΟΙΔΙΠΟΥΣ.

οὔκουν μ' ἐάσεις κἀκτὸς εἶ;

ΚΡΕΩΝ.

πορεύσομαι,
σοῦ μὲν τυχὼν ἀγνῶτος, ἐν δὲ τοῖσδ' ἴσος. [*Exit.*

ΧΟΡΟΣ.

ἀντ.

γύναι, τί μέλλεις κομίζειν δόμων τόνδ' ἔσω;

ΙΟΚΑΣΤΗ.

μαθοῦσά γ' ἥτις ἡ τύχη.

ΧΟΡΟΣ.

δόκησις ἀγνὼς λόγων ἦλθε, δάκνει δὲ καὶ τὸ μὴ 'νδικον.

ΙΟΚΑΣΤΗ.

ἀμφοῖν ἀπ' αὐτοῖν;

ΧΟΡΟΣ.

ναίχι.

ΙΟΚΑΣΤΗ.

καὶ τίς ἦν λόγος;

ΧΟΡΟΣ.

ἅλις ἔμοιγ', ἅλις, γᾶς προπονουμένας,
φαίνεται ἔνθ' ἔληξεν αὐτοῦ μένειν.

ΟΙΔΙΠΟΥΣ.

ὁρᾷς ἵν' ἥκεις, ἀγαθὸς ὢν γνώμην ἀνήρ,
τοὐμὸν παριεὶς καὶ καταμβλύνων κέαρ;

ΧΟΡΟΣ.

ἄναξ, εἶπον μὲν οὐχ ἅπαξ μόνον,
ἴσθι δὲ παραφρόνιμον, ἄπορον ἐπὶ φρόνιμα
πεφάνθαι μ' ἄν, εἴ σε νοσφίζομαι,
ὅς τ' ἐμὰν γᾶν φίλαν ἐν πόνοις
σαλεύουσαν κατ' ὀρθὸν οὔρισας,
τανῦν τ' εὔπομπος εἰ γένοιο.

ΙΟΚΑΣΤΗ.

πρὸς θεῶν δίδαξον κἄμ', ἄναξ, ὅτου ποτὲ
μῆνιν τοσήνδε πράγματος στήσας ἔχεις.

ΟΙΔΙΠΟΥΣ.

ἐρῶ· σὲ γὰρ τῶνδ' ἐς πλέον, γύναι, σέβω·
Κρέοντος, οἷά μοι βεβουλευκὼς ἔχει.

ΙΟΚΑΣΤΗ.

λέγ', εἰ σαφῶς τὸ νεῖκος ἐγκαλῶν ἐρεῖς.

ΟΙΔΙΠΟΥΣ.

φονέα μέ φησι Λαΐου καθεστάναι.

ΙΟΚΑΣΤΗ.

αὐτὸς ξυνειδώς, ἢ μαθὼν ἄλλου πάρα;

ΟΙΔΙΠΟΥΣ.

μάντιν μὲν οὖν κακοῦργον εἰσπέμψας, ἐπεὶ
τό γ' εἰς ἑαυτὸν πᾶν ἐλευθεροῖ στόμα.

ΙΟΚΑΣΤΗ.

σύ νυν ἀφεὶς σεαυτὸν ὧν λέγεις πέρι
ἐμοῦ 'πάκουσον καὶ μάθ' οὕνεκ' ἐστί σοι
βρότειον οὐδὲν μαντικῆς ἔχον τέχνης.
φανῶ δέ σοι σημεῖα τῶνδε σύντομα.
χρησμὸς γὰρ ἦλθε Λαΐῳ ποτ', οὐκ ἐρῶ
Φοίβου γ' ἀπ' αὐτοῦ, τῶν δ' ὑπηρετῶν ἄπο,
ὡς αὐτὸν ἥξοι μοῖρα πρὸς παιδὸς θανεῖν,
ὅστις γένοιτ' ἐμοῦ τε κἀκείνου πάρα.
καὶ τὸν μέν, ὥσπερ γ' ἡ φάτις, ξένοι ποτὲ
λῃσταὶ φονεύουσ' ἐν τριπλαῖς ἁμαξιτοῖς·
παιδὸς δὲ βλάστας οὐ διέσχον ἡμέραι
τρεῖς, καί νιν ἄρθρα κεῖνος ἐνζεύξας ποδοῖν
ἔρριψεν ἄλλων χερσὶν εἰς ἄβατον ὄρος.
κἀνταῦθ' Ἀπόλλων οὔτ' ἐκεῖνον ἤνυσεν
φονέα γενέσθαι πατρὸς οὔτε Λάϊον,
τὸ δεινὸν οὑφοβεῖτο, πρὸς παιδὸς θανεῖν.

τοιαῦτα φῆμαι μαντικαὶ διώρισαν,
ὧν ἐντρέπου σὺ μηδέν· ὧν γὰρ ἂν θεὸς
χρείαν ἐρευνᾷ ῥᾳδίως αὐτὸς φανεῖ.

ΟΙΔΙΠΟΥΣ.

οἷόν μ' ἀκούσαντ' ἀρτίως ἔχει, γύναι,
ψυχῆς πλάνημα κἀνακίνησις φρενῶν.

ΙΟΚΑΣΤΗ.

ποίας μερίμνης τοῦθ' ὑποστραφεὶς λέγεις;

ΟΙΔΙΠΟΥΣ.

ἔδοξ' ἀκοῦσαι σοῦ τόδ', ὡς ὁ Λάϊος
κατασφαγείη πρὸς τριπλαῖς ἁμαξιτοῖς.

ΙΟΚΑΣΤΗ.

ηὐδᾶτο γὰρ ταῦτ' οὐδέ πω λήξαντ' ἔχει.

ΟΙΔΙΠΟΥΣ.

καὶ ποῦ 'σθ' ὁ χῶρος οὗτος οὗ τόδ' ἦν πάθος;

ΙΟΚΑΣΤΗ.

Φωκὶς μὲν ἡ γῆ κλῄζεται, σχιστὴ δ' ὁδὸς
ἐς ταὐτὸ Δελφῶν κἀπὸ Δαυλίας ἄγει.

ΟΙΔΙΠΟΥΣ.

καὶ τίς χρόνος τοῖσδ' ἐστὶν οὑξεληλυθώς;

ΙΟΚΑΣΤΗ.

σχεδόν τι πρόσθεν ἢ σὺ τῆσδ' ἔχων χθονὸς
ἀρχὴν ἐφαίνου τοῦτ' ἐκηρύχθη πόλει.

ΟΙΔΙΠΟΥΣ.

ὦ Ζεῦ, τί μου δρᾶσαι βεβούλευσαι πέρι;

ΙΟΚΑΣΤΗ.

τί δ' ἐστί σοι τοῦτ', Οἰδίπους, ἐνθύμιον;

ΟΙΔΙΠΟΥΣ.

μήπω μ' ἐρώτα· τὸν δὲ Λάϊον φύσιν
τίν' εἶχε φράζε, τίνα δ' ἀκμὴν ἥβης ἔχων.

ΙΟΚΑΣΤΗ.

μέγας, χνοάζων ἄρτι λευκανθὲς κάρα,
μορφῆς δὲ τῆς σῆς οὐκ ἀπεστάτει πολύ.

ΟΙΔΙΠΟΥΣ.

οἴμοι τάλας· ἔοικ' ἐμαυτὸν εἰς ἀρὰς
δεινὰς προβάλλων ἀρτίως οὐκ εἰδέναι.

ΙΟΚΑΣΤΗ.

πῶς φῄς; ὀκνῶ τοι πρὸς σ' ἀποσκοποῦσ', ἄναξ.

ΟΙΔΙΠΟΥΣ.

δεινῶς ἀθυμῶ μὴ βλέπων ὁ μάντις ᾖ.
δείξεις δὲ μᾶλλον, ἢν ἓν ἐξείπῃς ἔτι.

ΙΟΚΑΣΤΗ.

καὶ μὴν ὀκνῶ μέν, ἃ δ' ἂν ἔρῃ μαθοῦσ' ἐρῶ.

ΟΙΔΙΠΟΥΣ.

πότερον ἐχώρει βαιός, ἢ πολλοὺς ἔχων
ἄνδρας λοχίτας, οἷ' ἀνὴρ ἀρχηγέτης;

ΙΟΚΑΣΤΗ.

πέντ' ἦσαν οἱ ξύμπαντες, ἐν δ' αὐτοῖσιν ἦν
κῆρυξ· ἀπήνη δ' ἦγε Λάϊον μία.

ΟΙΔΙΠΟΥΣ.

αἰαῖ, τάδ᾽ ἤδη διαφανῆ. τίς ἦν ποτε
ὁ τούσδε λέξας τοὺς λόγους ὑμῖν, γύναι;

ΙΟΚΑΣΤΗ.

οἰκεύς τις, ὅσπερ ἵκετ᾽ ἐκσωθεὶς μόνος.

ΟΙΔΙΠΟΥΣ.

ἦ κἀν δόμοισι τυγχάνει τανῦν παρών;

ΙΟΚΑΣΤΗ.

οὐ δῆτ᾽· ἀφ᾽ οὗ γὰρ κεῖθεν ἦλθε καὶ κράτη
σέ τ᾽ εἶδ᾽ ἔχοντα Λάϊόν τ᾽ ὀλωλότα,
ἐξικέτευσε τῆς ἐμῆς χειρὸς θιγὼν
ἀγρούς σφε πέμψαι κἀπὶ ποιμνίων νομάς,
ὡς πλεῖστον εἴη τοῦδ᾽ ἄποπτος ἄστεως.
κἄπεμψ᾽ ἐγώ νιν· ἄξιος γὰρ ὥς γ᾽ ἀνὴρ
δοῦλος φέρειν ἦν τῆσδε καὶ μείζω χάριν.

ΟΙΔΙΠΟΥΣ.

πῶς ἂν μόλοι δῆθ᾽ ἡμὶν ἐν τάχει πάλιν;

ΙΟΚΑΣΤΗ.

πάρεστιν. ἀλλὰ πρὸς τί τοῦτ᾽ ἐφίεσαι;

ΟΙΔΙΠΟΥΣ.

δέδοικ᾽ ἐμαυτόν, ὦ γύναι, μὴ πόλλ᾽ ἄγαν
εἰρημέν᾽ ᾖ μοι, δι᾽ ἅ νιν εἰσιδεῖν θέλω.

ΙΟΚΑΣΤΗ.

ἀλλ᾽ ἵξεται μέν· ἀξία δέ που μαθεῖν
κἀγὼ τά γ᾽ ἐν σοὶ δυσφόρως ἔχοντ᾽, ἄναξ.

ΟΙΔΙΠΟΥΣ.

κοὐ μὴ στερηθῇς γ' ἐς τοσοῦτον ἐλπίδων
ἐμοῦ βεβῶτος. τῷ γὰρ ἂν καὶ μείζονι
λέξαιμ' ἂν ἢ σοὶ διὰ τύχης τοιᾶσδ' ἰών;
ἐμοὶ πατὴρ μὲν Πόλυβος ἦν Κορίνθιος,
μήτηρ δὲ Μερόπη Δωρίς. ἠγόμην δ' ἀνὴρ
ἀστῶν μέγιστος τῶν ἐκεῖ, πρίν μοι τύχη
τοιάδ' ἐπέστη, θαυμάσαι μὲν ἀξία,
σπουδῆς γε μέντοι τῆς ἐμῆς οὐκ ἀξία.
ἀνὴρ γὰρ ἐν δείπνοις μ' ὑπερπλησθεὶς μέθῃ
καλεῖ παρ' οἴνῳ πλαστὸς ὡς εἴην πατρί.
κἀγὼ βαρυνθεὶς τὴν μὲν οὖσαν ἡμέραν
μόλις κατέσχον, θἀτέρᾳ δ' ἰὼν πέλας
μητρὸς πατρός τ' ἤλεγχον· οἱ δὲ δυσφόρως
τοὔνειδος ἦγον τῷ μεθέντι τὸν λόγον.
κἀγὼ τὰ μὲν κείνοιν ἐτερπόμην, ὅμως δ'
ἔκνιζέ μ' ἀεὶ τοῦθ'· ὑφεῖρπε γὰρ πολύ.
λάθρα δὲ μητρὸς καὶ πατρὸς πορεύομαι
Πυθώδε, καί μ' ὁ Φοῖβος ὧν μὲν ἱκόμην
ἄτιμον ἐξέπεμψεν, ἄλλα δ' ἄθλια
καὶ δεινὰ καὶ δύστηνα προυφάνη λέγων,
ὡς μητρὶ μὲν χρείη με μιχθῆναι, γένος δ'
ἄτλητον ἀνθρώποισι δηλώσοιμ' ὁρᾶν,
φονεὺς δ' ἐσοίμην τοῦ φυτεύσαντος πατρός.
κἀγὼ 'πακούσας ταῦτα τὴν Κορινθίαν
ἄστροις τὸ λοιπὸν ἐκμετρούμενος χθόνα
ἔφευγον, ἔνθα μήποτ' ὀψοίμην κακῶν
χρησμῶν ὀνείδη τῶν ἐμῶν τελούμενα.

στείχων δ' ἱκνοῦμαι τούσδε τοὺς χώρους ἐν οἷς
σὺ τὸν τύραννον τοῦτον ὄλλυσθαι λέγεις.
καί σοι, γύναι, τἀληθὲς ἐξερῶ. τριπλῆς
ὅτ' ἦ κελεύθου τῆσδ' ὁδοιπορῶν πέλας,
ἐνταῦθά μοι κῆρυξ τε κἀπὶ πωλικῆς
ἀνὴρ ἀπήνης ἐμβεβώς, οἷον σὺ φῄς,
ξυνηντίαζον· κἀξ ὁδοῦ μ' ὅ θ' ἡγεμὼν
αὐτός θ' ὁ πρέσβυς πρὸς βίαν ἠλαυνέτην.
κἀγὼ τὸν ἐκτρέποντα, τὸν τροχηλάτην,
παίω δι' ὀργῆς· καί μ' ὁ πρέσβυς ὡς ὁρᾷ,
ὄχου παραστείχοντα τηρήσας μέσον
κάρα διπλοῖς κέντροισί μου καθίκετο.
οὐ μὴν ἴσην γ' ἔτισεν, ἀλλὰ συντόμως
σκήπτρῳ τυπεὶς ἐκ τῆσδε χειρὸς ὕπτιος
μέσης ἀπήνης εὐθὺς ἐκκυλίνδεται·
κτείνω δὲ τοὺς ξύμπαντας. εἰ δὲ τῷ ξένῳ
τούτῳ προσήκει Λαΐῳ τι συγγενές,
τίς τοῦδέ γ' ἀνδρὸς ἔστιν ἀθλιώτερος ;
τίς ἐχθροδαίμων μᾶλλον ἂν γένοιτ' ἀνήρ ;
ᾧ μὴ ξένων ἔξεστι μηδ' ἀστῶν τινα
δόμοις δέχεσθαι, μηδὲ προσφωνεῖν τινα,
ὠθεῖν δ' ἀπ' οἴκων. καὶ τάδ' οὔτις ἄλλος ἦν
ἢ 'γὼ 'π' ἐμαυτῷ τάσδ' ἀρὰς ὁ προστιθείς.
λέχη δὲ τοῦ θανόντος ἐν χεροῖν ἐμαῖν
χραίνω, δι' ὧνπερ ὤλετ'. ἆρ' ἔφυν κακός ;
ἆρ' οὐχὶ πᾶς ἄναγνος, εἴ με χρὴ φυγεῖν,
καί μοι φυγόντι μήστι τοὺς ἐμοὺς ἰδεῖν
μηδ' ἐμβατεύειν πατρίδος, ἢ γάμοις με δεῖ

μητρὸς ζυγῆναι καὶ πατέρα κατακτανεῖν
Πόλυβον, ὃς ἐξέφυσε κἀξέθρεψέ με;
ἆρ' οὐκ ἀπ' ὠμοῦ ταῦτα δαίμονός τις ἂν
κρίνων ἐπ' ἀνδρὶ τῷδ' ἂν ὀρθοίη λόγον;
μὴ δῆτα, μὴ δῆτ', ὦ θεῶν ἁγνὸν σέβας,
ἴδοιμι ταύτην ἡμέραν, ἀλλ' ἐκ βροτῶν
βαίην ἄφαντος πρόσθεν ἢ τοιάνδ' ἰδεῖν
κηλῖδ' ἐμαυτῷ συμφορᾶς ἀφιγμένην.

ΧΟΡΟΣ.

ἡμῖν μέν, ὦναξ, ταῦτ' ὀκνήρ'· ἕως δ' ἂν οὖν
πρὸς τοῦ παρόντος ἐκμάθῃς, ἔχ' ἐλπίδα.

ΟΙΔΙΠΟΥΣ.

καὶ μὴν τοσοῦτόν γ' ἐστί μοι τῆς ἐλπίδος,
τὸν ἄνδρα τὸν βοτῆρα προσμεῖναι μόνον.

ΙΟΚΑΣΤΗ.

πεφασμένου δὲ τίς ποθ' ἡ προθυμία;

ΟΙΔΙΠΟΥΣ.

ἐγὼ διδάξω σ'· ἢν γὰρ εὑρεθῇ λέγων
σοὶ ταὔτ', ἔγωγ' ἂν ἐκπεφευγοίην πάθος.

ΙΟΚΑΣΤΗ.

ποῖον δέ μου περισσὸν ἤκουσας λόγον;

ΟΙΔΙΠΟΥΣ.

λῃστὰς ἔφασκες αὐτὸν ἄνδρας ἐννέπειν
ὥς νιν κατακτείναιεν. εἰ μὲν οὖν ἔτι
λέξει τὸν αὐτὸν ἀριθμόν, οὐκ ἐγὼ 'κτανον·

οὐ γὰρ γένοιτ' ἂν εἷς γε τοῖς πολλοῖς ἴσος·
εἰ δ' ἄνδρ' ἕν' οἰόζωνον αὐδήσει, σαφῶς
τοῦτ' ἐστὶν ἤδη τοὔργον εἰς ἐμὲ ῥέπον.

ΙΟΚΑΣΤΗ.

ἀλλ' ὡς φανέν γε τοὔπος ὧδ' ἐπίστασο,
κοὐκ ἔστιν αὐτῷ τοῦτό γ' ἐκβαλεῖν πάλιν·
πόλις γὰρ ἤκουσ', οὐκ ἐγὼ μόνη, τάδε.
εἰ δ' οὖν τι κἀκτρέποιτο τοῦ πρόσθεν λόγου,
οὔτοι ποτ', ὦναξ, τόν γε Λαΐου φόνον
φανεῖ δικαίως ὀρθόν, ὅν γε Λοξίας
διεῖπε χρῆναι παιδὸς ἐξ ἐμοῦ θανεῖν.
καίτοι νιν οὐ κεῖνός γ' ὁ δύστηνός ποτε
κατέκταν', ἀλλ' αὐτὸς πάροιθεν ὤλετο.
ὥστ' οὐχὶ μαντείας γ' ἂν οὔτε τῇδ' ἐγὼ
βλέψαιμ' ἂν οὕνεκ' οὔτε τῇδ' ἂν ὕστερον.

ΟΙΔΙΠΟΥΣ.

καλῶς νομίζεις. ἀλλ' ὅμως τὸν ἐργάτην
πέμψον τινὰ στελοῦντα μηδὲ τοῦτ' ἀφῇς.

ΙΟΚΑΣΤΗ.

πέμψω ταχύνασ'· ἀλλ' ἴωμεν ἐς δόμους.
οὐδὲν γὰρ ἂν πράξαιμ' ἂν ὧν οὐ σοὶ φίλον.

[*Exeunt* JOCASTA *et* ŒDIPUS.

ΧΟΡΟΣ.

στρ. ά.

εἴ μοι ξυνείη φέροντι μοῖρα τὰν εὔσεπτον ἁγνείαν λόγων
ἔργων τε πάντων, ὧν νόμοι πρόκεινται
ὑψίποδες, οὐρανίᾳ

αἰθέρι τεκνωθέντες, ὧν Ὄλυμπος
πατὴρ μόνος, οὐδέ νιν θνατὰ φύσις ἀνέρων
ἔτικτεν, οὐδὲ μή ποτε λάθα κατακοιμάσῃ·
μέγας ἐν τούτοις θεός, οὐδὲ γηράσκει.

ἀντ. α΄.

ὕβρις φυτεύει τύραννον· ὕβρις, εἰ πολλῶν ὑπερπλησθῇ μάταν,
ἃ μὴ 'πίκαιρα μηδὲ συμφέροντα,
ἀκρότατον εἰσαναβᾶσ'
ἀπότομον ὤρουσεν εἰς ἀνάγκαν,
ἔνθ' οὐ ποδὶ χρησίμῳ χρῆται. τὸ καλῶς δ' ἔχον
πόλει πάλαισμα μήποτε λῦσαι θεὸν αἰτοῦμαι.
θεὸν οὐ λήξω ποτὲ προστάταν ἴσχων.

στρ. β΄.

εἰ δέ τις ὑπέροπτα χερσὶν
ἢ λόγῳ πορεύεται,
Δίκας ἀφόβητος οὐδὲ
δαιμόνων ἕδη σέβων,
κακά νιν ἕλοιτο μοῖρα,
δυσπότμου χάριν χλιδᾶς,
εἰ μὴ τὸ κέρδος κερδανεῖ δικαίως
καὶ τῶν ἀσέπτων ἕρξεται,
ἢ τῶν ἀθίκτων ἕξεται ματᾴζων.
τίς ἔτι ποτ' ἐν τοῖσδ' ἀνὴρ θυμῶν βέλη
εὔξεται ψυχᾶς ἀμύνειν;
εἰ γὰρ αἱ τοιαίδε πράξεις τίμιαι,
τί δεῖ με χορεύειν;

ἀντ. β΄.

οὐκέτι τὸν ἄθικτον εἶμι
γᾶς ἐπ᾽ ὀμφαλὸν σέβων,
οὐδ᾽ ἐς τὸν Ἀβαῖσι ναόν,
οὐδὲ τὰν Ὀλυμπίαν,
εἰ μὴ τάδε χειρόδεικτα
πᾶσιν ἁρμόσει βροτοῖς.
ἀλλ᾽, ὦ κρατύνων, εἴπερ ὄρθ᾽ ἀκούεις,
Ζεῦ, πάντ᾽ ἀνάσσων, μὴ λάθοι
σε τάν τε σὰν ἀθάνατον αἰὲν ἀρχάν.
φθίνοντα γὰρ Πυθόχρηστα Λαΐου
θέσφατ᾽ ἐξαιροῦσιν ἤδη,
κοὐδαμοῦ τιμαῖς Ἀπόλλων ἐμφανής·
ἔρρει δὲ τὰ θεῖα.

ΙΟΚΑΣΤΗ.

χώρας ἄνακτες, δόξα μοι παρεστάθη [Introit.
ναοὺς ἱκέσθαι δαιμόνων, τάδ᾽ ἐν χεροῖν
στέφη λαβούσῃ κἀπιθυμιάματα.
ὑψοῦ γὰρ αἴρει θυμὸν Οἰδίπους ἄγαν
λύπαισι παντοίαισιν· οὐδ᾽ ὁποῖ᾽ ἀνὴρ
ἔννους τὰ καινὰ τοῖς πάλαι τεκμαίρεται,
ἀλλ᾽ ἔστι τοῦ λέγοντος, εἰ φόβους λέγῃ.
ὅτ᾽ οὖν παραινοῦσ᾽ οὐδὲν ἐς πλέον ποιῶ,
πρὸς σ᾽, ὦ Λύκει᾽ Ἄπολλον, ἄγχιστος γὰρ εἶ,
ἱκέτις ἀφῖγμαι τοῖσδε σὺν κατεύγμασιν,
ὅπως λύσιν τιν᾽ ἡμὶν εὐαγῆ πόρῃς·
ὡς νῦν ὀκνοῦμεν πάντες ἐκπεπληγμένον
κεῖνον βλέποντες ὡς κυβερνήτην νεώς.

ΑΓΓΕΛΟΣ.

ἆρ' ἂν παρ' ὑμῶν, ὦ ξένοι, μάθοιμ' ὅπου [Introit.
τὰ τοῦ τυράννου δώματ' ἐστὶν Οἰδίπου;
μάλιστα δ' αὐτὸν εἴπατ', εἰ κάτισθ' ὅπου.

ΧΟΡΟΣ.

στέγαι μὲν αἵδε, καὐτὸς ἔνδον, ὦ ξένε·
γυνὴ δὲ μήτηρ ἥδε τῶν κείνου τέκνων.

ΑΓΓΕΛΟΣ.

ἀλλ' ὀλβία τε καὶ ξὺν ὀλβίοις ἀεὶ
γένοιτ', ἐκείνου γ' οὖσα παντελὴς δάμαρ.

ΙΟΚΑΣΤΗ.

αὕτως δὲ καὶ σύ γ', ὦ ξέν'· ἄξιος γὰρ εἶ
τῆς εὐεπείας οὕνεκ'. ἀλλὰ φράζ' ὅτου
χρῄζων ἀφῖξαι χὤ τι σημῆναι θέλων.

ΑΓΓΕΛΟΣ.

ἀγαθὰ δόμοις τε καὶ πόσει τῷ σῷ, γύναι.

ΙΟΚΑΣΤΗ.

τὰ ποῖα ταῦτα; παρὰ τίνος δ' ἀφιγμένος;

ΑΓΓΕΛΟΣ.

ἐκ τῆς Κορίνθου. τὸ δ' ἔπος οὐξερῶ τάχα,
ἥδοιο μέν, πῶς δ' οὐκ ἄν, ἀσχάλλοις δ' ἴσως.

ΙΟΚΑΣΤΗ.

τί δ' ἔστι; ποίαν δύναμιν ὧδ' ἔχει διπλῆν;

ΑΓΓΕΛΟΣ.

τύραννον αὐτὸν οὑπιχώριοι χθονὸς
τῆς Ἰσθμίας στήσουσιν, ὡς ηὐδᾶτ᾽ ἐκεῖ.

ΙΟΚΑΣΤΗ.

τί δ᾽; οὐχ ὁ πρέσβυς Πόλυβος ἐγκρατὴς ἔτι;

ΑΓΓΕΛΟΣ.

οὐ δῆτ᾽, ἐπεί νιν θάνατος ἐν τάφοις ἔχει.

ΙΟΚΑΣΤΗ.

πῶς εἶπας; ἦ τέθνηκε Πόλυβος, ὦ γέρον;

ΑΓΓΕΛΟΣ.

εἰ μὴ λέγω τἀληθές, ἀξιῶ θανεῖν.

ΙΟΚΑΣΤΗ.

ὦ πρόσπολ᾽, οὐχὶ δεσπότῃ τάδ᾽ ὡς τάχος
μολοῦσα λέξεις; ὦ θεῶν μαντεύματα,
ἵν᾽ ἐστέ· τοῦτον Οἰδίπους πάλαι τρέμων
τὸν ἄνδρ᾽ ἔφευγε μὴ κτάνοι, καὶ νῦν ὅδε
πρὸς τῆς τύχης ὄλωλεν οὐδὲ τοῦδ᾽ ὕπο.

ΟΙΔΙΠΟΥΣ.

ὦ φίλτατον γυναικὸς Ἰοκάστης κάρα, [*Introit.*
τί μ᾽ ἐξεπέμψω δεῦρο τῶνδε δωμάτων;

ΙΟΚΑΣΤΗ.

ἄκουε τἀνδρὸς τοῦδε, καὶ σκόπει κλύων
τὰ σέμν᾽ ἵν᾽ ἥκει τοῦ θεοῦ μαντεύματα.

ΟΙΔΙΠΟΥΣ.

οὗτος δὲ τίς ποτ' ἐστὶ καὶ τί μοι λέγει;

ΙΟΚΑΣΤΗ.

ἐκ τῆς Κορίνθου, πατέρα τὸν σὸν ἀγγελῶν
ὡς οὐκέτ' ὄντα Πόλυβον, ἀλλ' ὀλωλότα.

ΟΙΔΙΠΟΥΣ.

τί φῄς, ξέν'; αὐτός μοι σὺ σημήνας γενοῦ.

ΑΓΓΕΛΟΣ.

εἰ τοῦτο πρῶτον δεῖ μ' ἀπαγγεῖλαι σαφῶς,
εὖ ἴσθ' ἐκεῖνον θανάσιμον βεβηκότα.

ΟΙΔΙΠΟΥΣ.

πότερα δόλοισιν, ἢ νόσου ξυναλλαγῇ;

ΑΓΓΕΛΟΣ.

σμικρὰ παλαιὰ σώματ' εὐνάζει ῥοπή.

ΟΙΔΙΠΟΥΣ.

νόσοις ὁ τλήμων, ὡς ἔοικεν, ἔφθιτο.

ΑΓΓΕΛΟΣ.

καὶ τῷ μακρῷ γε συμμετρούμενος χρόνῳ.

ΟΙΔΙΠΟΥΣ.

φεῦ φεῦ, τί δῆτ' ἄν, ὦ γύναι, σκοποῖτό τις
τὴν Πυθόμαντιν ἑστίαν, ἢ τοὺς ἄνω
κλάζοντας ὄρνις, ὧν ὑφηγητῶν ἐγὼ
κτανεῖν ἔμελλον πατέρα τὸν ἐμόν; ὁ δὲ θανὼν

κεύθει κάτω δὴ γῆς· ἐγὼ δ' ὅδ' ἐνθάδε
ἄψαυστος ἔγχους, εἴ τι μὴ τὠμῷ πόθῳ
κατέφθιθ'· οὕτω δ' ἂν θανὼν εἴη 'ξ ἐμοῦ.
τὰ δ' οὖν παρόντα συλλαβὼν θεσπίσματα
κεῖται παρ' Ἅιδῃ Πόλυβος ἄξι' οὐδενός.

ΙΟΚΑΣΤΗ.

οὔκουν ἐγώ σοι ταῦτα προὔλεγον πάλαι;

ΟΙΔΙΠΟΥΣ.

ηὔδας· ἐγὼ δὲ τῷ φόβῳ παρηγόμην.

ΙΟΚΑΣΤΗ.

μὴ νῦν ἔτ' αὐτῶν μηδὲν ἐς θυμὸν βάλῃς.

ΟΙΔΙΠΟΥΣ.

καὶ πῶς τὸ μητρὸς λέκτρον οὐκ ὀκνεῖν με δεῖ;

ΙΟΚΑΣΤΗ.

τί δ' ἂν φοβοῖτ' ἄνθρωπος, ᾧ τὰ τῆς τύχης
κρατεῖ, πρόνοια δ' ἐστὶν οὐδενὸς σαφής;
εἰκῇ κράτιστον ζῆν, ὅπως δύναιτό τις.
σὺ δ' εἰς τὰ μητρὸς μὴ φοβοῦ νυμφεύματα·
πολλοὶ γὰρ ἤδη κἀν ὀνείρασιν βροτῶν
μητρὶ ξυνευνάσθησαν. ἀλλὰ ταῦθ' ὅτῳ
παρ' οὐδέν ἐστι, ῥᾷστα τὸν βίον φέρει.

ΟΙΔΙΠΟΥΣ.

καλῶς ἅπαντα ταῦτ' ἂν ἐξείρητό σοι,
εἰ μὴ 'κύρει ζῶσ' ἡ τεκοῦσα· νῦν δ' ἐπεὶ
ζῇ, πᾶσ' ἀνάγκη, κεἰ καλῶς λέγεις, ὀκνεῖν.

ΙΟΚΑΣΤΗ.

καὶ μὴν μέγας γ᾽ ὀφθαλμὸς οἱ πατρὸς τάφοι.

ΟΙΔΙΠΟΥΣ.

μέγας, ξυνίημ᾽· ἀλλὰ τῆς ζώσης φόβος.

ΑΓΓΕΛΟΣ.

ποίας δὲ καὶ γυναικὸς ἐκφοβεῖσθ᾽ ὕπερ;

ΟΙΔΙΠΟΥΣ.

Μερόπης, γεραιέ, Πόλυβος ἧς ᾤκει μέτα.

ΑΓΓΕΛΟΣ.

τί δ᾽ ἔστ᾽ ἐκείνης ὑμὶν ἐς φόβον φέρον;

ΟΙΔΙΠΟΥΣ.

θεήλατον μάντευμα δεινόν, ὦ ξένε.

ΑΓΓΕΛΟΣ.

ἦ ῥητόν; ἢ οὐχὶ θεμιτὸν ἄλλον εἰδέναι;

ΟΙΔΙΠΟΥΣ.

μάλιστά γ᾽· εἶπε γάρ με Λοξίας ποτὲ
χρῆναι μιγῆναι μητρὶ τἠμαυτοῦ, τό τε
πατρῷον αἷμα χερσὶ ταῖς ἐμαῖς ἑλεῖν.
ὧν οὕνεχ᾽ ἡ Κόρινθος ἐξ ἐμοῦ πάλαι
μακρὰν ἀπῳκεῖτ᾽· εὐτυχῶς μέν, ἀλλ᾽ ὅμως
τὰ τῶν τεκόντων ὄμμαθ᾽ ἥδιστον βλέπειν.

ΑΓΓΕΛΟΣ.

ἦ γὰρ τάδ᾽ ὀκνῶν κεῖθεν ἦσθ᾽ ἀπόπτολις;

ΟΙΔΙΠΟΥΣ.

πατρός τε χρῄζων μὴ φονεὺς εἶναι, γέρον.

ΑΓΓΕΛΟΣ.

τί δῆτ' ἐγὼ οὐχὶ τοῦδε τοῦ φόβου σ', ἄναξ,
ἐπείπερ εὔνους ἦλθον, ἐξελυσάμην;

ΟΙΔΙΠΟΥΣ.

καὶ μὴν χάριν γ' ἂν ἀξίαν λάβοις ἐμοῦ.

ΑΓΓΕΛΟΣ.

καὶ μὴν μάλιστα τοῦτ' ἀφικόμην, ὅπως
σοῦ πρὸς δόμους ἐλθόντος εὖ πράξαιμί τι.

ΟΙΔΙΠΟΥΣ.

ἀλλ' οὔποτ' εἶμι τοῖς φυτεύσασίν γ' ὁμοῦ.

ΑΓΓΕΛΟΣ.

ὦ παῖ, καλῶς εἶ δῆλος οὐκ εἰδὼς τί δρᾷς.

ΟΙΔΙΠΟΥΣ.

πῶς, ὦ γεραιέ; πρὸς θεῶν δίδασκέ με.

ΑΓΓΕΛΟΣ.

εἰ τῶνδε φεύγεις οὕνεκ' εἰς οἴκους μολεῖν.

ΟΙΔΙΠΟΥΣ.

ταρβῶ γε μή μοι Φοῖβος ἐξέλθῃ σαφής.

ΑΓΓΕΛΟΣ.

ἦ μὴ μίασμα τῶν φυτευσάντων λάβῃς;

ΟΙΔΙΠΟΥΣ.

τοῦτ' αὐτό, πρέσβυ, τοῦτό μ' εἰσαεὶ φοβεῖ.

ΑΓΓΕΛΟΣ.

ἆρ' οἶσθα δῆτα πρὸς δίκης οὐδὲν τρέμων;

ΟΙΔΙΠΟΥΣ.

πῶς δ' οὐχί, παῖς γ' εἰ τῶνδε γεννητῶν ἔφυν;

ΑΓΓΕΛΟΣ.

ὁθούνεκ' ἦν σοι Πόλυβος οὐδὲν ἐν γένει.

ΟΙΔΙΠΟΥΣ.

πῶς εἶπας; οὐ γὰρ Πόλυβος ἐξέφυσέ με;

ΑΓΓΕΛΟΣ.

οὐ μᾶλλον οὐδὲν τοῦδε τἀνδρός, ἀλλ' ἴσον.

ΟΙΔΙΠΟΥΣ.

καὶ πῶς ὁ φύσας ἐξ ἴσου τῷ μηδενί;

ΑΓΓΕΛΟΣ.

ἀλλ' οὔ σ' ἐγείνατ' οὔτ' ἐκεῖνος οὔτ' ἐγώ.

ΟΙΔΙΠΟΥΣ.

ἀλλ' ἀντὶ τοῦ δὴ παῖδά μ' ὠνομάζετο;

ΑΓΓΕΛΟΣ.

δῶρόν ποτ', ἴσθι, τῶν ἐμῶν χειρῶν λαβών.

ΟΙΔΙΠΟΥΣ.

κᾆθ' ὧδ' ἀπ' ἄλλης χειρὸς ἔστερξεν μέγα;

ΑΓΓΕΛΟΣ.

ἡ γὰρ πρὶν αὐτὸν ἐξέπεισ' ἀπαιδία.

ΟΙΔΙΠΟΥΣ.

σὺ δ' ἐμπολήσας, ἢ τεκών μ' αὐτῷ δίδως;

ΑΓΓΕΛΟΣ.

εὑρὼν ναπαίαις ἐν Κιθαιρῶνος πτυχαῖς.

ΟΙΔΙΠΟΥΣ.

ὡδοιπόρεις δὲ πρὸς τί τούσδε τοὺς τόπους;

ΑΓΓΕΛΟΣ.

ἐνταῦθ' ὀρείοις ποιμνίοις ἐπεστάτουν.

ΟΙΔΙΠΟΥΣ.

ποιμὴν γὰρ ἦσθα κἀπὶ θητείᾳ πλάνης;

ΑΓΓΕΛΟΣ.

σοῦ δ', ὦ τέκνον, σωτήρ γε τῷ τότ' ἐν χρόνῳ.

ΟΙΔΙΠΟΥΣ.

τί δ' ἄλγος ἴσχοντ' ἐν κακοῖς με λαμβάνεις;

ΑΓΓΕΛΟΣ.

ποδῶν ἂν ἄρθρα μαρτυρήσειεν τὰ σά.

ΟΙΔΙΠΟΥΣ.

οἴμοι, τί τοῦτ' ἀρχαῖον ἐννέπεις κακόν;

ΑΓΓΕΛΟΣ.

λύω σ' ἔχοντα διατόρους ποδοῖν ἀκμάς.

ΟΙΔΙΠΟΥΣ.

δεινόν γ' ὄνειδος σπαργάνων ἀνειλόμην.

ΑΓΓΕΛΟΣ.

ὥστ' ὠνομάσθης ἐκ τύχης ταύτης ὃς εἶ.

ΟΙΔΙΠΟΥΣ.

ὦ πρὸς θεῶν, πρὸς μητρός, ἢ πατρός, φράσον.

ΑΓΓΕΛΟΣ.

οὐκ οἶδ'· ὁ δοὺς δὲ ταῦτ' ἐμοῦ λῷον φρονεῖ.

ΟΙΔΙΠΟΥΣ.

ἦ γὰρ παρ' ἄλλου μ' ἔλαβες οὐδ' αὐτὸς τυχών;

ΑΓΓΕΛΟΣ.

οὔκ, ἀλλὰ ποιμήν ἄλλος ἐκδίδωσί μοι.

ΟΙΔΙΠΟΥΣ.

τίς οὗτος; ἦ κάτοισθα δηλῶσαι λόγῳ;

ΑΓΓΕΛΟΣ.

τῶν Λαΐου δήπου τις ὠνομάζετο.

ΟΙΔΙΠΟΥΣ.

ἦ τοῦ τυράννου τῆσδε γῆς πάλαι ποτέ;

ΑΓΓΕΛΟΣ.

μάλιστα· τούτου τἀνδρὸς οὗτος ἦν βοτήρ.

ΟΙΔΙΠΟΥΣ.

ἦ κἄστ' ἔτι ζῶν οὗτος, ὥστ' ἰδεῖν ἐμέ;

ΑΓΓΕΛΟΣ.

ὑμεῖς γ' ἄριστ' εἰδεῖτ' ἂν οὑπιχώριοι.

ΟΙΔΙΠΟΥΣ.

ἔστιν τις ὑμῶν τῶν παρεστώτων πέλας,
ὅστις κάτοιδε τὸν βοτῆρ', ὃν ἐννέπει,
εἴτ' οὖν ἐπ' ἀγρῶν εἴτε κἀνθάδ' εἰσιδών;
σημήναθ', ὡς ὁ καιρὸς εὑρῆσθαι τάδε.

ΧΟΡΟΣ.

οἶμαι μὲν οὐδέν' ἄλλον ἢ τὸν ἐξ ἀγρῶν,
ὃν κἀμάτευες πρόσθεν εἰσιδεῖν· ἀτὰρ
ἥδ' ἂν τάδ' οὐχ ἥκιστ' ἂν Ἰοκάστη λέγοι.

ΟΙΔΙΠΟΥΣ.

γύναι, νοεῖς ἐκεῖνον, ὅντιν' ἀρτίως
μολεῖν ἐφιέμεσθα; τόνδ' οὗτος λέγει;

ΙΟΚΑΣΤΗ.

τί δ' ὅντιν' εἶπε; μηδὲν ἐντραπῇς. τὰ δὲ
ῥηθέντα βούλου μηδὲ μεμνῆσθαι μάτην.

ΟΙΔΙΠΟΥΣ.

οὐκ ἂν γένοιτο τοῦθ', ὅπως ἐγὼ λαβὼν
σημεῖα τοιαῦτ' οὐ φανῶ τοὐμὸν γένος.

ΙΟΚΑΣΤΗ.

μὴ πρὸς θεῶν, εἴπερ τι τοῦ σαυτοῦ βίου
κήδει, ματεύσῃς τοῦθ'· ἅλις νοσοῦσ' ἐγώ.

ΟΙΔΙΠΟΥΣ.

θάρσει. σὺ μὲν γὰρ οὐδ' ἐὰν τρίτης ἐγὼ
μητρὸς φανῶ τρίδουλος, ἐκφανεῖ κακή.

ΙΟΚΑΣΤΗ.

ὅμως πιθοῦ μοι, λίσσομαι· μὴ δρᾶ τάδε.

ΟΙΔΙΠΟΥΣ.

οὐκ ἂν πιθοίμην μὴ οὐ τάδ' ἐκμαθεῖν σαφῶς.

ΙΟΚΑΣΤΗ.

καὶ μὴν φρονοῦσά γ' εὖ τὰ λῷστά σοι λέγω.

ΟΙΔΙΠΟΥΣ.

τὰ λῷστα τοίνυν ταῦτά μ' ἀλγύνει πάλαι.

ΙΟΚΑΣΤΗ.

ὦ δύσποτμ', εἴθε μήποτε γνοίης ὃς εἶ.

ΟΙΔΙΠΟΥΣ.

ἄξει τις ἐλθὼν δεῦρο τὸν βοτῆρά μοι;
ταύτην δ' ἐᾶτε πλουσίῳ χαίρειν γένει.

ΙΟΚΑΣΤΗ.

ἰοὺ ἰού, δύστηνε· τοῦτο γάρ σ' ἔχω
μόνον προσειπεῖν, ἄλλο δ' οὔποθ' ὕστερον. [*Exit.*

ΧΟΡΟΣ.

τί ποτε βέβηκεν, Οἰδίπους, ὑπ' ἀγρίας
ᾄξασα λύπης ἡ γυνή; δέδοιχ' ὅπως
μὴ 'κ τῆς σιωπῆς τῆσδ' ἀναρρήξει κακά.

ΟΙΔΙΠΟΥΣ.

ὁποῖα χρῄζει ῥηγνύτω· τοὐμὸν δ' ἐγώ,
κεἰ σμικρόν ἐστι, σπέρμ' ἰδεῖν βουλήσομαι.

αὕτη δ' ἴσως, φρονεῖ γὰρ ὡς γυνὴ μέγα,
τὴν δυσγένειαν τὴν ἐμὴν αἰσχύνεται.
ἐγὼ δ' ἐμαυτὸν παῖδα τῆς Τύχης νέμων
τῆς εὖ διδούσης οὐκ ἀτιμασθήσομαι.
τῆς γὰρ πέφυκα μητρός· οἱ δὲ συγγενεῖς
μῆνές με μικρὸν καὶ μέγαν διώρισαν.
τοιόσδε δ' ἐκφὺς οὐκ ἂν ἐξέλθοιμ' ἔτι
ποτ' ἄλλος, ὥστε μὴ 'κμαθεῖν τοὐμὸν γένος.

ΧΟΡΟΣ.

στρ.

εἴπερ ἐγὼ μάντις εἰμὶ καὶ κατὰ γνώμαν ἴδρις,
οὐ τὸν Ὄλυμπον ἀπείρων, ὦ Κιθαιρών,
οὐκ ἔσῃ τὰν αὔριον πανσέληνον, μὴ οὐ σέ γε
καὶ πατριώταν Οἰδίπου
καὶ τροφὸν καὶ ματέρ' αὔξειν,
καὶ χορεύεσθαι πρὸς ἡμῶν, ὡς ἐπίηρα φέροντα τοῖς ἐμοῖς
τυράννοις.
ἰήϊε Φοῖβε, σοὶ δὲ
ταῦτ' ἀρέστ' εἴη.

ἀντ.

τίς σε, τέκνον, τίς σ' ἔτικτε τᾶν μακραιώνων κορᾶν,
Πανὸς ὀρεσσιβάτα πατρὸς πελασθεῖσ',
ἤ σέ γ' εὐνάτειρά τις Λοξίου; τῷ γὰρ πλάκες
ἀγρόνομοι πᾶσαι φίλαι·
εἴθ' ὁ Κυλλάνας ἀνάσσων,
εἴθ' ὁ Βακχεῖος θεὸς ναίων ἐπ' ἄκρων ὀρέων εὕρημα δέξατ'
ἔκ του

Νυμφᾶν Ἑλικωνίδων, αἷς
πλεῖστα συμπαίζει.

ΟΙΔΙΠΟΥΣ.

εἰ χρή τι κἀμὲ μὴ συναλλάξαντά πω,
πρέσβεις, σταθμᾶσθαι, τὸν βοτῆρ' ὁρᾶν δοκῶ,
ὅνπερ πάλαι ζητοῦμεν. ἔν τε γὰρ μακρῷ
γήρᾳ ξυνᾴδει τῷδε τἀνδρὶ σύμμετρος,
ἄλλως τε τοὺς ἄγοντας ὥσπερ οἰκέτας
ἔγνωκ' ἐμαυτοῦ· τῇ δ' ἐπιστήμῃ σύ μου
προὔχοις τάχ' ἄν που, τὸν βοτῆρ' ἰδὼν πάρος.

ΧΟΡΟΣ.

ἔγνωκα γάρ, σάφ' ἴσθι· Λαΐου γὰρ ἦν
εἴπερ τις ἄλλος πιστὸς ὡς νομεὺς ἀνήρ.

ΟΙΔΙΠΟΥΣ.

σὲ πρῶτ' ἐρωτῶ, τὸν Κορίνθιον ξένον,
ἦ τόνδε φράζεις;

ΑΓΓΕΛΟΣ.

τοῦτον, ὅνπερ εἰσορᾷς.

ΟΙΔΙΠΟΥΣ.

οὗτος σύ, πρέσβυ, δεῦρό μοι φώνει βλέπων [*Introit*
ὅσ' ἄν σ' ἐρωτῶ. Λαΐου ποτ' ἦσθα σύ; *pastor* LAII.

ΘΕΡΑΠΩΝ.

ἦ δοῦλος οὐκ ὠνητός, ἀλλ' οἴκοι τραφείς.

ΟΙΔΙΠΟΥΣ.

ἔργον μεριμνῶν ποῖον ἢ βίον τίνα;

ΘΕΡΑΠΩΝ.

ποίμναις τὰ πλεῖστα τοῦ βίου συνειπόμην.

ΟΙΔΙΠΟΥΣ.

χώροις μάλιστα πρὸς τίσι ξύναυλος ὤν;

ΘΕΡΑΠΩΝ.

ἦν μὲν Κιθαιρών, ἦν δὲ πρόσχωρος τόπος.

ΟΙΔΙΠΟΥΣ.

τὸν ἄνδρα τόνδ᾽ οὖν οἶσθα τῇδέ που μαθών;

ΘΕΡΑΠΩΝ.

τί χρῆμα δρῶντα; ποῖον ἄνδρα καὶ λέγεις;

ΟΙΔΙΠΟΥΣ.

τόνδ᾽ ὃς πάρεστιν· ἦ ξυνήλλαξας τί πω;

ΘΕΡΑΠΩΝ.

οὐχ ὥστε γ᾽ εἰπεῖν ἐν τάχει μνήμης ὕπο.

ΑΓΓΕΛΟΣ.

κοὐδέν γε θαῦμα, δέσποτ᾽. ἀλλ᾽ ἐγὼ σαφῶς
ἀγνῶτ᾽ ἀναμνήσω νιν. εὖ γὰρ οἶδ᾽ ὅτι
κάτοιδεν ἦμος τὸν Κιθαιρῶνος τόπον
ὁ μὲν διπλοῖσι ποιμνίοις, ἐγὼ δ᾽ ἑνὶ
ἐπλησίαζον τῷδε τἀνδρὶ τρεῖς ὅλους
ἐξ ἦρος εἰς ἀρκτοῦρον ἐκμήνους χρόνους·

χειμῶνα δ' ἤδη τἀμά τ' εἰς ἔπαυλ' ἐγὼ
ἤλαυνον οὗτός τ' εἰς τὰ Λαΐου σταθμά.
λέγω τι τούτων, ἢ οὐ λέγω πεπραγμένον;

ΘΕΡΑΠΩΝ.

λέγεις ἀληθῆ, καίπερ ἐκ μακροῦ χρόνου.

ΑΓΓΕΛΟΣ.

φέρ' εἰπὲ νῦν, τότ' οἶσθα παῖδά μοί τινα
δούς, ὡς ἐμαυτῷ θρέμμα θρεψαίμην ἐγώ;

ΘΕΡΑΠΩΝ.

τί δ' ἐστὶ — πρὸς τί τοῦτο τοὔπος ἱστορεῖς;

ΑΓΓΕΛΟΣ.

ὅδ' ἐστίν, ὦ τᾶν, κεῖνος ὃς τότ' ἦν νέος.

ΘΕΡΑΠΩΝ.

οὐκ εἰς ὄλεθρον; οὐ σιωπήσας ἔσει;

ΟΙΔΙΠΟΥΣ.

ἆ, μὴ κόλαζε, πρέσβυ, τόνδ', ἐπεὶ τὰ σὰ
δεῖται κολαστοῦ μᾶλλον ἢ τὰ τοῦδ' ἔπη.

ΘΕΡΑΠΩΝ.

τί δ', ὦ φέριστε δεσποτῶν, ἁμαρτάνω;

ΟΙΔΙΠΟΥΣ.

οὐκ ἐννέπων τὸν παῖδ' ὃν οὗτος ἱστορεῖ.

ΘΕΡΑΠΩΝ.

λέγει γὰρ εἰδὼς οὐδέν, ἀλλ' ἄλλως πονεῖ.

ΟΙΔΙΠΟΥΣ.

σὺ πρὸς χάριν μὲν οὐκ ἐρεῖς, κλαίων δ' ἐρεῖς.

ΘΕΡΑΠΩΝ.

μὴ δῆτα, πρὸς θεῶν, τὸν γέροντά μ' αἰκίσῃ.

ΟΙΔΙΠΟΥΣ.

οὐχ ὡς τάχος τις τοῦδ' ἀποστρέψει χέρας;

ΘΕΡΑΠΩΝ.

δύστηνος, ἀντὶ τοῦ; τί προσχρῄζων μαθεῖν;

ΟΙΔΙΠΟΥΣ.

τὸν παῖδ' ἔδωκας τῷδ' ὃν οὗτος ἱστορεῖ;

ΘΕΡΑΠΩΝ.

ἔδωκ'· ὀλέσθαι δ' ὤφελον τῇδ' ἡμέρᾳ.

ΟΙΔΙΠΟΥΣ.

ἀλλ' εἰς τόδ' ἥξεις μὴ λέγων γε τοὔνδικον.

ΘΕΡΑΠΩΝ.

πολλῷ γε μᾶλλον, ἢν φράσω, διόλλυμαι.

ΟΙΔΙΠΟΥΣ.

ἁνὴρ ὅδ', ὡς ἔοικεν, ἐς τριβὰς ἐλᾷ.

ΘΕΡΑΠΩΝ.

οὐ δῆτ' ἔγωγ', ἀλλ' εἶπον ὡς δοίην πάλαι.

ΟΙΔΙΠΟΥΣ.

πόθεν λαβών; οἰκεῖον, ἢ 'ξ ἄλλου τινός;

ΘΕΡΑΠΩΝ.

ἐμὸν μὲν οὐκ ἔγωγ᾽, ἐδεξάμην δέ του.

ΟΙΔΙΠΟΥΣ.

τίνος πολιτῶν τῶνδε κἀκ ποίας στέγης;

ΘΕΡΑΠΩΝ.

μὴ πρὸς θεῶν, μή, δέσποθ᾽, ἱστόρει πλέον.

ΟΙΔΙΠΟΥΣ.

ὄλωλας, εἴ σε ταῦτ᾽ ἐρήσομαι πάλιν.

ΘΕΡΑΠΩΝ.

τῶν Λαΐου τοίνυν τις ἦν γεννημάτων.

ΟΙΔΙΠΟΥΣ.

ἦ δοῦλος, ἢ κείνου τις ἐγγενὴς γεγώς;

ΘΕΡΑΠΩΝ.

οἴμοι, πρὸς αὐτῷ γ᾽ εἰμὶ τῷ δεινῷ λέγειν.

ΟΙΔΙΠΟΥΣ.

κἄγωγ᾽ ἀκούειν· ἀλλ᾽ ὅμως ἀκουστέον.

ΘΕΡΑΠΩΝ.

κείνου γέ τοι δὴ παῖς ἐκλῄζεθ᾽· ἡ δ᾽ ἔσω
κάλλιστ᾽ ἂν εἴποι σὴ γυνὴ τάδ᾽ ὡς ἔχει.

ΟΙΔΙΠΟΥΣ.

ἦ γὰρ δίδωσιν ἥδε σοι;

ΘΕΡΑΠΩΝ.

μάλιστ᾽, ἄναξ.

ΟΙΔΙΠΟΥΣ.

ὡς πρὸς τί χρείας;

ΘΕΡΑΠΩΝ.

ὡς ἀναλώσαιμί νιν.

ΟΙΔΙΠΟΥΣ.

τεκοῦσα τλήμων;

ΘΕΡΑΠΩΝ.

θεσφάτων γ' ὄκνῳ κακῶν.

ΟΙΔΙΠΟΥΣ.

ποίων;

ΘΕΡΑΠΩΝ.

κτενεῖν νιν τοὺς τεκόντας ἦν λόγος.

ΟΙΔΙΠΟΥΣ.

πῶς δῆτ' ἀφῆκας τῷ γέροντι τῷδε σύ;

ΘΕΡΑΠΩΝ.

κατοικτίσας, ὦ δέσποθ', ὡς ἄλλην χθόνα
δοκῶν ἀποίσειν, αὐτὸς ἔνθεν ἦν· ὁ δὲ
κάκ' ἐς μέγιστ' ἔσωσεν. εἰ γὰρ οὗτος εἶ
ὅν φησιν οὗτος, ἴσθι δύσποτμος γεγώς.

ΟΙΔΙΠΟΥΣ.

ἰοὺ ἰού· τὰ πάντ' ἂν ἐξήκοι σαφῆ.
ὦ φῶς, τελευταῖόν σε προσβλέψαιμι νῦν,
ὅστις πέφασμαι φύς τ' ἀφ' ὧν οὐ χρῆν, ξὺν οἷς τ'
οὐ χρῆν ὁμιλῶν, οὕς τέ μ' οὐκ ἔδει κτανών.

[*Exeunt.*

ΧΟΡΟΣ.

στρ. ά.

ἰὼ γενεαὶ βροτῶν,
ὡς ὑμᾶς ἴσα καὶ τὸ μηδὲν ζώσας ἐναριθμῶ.
τίς γάρ, τίς ἀνὴρ πλέον
τᾶς εὐδαιμονίας φέρει
ἢ τοσοῦτον ὅσον δοκεῖν
καὶ δόξαντ᾽ ἀποκλῖναι;
τὸ σόν τοι παράδειγμ᾽ ἔχων,
τὸν σὸν δαίμονα, τὸν σόν, ὦ τλάμων Οἰδιπόδα, βροτῶν
οὐδὲν μακαρίζω·

ἀντ. ά.

ὅστις καθ᾽ ὑπερβολὰν
τοξεύσας ἐκράτησας τοῦ πάντ᾽ εὐδαίμονος ὄλβου,
ὦ Ζεῦ, κατὰ μὲν φθίσας
τὰν γαμψώνυχα παρθένον
χρησμῳδόν· θανάτων δ᾽ ἐμᾷ
χώρᾳ πύργος ἀνέστας·
ἐξ οὗ καὶ βασιλεὺς καλεῖ
ἐμός, καὶ τὰ μέγιστ᾽ ἐτιμάθης, ταῖς μεγάλαισιν ἐν
Θήβαισιν ἀνάσσων.

στρ. β΄.

ταννῦν δ᾽ ἀκούειν τίς ἀθλιώτερος;
τίς ἄταις ἐν ἀγρίαις, τίς ἐν πόνοις
ξύνοικος ἀλλαγᾷ βίου;
ἰὼ κλεινὸν Οἰδίπου κάρα,
ᾧ μέγας λιμὴν
αὑτὸς ἤρκεσεν
παιδὶ καὶ πατρὶ θαλαμηπόλῳ πεσεῖν,

πῶς ποτε πῶς ποθ' αἱ πατρῷαί σ' ἄλοκες φέρειν,
τάλας,
σῖγ' ἐδυνάσθησαν ἐς τοσόνδε;

ἀντ. β'.

ἐφεῦρέ σ' ἄκονθ' ὁ πάνθ' ὁρῶν χρόνος,
δικάζει τὸν ἄγαμον γάμον πάλαι,
τεκνοῦντα καὶ τεκνούμενον.
ἰώ, Λαΐειον ὦ τέκνον,
εἴθε σ', εἴθε σε
μήποτ' εἰδόμαν.
δύρομαι γὰρ ὡς περίαλλ' ἰακχίων
ἐκ στομάτων. τὸ δ' ὀρθὸν εἰπεῖν, ἀνέπνευσά τ' ἐκ
σέθεν
καὶ κατεκοίμησα τοὐμὸν ὄμμα.

ΕΞΑΓΓΕΛΟΣ.

ὦ γῆς μέγιστα τῆσδ' ἀεὶ τιμώμενοι, [*Introit.*
οἷ' ἔργ' ἀκούσεσθ', οἷα δ' εἰσόψεσθ', ὅσον δ'
ἀρεῖσθε πένθος, εἴπερ ἐγγενῶς ἔτι
τῶν Λαβδακείων ἐντρέπεσθε δωμάτων.
οἶμαι γὰρ οὔτ' ἂν Ἴστρον οὔτε Φᾶσιν ἂν
νίψαι καθαρμῷ τήνδε τὴν στέγην, ὅσα
κεύθει, τὰ δ' αὐτίκ' εἰς τὸ φῶς φανεῖ κακὰ
ἑκόντα κοὐκ ἄκοντα. τῶν δὲ πημονῶν
μάλιστα λυποῦσ' αἳ φανῶσ' αὐθαίρετοι.

ΧΟΡΟΣ.

λείπει μὲν οὐδ' ἃ πρόσθεν ᾔδεμεν τὸ μὴ οὐ
βαρύστον' εἶναι· πρὸς δ' ἐκείνοισιν τί φῇς;

ΕΞΑΓΓΕΛΟΣ.

ὁ μὲν τάχιστος τῶν λόγων εἰπεῖν τε καὶ
μαθεῖν, τέθνηκε θεῖον Ἰοκάστης κάρα.

ΧΟΡΟΣ.

ὦ δυστάλαινα, πρὸς τίνος ποτ' αἰτίας;

ΕΞΑΓΓΕΛΟΣ.

αὐτὴ πρὸς αὐτῆς· τῶν δὲ πραχθέντων τὰ μὲν
ἄλγιστ' ἄπεστιν· ἡ γὰρ ὄψις οὐ πάρα.
ὅμως δ', ὅσον γε κἀν ἐμοὶ μνήμης ἔνι,
πεύσει τὰ κείνης ἀθλίας παθήματα.
ὅπως γὰρ ὀργῇ χρωμένη παρῆλθ' ἔσω
θυρῶνος, ἵετ' εὐθὺ πρὸς τὰ νυμφικὰ
λέχη, κόμην σπῶσ' ἀμφιδεξίοις ἀκμαῖς.
πύλας δ' ὅπως εἰσῆλθ' ἐπιρράξασ' ἔσω
καλεῖ τὸν ἤδη Λάϊον πάλαι νεκρόν,
μνήμην παλαιῶν σπερμάτων ἔχουσ', ὑφ' ὧν
θάνοι μὲν αὐτός, τὴν δὲ τίκτουσαν λίποι
τοῖς οἷσιν αὐτοῦ δύστεκνον παιδουργίαν.
γοᾶτο δ' εὐνάς, ἔνθα δύστηνος διπλοῦς
ἐξ ἀνδρὸς ἄνδρα καὶ τέκν' ἐκ τέκνων τέκοι.
χὤπως μὲν ἐκ τῶνδ' οὐκέτ' οἶδ' ἀπόλλυται·
βοῶν γὰρ εἰσέπαισεν Οἰδίπους, ὑφ' οὗ
οὐκ ἦν τὸ κείνης ἐκθεάσασθαι κακόν,
ἀλλ' εἰς ἐκεῖνον περιπολοῦντ' ἐλεύσσομεν.
φοιτᾷ γὰρ ἡμᾶς ἔγχος ἐξαιτῶν πορεῖν,
γυναῖκά τ' οὐ γυναῖκα, μητρῴαν δ' ὅπου
κίχοι διπλῆν ἄρουραν οὗ τε καὶ τέκνων.

λυσσῶντι δ' αὐτῷ δαιμόνων δείκνυσί τις·
οὐδεὶς γὰρ ἀνδρῶν, οἳ παρῆμεν ἐγγύθεν.
δεινὸν δ' ἀΰσας ὡς ὑφηγητοῦ τινος
πύλαις διπλαῖς ἐνήλατ', ἐκ δὲ πυθμένων
ἔκλινε κοῖλα κλῇθρα κἀμπίπτει στέγῃ.
οὗ δὴ κρεμαστὴν τὴν γυναῖκ' ἐσείδομεν,
πλεκταῖσιν αἰώραισιν ἐμπεπληγμένην.
ὁ δ' ὡς ὁρᾷ νιν, δεινὰ βρυχηθεὶς τάλας,
χαλᾷ κρεμαστὴν ἀρτάνην. ἐπεὶ δὲ γῇ
ἔκειτο τλήμων, δεινὰ δ' ἦν τἀνθένδ' ὁρᾶν.
ἀποσπάσας γὰρ εἱμάτων χρυσηλάτους
περόνας ἀπ' αὐτῆς, αἷσιν ἐξεστέλλετο,
ἄρας ἔπαισεν ἄρθρα τῶν αὑτοῦ κύκλων,
αὐδῶν τοιαῦθ', ὁθούνεκ' οὐκ ὄψοιντό νιν
οὔθ' οἷ' ἔπασχεν οὔθ' ὁποῖ' ἔδρα κακά,
ἀλλ' ἐν σκότῳ τὸ λοιπὸν οὓς μὲν οὐκ ἔδει
ὀψοίαθ', οὓς δ' ἔχρῃζεν οὐ γνωσοίατο.
τοιαῦτ' ἐφυμνῶν πολλάκις τε κοὐχ ἅπαξ
ἤρασσ' ἐπαίρων βλέφαρα. φοίνιαι δ' ὁμοῦ
γλῆναι γένει' ἔτεγγον, οὐδ' ἀνίεσαν
φόνου μυδώσας σταγόνας, ἀλλ' ὁμοῦ μέλας
ὄμβρος χαλάζης αἱματοῦς ἐτέγγετο.
τάδ' ἐκ δυοῖν ἔρρωγεν, οὐ μόνου κακά,
ἀλλ' ἀνδρὶ καὶ γυναικὶ συμμιγῆ κακά.
ὁ πρὶν παλαιὸς δ' ὄλβος ἦν πάροιθε μὲν
ὄλβος δικαίως· νῦν δὲ τῇδε θἠμέρᾳ
στεναγμός, ἄτη, θάνατος, αἰσχύνη, κακῶν
ὅσ' ἐστὶ πάντων ὀνόματ', οὐδέν ἐστ' ἀπόν.

ΧΟΡΟΣ.

νῦν δ' ἔσθ' ὁ τλήμων ἔν τινι σχολῇ κακοῦ;

ΕΞΑΓΓΕΛΟΣ.

βοᾷ διοίγειν κλῇθρα καὶ δηλοῦν τινα
τοῖς πᾶσι Καδμείοισι τὸν πατροκτόνον,
τὸν μητρὸς — αὐδῶν ἀνόσι' οὐδὲ ῥητά μοι,
ὡς ἐκ χθονὸς ῥίψων ἑαυτόν, οὐδ' ἔτι
μενῶν δόμοις ἀραῖος, ὡς ἠράσατο.
ῥώμης γε μέντοι καὶ προηγητοῦ τινος
δεῖται· τὸ γὰρ νόσημα μεῖζον ἢ φέρειν.
δείξει δὲ καὶ σοί. κλῇθρα γὰρ πυλῶν τάδε
διοίγεται· θέαμα δ' εἰσόψει τάχα
τοιοῦτον οἷον καὶ στυγοῦντ' ἐποικτίσαι.

ΧΟΡΟΣ.

ὦ δεινὸν ἰδεῖν πάθος ἀνθρώποις, [*Introit* Œd.
ὦ δεινότατον πάντων ὅσ' ἐγὼ
προσέκυρσ' ἤδη. τίς σ', ὦ τλῆμον,
προσέβη μανία; τίς ὁ πηδήσας
μείζονα δαίμων τῶν μακίστων
πρὸς σῇ δυσδαίμονι μοίρᾳ;
φεῦ φεῦ, δύσταν'· ἀλλ' οὐδ' ἐσιδεῖν
δύναμαί σε, θέλων πόλλ' ἀνερέσθαι,
πολλὰ πυθέσθαι, πολλὰ δ' ἀθρῆσαι·
τοίαν φρίκην παρέχεις μοι.

ΟΙΔΙΠΟΥΣ.

αἰαῖ αἰαῖ, δύστανος ἐγώ,
ποῖ γᾶς φέρομαι τλάμων; πᾶ μοι

φθογγὰ δι' ἄλας πέταται φοράδην;
ἰὼ δαῖμον, ἵν' ἐξήλλου.

ΧΟΡΟΣ.

ἐς δεινόν, οὐδ' ἀκουστόν, οὐδ' ἐπόψιμον.

ΟΙΔΙΠΟΥΣ.

στρ. ά.

ἰὼ σκότου
νέφος ἐμὸν ἀπότροπον, ἐπιπλόμενον ἄφατον,
ἀδάματόν τε καὶ δυσούριστον ὄν.
οἴμοι,
οἴμοι μάλ' αὖθις· οἷον εἰσέδυ μ' ἅμα
κέντρων τε τῶνδ' οἴστρημα καὶ μνήμη κακῶν.

ΧΟΡΟΣ.

καὶ θαῦμά γ' οὐδὲν ἐν τοσοῖσδε πήμασιν
διπλᾶ σε πενθεῖν καὶ διπλᾶ φέρειν κακά.

ΟΙΔΙΠΟΥΣ.

ἀντ. ά.

ἰὼ φίλος,
σὺ μὲν ἐμὸς ἐπίπολος ἔτι μόνιμος· ἔτι γὰρ
ὑπομένεις με τὸν τυφλὸν κηδεύων.
φεῦ φεῦ.
οὐ γάρ με λήθεις, ἀλλὰ γιγνώσκω σαφῶς,
καίπερ σκοτεινός, τήν γε σὴν αὐδὴν ὅμως.

ΧΟΡΟΣ.

ὦ δεινὰ δράσας, πῶς ἔτλης τοιαῦτα σὰς
ὄψεις μαρᾶναι; τίς σ' ἐπῆρε δαιμόνων;

ΟΙΔΙΠΟΥΣ.

στρ. β'.

Ἀπόλλων τάδ' ἦν, Ἀπόλλων, φίλοι,
ὁ κακὰ κακὰ τελῶν ἐμὰ τάδ' ἐμὰ πάθεα.
ἔπαισε δ' αὐτόχειρ νιν οὔτις, ἀλλ' ἐγὼ τλάμων.
τί γὰρ ἔδει μ' ὁρᾶν,
ὅτῳ γ' ὁρῶντι μηδὲν ἦν ἰδεῖν γλυκύ;

ΧΟΡΟΣ.

ἦν ταῦθ' ὅπωσπερ καὶ σὺ φῄς.

ΟΙΔΙΠΟΥΣ.

τί δῆτ' ἐμοὶ βλεπτόν, ἢ στερκτόν, ἢ προσήγορον
ἔτ' ἔστ' ἀκούειν ἁδονᾷ, φίλοι;
ἀπάγετ' ἐκτόπιον ὅτι τάχιστά με,
ἀπάγετ', ὦ φίλοι, τὸν μέγ' ὀλέθριον,
τὸν καταρατότατον, ἔτι δὲ καὶ θεοῖς
ἐχθρότατον βροτῶν.

ΧΟΡΟΣ.

δείλαιε τοῦ νοῦ τῆς τε συμφορᾶς ἴσον,
ὥς σ' ἠθέλησα μήδ' ἀναγνῶναί ποτ' ἄν.

ΟΙΔΙΠΟΥΣ.

ἀντ. β'.

ὄλοιθ' ὅστις ἦν ὃς ἀγρίας πέδας
νομάδ' ἐπιποδίας ἔλαβέ μ' ἀπό τε φόνου
ἔρυτο κἀνέσωσεν, οὐδὲν εἰς χάριν πράσσων.
τότε γὰρ ἂν θανὼν
οὐκ ἦν φίλοισιν οὐδ' ἐμοὶ τοσόνδ' ἄχος.

ΧΟΡΟΣ.

θέλοντι κἀμοὶ τοῦτ' ἂν ἦν.

ΟΙΔΙΠΟΥΣ.

οὔκουν πατρός γ' ἂν φονεὺς ἦλθον, οὐδὲ νυμφίος
βροτοῖς ἐκλήθην ὧν ἔφυν ἄπο.
νῦν δ' ἄθεος μέν εἰμ', ἀνοσίων δὲ παῖς,
ὁμογενὴς δ' ἀφ' ὧν αὐτὸς ἔφυν τάλας.
εἰ δέ τι πρεσβύτερον ἔτι κακοῦ κακόν,
τοῦτ' ἔλαχ' Οἰδίπους.

ΧΟΡΟΣ.

οὐκ οἶδ' ὅπως σε φῶ βεβουλεῦσθαι καλῶς.
κρείσσων γὰρ ἦσθα μηκέτ' ὢν ἢ ζῶν τυφλός.

ΟΙΔΙΠΟΥΣ.

ὡς μὲν τάδ' οὐχ ὧδ' ἔστ' ἄριστ' εἰργασμένα,
μή μ' ἐκδίδασκε, μηδὲ συμβούλευ' ἔτι.
ἐγὼ γὰρ οὐκ οἶδ' ὄμμασιν ποίοις βλέπων
πατέρα ποτ' ἂν προσεῖδον εἰς Ἅιδου μολών,
οὐδ' αὖ τάλαιναν μητέρ', οἶν ἐμοὶ δυοῖν
ἔργ' ἐστὶ κρείσσον' ἀγχόνης εἰργασμένα.
ἀλλ' ἡ τέκνων δῆτ' ὄψις ἦν ἐφίμερος,
βλαστοῦσ' ὅπως ἔβλαστε, προσλεύσσειν ἐμοί;
οὐ δῆτα τοῖς γ' ἐμοῖσιν ὀφθαλμοῖς ποτε·
οὐδ' ἄστυ γ', οὐδὲ πύργος, οὐδὲ δαιμόνων
ἀγάλμαθ' ἱρά, τῶν ὁ παντλήμων ἐγὼ
κάλλιστ' ἀνὴρ εἷς ἔν γε ταῖς Θήβαις τραφεὶς
ἀπεστέρησ' ἐμαυτόν, αὐτὸς ἐννέπων

ὠθεῖν ἅπαντας τὸν ἀσεβῆ, τὸν ἐκ θεῶν
φανέντ' ἄναγνον καὶ γένους τοῦ Λαΐου.
τοιάνδ' ἐγὼ κηλῖδα μηνύσας ἐμὴν
ὀρθοῖς ἔμελλον ὄμμασιν τούτους ὁρᾶν;
ἥκιστά γ'· ἀλλ' εἰ τῆς ἀκουούσης ἔτ' ἦν
πηγῆς δι' ὤτων φραγμός, οὐκ ἂν ἐσχόμην
τὸ μήποκλῇσαι τοὐμὸν ἄθλιον δέμας,
ἵν' ἦν τυφλός τε καὶ κλύων μηδέν· τὸ γὰρ
τὴν φροντίδ' ἔξω τῶν κακῶν οἰκεῖν γλυκύ.
ἰὼ Κιθαιρών, τί μ' ἐδέχου; τί μ' οὐ λαβὼν
ἔκτεινας εὐθύς, ὡς ἔδειξα μήποτε
ἐμαυτὸν ἀνθρώποισιν ἔνθεν ἦν γεγώς;
ὦ Πόλυβε καὶ Κόρινθε καὶ τὰ πάτρια
λόγῳ παλαιὰ δώμαθ', οἷον ἆρά με
κάλλος κακῶν ὕπουλον ἐξεθρέψατε.
νῦν γὰρ κακός τ' ὢν κάκ κακῶν εὑρίσκομαι.
ὦ τρεῖς κέλευθοι καὶ κεκρυμμένη νάπη
δρυμός τε καὶ στενωπὸς ἐν τριπλαῖς ὁδοῖς,
αἳ τοὐμὸν αἷμα τῶν ἐμῶν χειρῶν ἄπο
ἐπίετε πατρός, ἆρά μου μέμνησθέ τι,
οἷ' ἔργα δράσας ὑμὶν εἶτα δεῦρ' ἰὼν
ὁποῖ' ἔπρασσον αὖθις; ὦ γάμοι γάμοι,
ἐφύσαθ' ἡμᾶς, καὶ φυτεύσαντες πάλιν
ἀνεῖτε ταὐτὸν σπέρμα, κἀπεδείξατε
πατέρας, ἀδελφούς, παῖδας, αἷμ' ἐμφύλιον,
νύμφας, γυναῖκας, μητέρας τε, χὠπόσα
αἴσχιστ' ἐν ἀνθρώποισιν ἔργα γίγνεται.
ἀλλ' — οὐ γὰρ αὐδᾶν ἔσθ' ἃ μηδὲ δρᾶν καλόν —

ὅπως τάχιστα πρὸς θεῶν ἔξω μέ που
καλύψατ', ἢ φονεύσατ', ἢ θαλάσσιον
ἐκρίψατ', ἔνθα μήποτ' εἰσόψεσθ' ἔτι.
ἴτ', ἀξιώσατ' ἀνδρὸς ἀθλίου θιγεῖν.
πίθεσθε, μὴ δείσητε. τἀμὰ γὰρ κακὰ
οὐδεὶς οἷός τε πλὴν ἐμοῦ φέρειν βροτῶν.

ΧΟΡΟΣ.

ἀλλ' ὧν ἐπαιτεῖς ἐς δέον πάρεσθ' ὅδε
Κρέων τὸ πράσσειν καὶ τὸ βουλεύειν, ἐπεὶ
χώρας λέλειπται μοῦνος ἀντὶ σοῦ φύλαξ.

ΟΙΔΙΠΟΥΣ.

οἴμοι, τί δῆτα λέξομεν πρὸς τόνδ' ἔπος;
τίς μοι φανεῖται πίστις ἔνδικος; τὰ γὰρ
πάρος πρὸς αὐτὸν πάντ' ἐφεύρημαι κακός.

ΚΡΕΩΝ.

οὔθ' ὡς γελαστής, Οἰδίπους, ἐλήλυθα, [*Introit.*
οὔθ' ὡς ὀνειδιῶν τι τῶν πάρος κακῶν.
ἀλλ' εἰ τὰ θνητῶν μὴ καταισχύνεσθ' ἔτι
γένεθλα, τὴν γοῦν πάντα βόσκουσαν φλόγα
αἰδεῖσθ' ἄνακτος Ἡλίου, τοιόνδ' ἄγος
ἀκάλυπτον οὕτω δεικνύναι, τὸ μήτε γῆ
μήτ' ὄμβρος ἱρὸς μήτε φῶς προσδέξεται.
ἀλλ' ὡς τάχιστ' ἐς οἶκον ἐσκομίζετε·
τοῖς ἐν γένει γὰρ τἀγγενῆ μάλισθ' ὁρᾶν
μόνοις τ' ἀκούειν εὐσεβῶς ἔχει κακά.

ΟΙΔΙΠΟΥΣ.

πρὸς θεῶν, ἐπείπερ ἐλπίδος μ' ἀπέσπασας,
ἄριστος ἐλθὼν πρὸς κάκιστον ἄνδρ' ἐμέ,
πιθοῦ τί μοι· πρὸς σοῦ γάρ, οὐδ' ἐμοῦ, φράσω.

ΚΡΕΩΝ.

καὶ τοῦ με χρείας ὧδε λιπαρεῖς τυχεῖν;

ΟΙΔΙΠΟΥΣ.

ῥῖψόν με γῆς ἐκ τῆσδ' ὅσον τάχισθ', ὅπου
θνητῶν φανοῦμαι μηδενὸς προσήγορος.

ΚΡΕΩΝ.

ἔδρασ' ἂν εὖ τοῦτ' ἴσθ' ἄν, εἰ μὴ τοῦ θεοῦ
πρώτιστ' ἔχρῃζον ἐκμαθεῖν τί πρακτέον.

ΟΙΔΙΠΟΥΣ.

ἀλλ' ἥ γ' ἐκείνου πᾶσ' ἐδηλώθη φάτις,
τὸν πατροφόντην, τὸν ἀσεβῆ μ' ἀπολλύναι.

ΚΡΕΩΝ.

οὕτως ἐλέχθη ταῦθ'· ὅμως δ', ἵν' ἕσταμεν
χρείας, ἄμεινον ἐκμαθεῖν τί δραστέον.

ΟΙΔΙΠΟΥΣ.

οὕτως ἄρ' ἀνδρὸς ἀθλίου πεύσεσθ' ὕπερ;

ΚΡΕΩΝ.

καὶ γὰρ σὺ νῦν τἂν τῷ θεῷ πίστιν φέροις.

ΟΙΔΙΠΟΥΣ.

καὶ σοί γ᾽ ἐπισκήπτω τε καὶ προτρέψομαι,
τῆς μὲν κατ᾽ οἴκους αὐτὸς ὃν θέλεις τάφον
θοῦ· καὶ γὰρ ὀρθῶς τῶν γε σῶν τελεῖς ὕπερ·
ἐμοῦ δὲ μήποτ᾽ ἀξιωθήτω τόδε
πατρῷον ἄστυ ζῶντος οἰκητοῦ τυχεῖν,
ἀλλ᾽ ἔα με ναίειν ὄρεσιν, ἔνθα κλῄζεται
οὑμὸς Κιθαιρὼν οὗτος, ὃν μήτηρ τέ μοι
πατήρ τ᾽ ἐθέσθην ζῶντε κύριον τάφον,
ἵν᾽ ἐξ ἐκείνων, οἵ μ᾽ ἀπωλλύτην, θάνω.
καίτοι τοσοῦτόν γ᾽ οἶδα, μήτε μ᾽ ἂν νόσον
μήτ᾽ ἄλλο πέρσαι μηδέν· οὐ γὰρ ἄν ποτε
θνήσκων ἐσώθην, μὴ ᾽πί τῳ δεινῷ κακῷ.
ἀλλ᾽ ἡ μὲν ἡμῶν μοῖρ᾽, ὅποιπερ εἶσ᾽, ἴτω·
παίδων δὲ τῶν μὲν ἀρσένων μή μοι, Κρέον,
προσθῇ μέριμναν· ἄνδρες εἰσίν, ὥστε μὴ
σπάνιν ποτὲ σχεῖν, ἔνθ᾽ ἂν ὦσι, τοῦ βίου·
ταῖν δ᾽ ἀθλίαιν οἰκτραῖν τε παρθένοιν ἐμαῖν,
αἶν οὔποθ᾽ ἡμὴ χωρὶς ἐστάθη βορᾶς
τράπεζ᾽ ἄνευ τοῦδ᾽ ἀνδρός, ἀλλ᾽ ὅσων ἐγὼ
ψαύοιμι, πάντων τῶνδ᾽ ἀεὶ μετειχέτην·
αἷν μοι μέλεσθαι· καὶ μάλιστα μὲν χεροῖν
ψαῦσαί μ᾽ ἔασον κἀποκλαύσασθαι κακά.
ἴθ᾽ ὦναξ,
ἴθ᾽ ὦ γονῇ γενναῖε. χερσί τἂν θιγὼν
δοκοῖμ᾽ ἔχειν σφᾶς, ὥσπερ ἡνίκ᾽ ἔβλεπον.
τί φημί;
οὐ δὴ κλύω που πρὸς θεῶν τοῖν μοι φίλοιν

δακρυρροοῦντοιν, καί μ' ἐποικτείρας Κρέων
ἔπεμψέ μοι τὰ φίλτατ' ἐκγόνοιν ἐμοῖν;
λέγω τι;

ΚΡΕΩΝ.

λέγεις· ἐγὼ γάρ εἰμ' ὁ πορσύνας τάδε,
γνοὺς τὴν παροῦσαν τέρψιν, ἥ σ' εἶχεν πάλαι.

ΟΙΔΙΠΟΥΣ.

ἀλλ' εὐτυχοίης, καί σε τῆσδε τῆς ὁδοῦ
δαίμων ἄμεινον ἢ 'μὲ φρουρήσας τύχοι.
ὦ τέκνα, ποῦ ποτ' ἐστέ; δεῦρ' ἴτ', ἔλθετε
ὡς τὰς ἀδελφὰς τάσδε τὰς ἐμὰς χέρας,
αἳ τοῦ φυτουργοῦ πατρὸς ὑμὶν ὧδ' ὁρᾶν
τὰ πρόσθε λαμπρὰ προυξένησαν ὄμματα·
ὃς ὑμίν, ὦ τέκν', οὔθ' ὁρῶν οὔθ' ἱστορῶν
πατὴρ ἐφάνθην ἔνθεν αὐτὸς ἠρόθην.
καὶ σφὼ δακρύω — προσβλέπειν γὰρ οὐ σθένω —
νοούμενος τὰ λοιπὰ τοῦ πικροῦ βίου,
οἷον βιῶναι σφὼ πρὸς ἀνθρώπων χρεών.
ποίας γὰρ ἀστῶν ἥξετ' εἰς ὁμιλίας,
ποίας δ' ἑορτάς, ἔνθεν οὐ κεκλαυμέναι
πρὸς οἶκον ἵξεσθ' ἀντὶ τῆς θεωρίας;
ἀλλ' ἡνίκ' ἂν δὴ πρὸς γάμων ἥκητ' ἀκμάς,
τίς οὗτος ἔσται, τίς παραρρίψει, τέκνα,
τοιαῦτ' ὀνείδη λαμβάνων, ἃ τοῖς ἐμοῖς
γονεῦσιν ἔσται σφῷν θ' ὁμοῦ δηλήματα;
τί γὰρ κακῶν ἄπεστι; τὸν πατέρα πατὴρ
ὑμῶν ἔπεφνε· τὴν τεκοῦσαν ἤροσεν,

ὅθεν περ αὐτὸς ἐσπάρη, κἀκ τῶν ἴσων
ἐκτήσαθ' ὑμᾶς, ὧνπερ αὐτὸς ἐξέφυ.
τοιαῦτ' ὀνειδιεῖσθε. κᾆτα τίς γαμεῖ;
οὐκ ἔστιν οὐδείς, ὦ τέκν', ἀλλὰ δηλαδὴ
χέρσους φθαρῆναι κἀγάμους ὑμᾶς χρεών.
ὦ παῖ Μενοικέως, ἀλλ' ἐπεὶ μόνος πατὴρ
ταύταιν λέλειψαι, νὼ γάρ, ὣ 'φυτεύσαμεν,
ὀλώλαμεν δύ' ὄντε, μή σφε περιίδῃς
πτωχὰς ἀνάνδρους ἐγγενεῖς ἀλωμένας,
μηδ' ἐξισώσῃς τάσδε τοῖς ἐμοῖς κακοῖς.
ἀλλ' οἴκτισόν σφας, ὧδε τηλικάσδ' ὁρῶν
πάντων ἐρήμους, πλὴν ὅσον τὸ σὸν μέρος.
ξύννευσον, ὦ γενναῖε, σῇ ψαύσας χερί.
σφῷν δ', ὦ τέκν', εἰ μὲν εἰχέτην ἤδη φρένας,
πόλλ' ἂν παρῄνουν· νῦν δὲ τοῦτ' εὔχεσθέ μοι,
οὗ καιρὸς ἀεὶ ζῆν, βίου δὲ λῴονος
ὑμᾶς κυρῆσαι τοῦ φυτεύσαντος πατρός.

ΚΡΕΩΝ.

ἅλις, ἵν' ἐξήκεις δακρύων· ἀλλ' ἴθι στέγης ἔσω.

ΟΙΔΙΠΟΥΣ.

πειστέον, κεἰ μηδὲν ἡδύ.

ΚΡΕΩΝ.

πάντα γὰρ καιρῷ καλά.

ΟΙΔΙΠΟΥΣ.

οἶσθ' ἐφ' οἷς οὖν εἶμι;

ΚΡΕΩΝ.

λέξεις, καὶ τότ᾽ εἴσομαι κλύων.

ΟΙΔΙΠΟΥΣ.

γῆς μ᾽ ὅπως πέμψεις ἄποικον.

ΚΡΕΩΝ.

τοῦ θεοῦ μ᾽ αἰτεῖς δόσιν.

ΟΙΔΙΠΟΥΣ.

ἀλλὰ θεοῖς γ᾽ ἔχθιστος ἥκω.

ΚΡΕΩΝ.

τοιγαροῦν τεύξει τάχα.

ΟΙΔΙΠΟΥΣ.

φῂς τάδ᾽ οὖν;

ΚΡΕΩΝ.

ἃ μὴ φρονῶ γὰρ οὐ φιλῶ λέγειν μάτην.

ΟΙΔΙΠΟΥΣ.

ἄπαγέ νύν μ᾽ ἐντεῦθεν ἤδη.

ΚΡΕΩΝ.

στεῖχέ νυν, τέκνων δ᾽ ἀφοῦ.

ΟΙΔΙΠΟΥΣ.

μηδαμῶς ταύτας γ᾽ ἕλῃ μου.

ΚΡΕΩΝ.

πάντα μὴ βούλου κρατεῖν·
καὶ γὰρ ἁκράτησας οὔ σοι τῷ βίῳ ξυνέσπετο. [*Exeunt.*

ΧΟΡΟΣ.

ὦ πάτρας Θήβης ἔνοικοι, λεύσσετ', Οἰδίπους ὅδε,
ὃς τὰ κλείν' αἰνίγματ' ᾔδη καὶ κράτιστος ἦν ἀνήρ,
ὅςτις οὐ ζήλῳ πολιτῶν καὶ τύχαις ἐπιβλέπων,
εἰς ὅσον κλύδωνα δεινῆς συμφορᾶς ἐλήλυθεν.
ὥστε, θνητὸν ὄντ', ἐκείνην τὴν τελευταίαν ἰδεῖν
ἡμέραν ἐπισκοποῦντα, μηδέν' ὀλβίζειν, πρὶν ἂν
τέρμα τοῦ βίου περάσῃ μηδὲν ἀλγεινὸν παθών.

[*Exit* Chorus.

NOTES.

TABLE OF ABBREVIATIONS.

Camp. ....Campbell.
Cf.......................*Confer*, i. e. *compare*.
Dind.......... ....Dindorf.
G.........................Goodwin's Elementary Greek Grammar.
H........................Hadley's Greek Grammar.
κ. τ. λ....................καὶ τὰ λοιπά, *et cetera*.
Lex.......................Liddell and Scott's Greek-English Lexicon, Sixth Oxford Edition, 1869.
Lexx....................The above, and Dr. Drisler's edition of the same, 1846. The references before the colon are to the former; after it, to the latter.
M........................Goodwin's Syntax of the Moods and Tenses of the Greek Verb.
Mitch...................Mitchell.
Ox.......................Oxford Pocket Edition of the Œdipus Tyrannus.
Schn. or Schneid. ...Schneidewin.
Schol. ....*Scholium*, *Scholia*, or *Scholiast*. The *Scholia Antiqua* are meant, quoted from Elmsley.
Schol. Min.............*Scholia Minora*, quoted from Erfurdt.
Wund..................Wunder.

NOTES.

Suggestion. — It is suggested that the student read either pp. 134–184 inclusive of J. L. Klein's Geschichte des Drama's, Vol. I., Leipzig, T. O. Weigel, 1865; or Chapter VII. (on the Representation of Greek Plays) of J. W. Donaldson's Treatise on the History and Exhibition of the Greek Drama, to be found in his Theatre of the Greeks, seventh edition, London, Longman, 1860; or the article Theatrum, in the Dictionary of Antiquities. The *Introduction* should be read at the outset, and then re-read with the progress of the drama.

The characters are distributed among the actors as follows: —

Protagonistes: ΟΙΔΙΠΟΥΣ.
Deuteragonistes: ΙΕΡΕΥΣ, ΙΟΚΑΣΤΗ, ΘΕΡΑΠΩΝ, ΕΞΑΓΓΕΛΟΣ.
Tritagonistes: ΚΡΕΩΝ, ΤΕΙΡΕΣΙΑΣ, ΑΓΓΕΛΟΣ.

1. Note the antithesis of the words **πάλαι**, *ancient* (G. 141, N. 3; H. 492, f), and **νέα**, *last-born*, heightened by their juxtaposition. The latter is not used absolutely. Only in contrast with old-time Cadmus could a part of the suppliants at least, the priests, be considered *youthful*. The poet has in mind also rather his own age than that of Œdipus when he calls Cadmus *ancient*. In fact these two both belonged to the heroic age of the Greeks, and lived but three generations apart. The line of descent was Cadmus, Polydorus, Labdacus, Laius, Œdipus.

2. The eager gestures of the suppliants justify the use of **θοάζετε**, in which the sense of rapid motion (from θοός, *quick*) is inherent: *what petitions pray do you urge upon me here?* **ἕδρας**, lit. *sittings*, acquires the meaning of *petitions* from the posture of the suppliants. For another interpretation of ἕδρας θοάζετε, see lexx., θοάζω, II., according to which another simpler expression of the thought is διὰ τί ποτε τάσδε τὰς ἕδρας μοι κάθησθε;

3. **κλάδοισιν** (G. 188, 1; H. 607). — **ἐξεστεμμένοι**, *furnished* (τὸ δὲ ἐξεστεμμένοι, ἀντὶ τοῦ κεκοσμημένοι: Schol.), for the suppliants were not themselves *crowned*, unless perhaps the priests. The reference is to the fillets upon

the olive branches. These *suppliant boughs* were placed on the altars, from which they were removed if the prayer was granted. See 143.

4, 5. *While the city is at the same time full of incense and of wailings which yet mingle with the strains of the hopeful pæan.* Although the tone of interrogation is dropped, the statements are virtually questions. — Notwithstanding Œdipus asks the occasion of the ascending incense and the reason for the prayers and lamentations heard in the city, he certainly was as fully acquainted with the calamity under which his people were laboring as any one before him. See 58. But for the purposes of the drama he leads them to relate their distress, and then assures them of all possible help. — The antithesis here is not exact. The poet begins with the contrast between *θυμιαμάτων*, offered to the gods with hope of their removing the plague, and *στεναγμάτων*, indicating the despair of the people, when a word much stronger than the former, *παιάνων*, suggests itself. The pæan here is a song of hope. — **θυμιαμάτων** (G. 172, 1; H. 575). The plural is used where we should employ the singular to denote that incense is offered in many different places. — The repetition of *ὁμοῦ* is emphatic, heightening the antithesis.

6. **ἀγώ** (G. 11 and N. 1; H. 68 and rem. b). — **ἅ,** *which things*, i. e. the reason of them. — **δικαιῶν** (G. 277, 2; H. 789, c). — **μή** (G. 283, 3; H. 837).

7. **ἀγγέλων ἄλλων** : said with poetic freedom, since it is evident that Œdipus does not in fact belong to the class of which by the form of expression he is made a member. Cf. —

> So hand in hand they passed, the loveliest pair
> That ever since in love's embraces met;
> Adam, the goodliest man of men since born,
> His sons; the fairest of her daughters, Eve.
>
> PARADISE LOST, IV., 321-324.

8. **πᾶσι,** *in the judgment of all* (H. 601). So that *πᾶσι κλεινός* is *world-renowned.*

9. He addresses the priest of Zeus.

10. **φωνεῖν** (G. 261, 1, N.; H. 767; M. 93, 1, N. 2, (a), third ex.). — **τίνι, κ. τ. λ.,** *in what temper sit ye here?*

11. **(τί) δείσαντες ἢ (τί) στέρξαντες;** *στέργω*, in the sense of *to desire.* So Dind., who however makes the form of the epexegesis of *τίνι τρόπῳ* different, namely (*πότερον*) *δείσαντες ἢ στέρξαντες;* Nam hoc dicit: *utrum deorum iram atque pœnam ob impium aliquod facinus metuentes, an auxilium in præsente calamitate desiderantes?* — **θέλοντος ἄν** (G. 278, 1; 277, 2, and N. 2, and 211; H. 790, c; 795, e, and 803, a).

12, 13. The object of **προσαρκεῖν** is *ὑμῖν* understood. Cf. 141. — **δυσάλ-**

γητος, κ. τ. λ., *for hard-hearted should I be not to compassionate such supplication.* —**ἂν εἴην** (G. 224; H. 748). —**κατοικτείρων** (G. 226, 1, and 283, 4; H. 751 and 839). —**οὐ** follows *μή*, because of the negative idea involved in *δυσάλγητος* (M. 95, 2, N. 1, b, ad fin., where note the use of *χαλεπαί* in the last example).

14. The aged priest of Zeus, who had been singled out from the others and personally addressed, now rises, as respect for his sovereign requires, and replies. — **Οἰδίπους** : for its declension see lexx. and G. 60, 1; H. 191. —**χώρας** (G. 171, 3; H. 581, a).

15. ὁρᾷς μὲν ἡμᾶς : *μέν* corresponds to *δέ* in 19 ; *μέν* in 16 to *δέ* in 17, and *μέν* in 18 to *δέ* in the same line. This correlation is possible. See, however, the note given below on **μέν** in verse 18.

16. βωμοῖσι (G. 187 and 44 ; H. 605 and 143). The altars were those of Apollo and other deities before the king's palace. See on 159. — **οἱ μέν** (G. 143, 1 ; H. 525, a). Together with *οἱ δέ* in 17 and *οἱ δέ* in 18, in partitive apposition with the relative *ἥλικοι*. — The children are likened to birds not yet strong of wing.

17. οἱ δέ, κ. τ. λ., *others weighed down by old age.* The feeble because of youth are contrasted with the feeble because of years.

18. ἱερῆς (G. 53, 3, N. 2 ; H. 190, d). An appositive to the preceding *οἱ δέ*.—**ἐγὼ μὲν Ζηνός** : this does not introduce a new class. The speaker belonged to the second one mentioned, that of the priests. — **μέν** : instead of the correlation given under 15, *μέν* is perhaps better considered the correlative to *οἱ δέ* in the phrase *οἱ δὲ ἄλλων θεῶν* to be supplied, *ἐγὼ μέν* and *οἱ δέ* in such an expression being the terms necessary to distribute fully *ἱερῆς*. *οἱ δέ* expressed in 18 is then along with *οἱ δέ* in 17 correlative to *οἱ μέν* in 16. These three terms distribute *ἥλικοι*. See lex., *μέν*, A, II., 2. —**ἐπί** : cf. on 183. — **ἠθέων λεκτοί** = *λεκτοὶ ἤθεοι*.

19. τὸ δ' ἄλλο (G. 142, 2, N. 3; H. 538, e). —This one before the palace was but one of the crowds of suppliants. There was, beside this, one in each of the two market-places, one at each temple of Pallas, and another at the temple of Apollo on the river Ismenus.

20. ἀγοραῖσι (G. 190 and 39; H. 612 and 129).

21. μαντείᾳ σποδῷ, *oracular ashes,* those of burnt sacrifices through which divination was practised. — The gen. depends on **ἐπί**, while the dat. *σποδῷ* is governed by **πρός**, like *ναοῖς*.

22–24. The English order is : *πόλις γάρ* (H. 530, b), *ὥσπερ καὐτὸς εἰσορᾷς, σαλεύει ἤδη ἄγαν καί* (*ἐστι*) *οὐκ ἔτι οἵα τε* (G. 151, N. 4, and 261, 1 and N. ; H. 814 and 856, a) *ἀνακουφίσαι κάρα βυθῶν* (G. 174; H. 580) *φοινίου σάλου.* — **φοινίου σάλου,** *the ensanguined sea,* red with the blood of so many dead.

25. **κάλυξιν** (G. 188, 1, N. 1; H. 609).

26. **βουνόμοις** = *βοῶν νεμομένων*. — **τόκοισί τε ἀγόνοις**: travail that causes the death of the mother before the child is born. Cf. II. Kings, xix., 3.

27. **ἐν**, *in among them* (as if *ἐν τούτοις*), adverbially. Possibly to be connected with *σκήψας* by tmesis. — **πυρφόρος**, *fever bringing*, from ΠΥ̂Ρ = *πυρετός* and ΦΕ΄ΡΩ. Less probable the interpretation of Schn., who says the plague was so designated because keeping continually ablaze the funeral pyres. — **θεός**: the plague is called a *god*, as indeed among the Greeks was almost anything that was mighty in its operation.

28. **ἐλαύνει**, *agitat.*

29. **δῶμα Καδμεῖον**, *the home of Cadmus*, i. e. Thebes.

30. **στεναγμοῖς—γόοις**: "Effectum pro efficienti. The dead are poetically represented by the cries of those they have left behind them." Wolff. For the case, see *κλάδοισιν* in 3. — **πλουτίζεται**: in contrast to *κενοῦται*, in the preceding line.

31 sqq. *Therefore I and these youths beseech thy aid, not because we judge thee equal to the gods indeed, but,* etc. — **θεοῖσι** (G. 186; H. 603). — **νύν**, *since the city is in such dire plight.* — **ἰσούμενον** (G. 280; H. 799).

32. **παῖδες**: the other aged priests, who were probably near him, he regards as one with himself, and so does not include them in the term of reference. With the utterance of the word *παῖδες*, he makes a gesture toward the children and young men. — **ἑζόμεσθα** (G. 122, 2; H. 355, D, d).

33, 34. **ἀνδρῶν** (G. 168; H. 559). — **ἔν τε, κ. τ. λ.**, *both in the case of the common accidents of life, and in those greater events where a god's help is needed.* The speaker has in mind the overthrow of the Sphinx by Œdipus, aided by divine power. See 38.

35. **τέ** finds its correlative in 40. — **ἐξέλυσας**: see lexx., II. — **ἄστυ** (G. 162; H. 551).

36. **σκληρᾶς ἀοιδοῦ**: the Sphinx is so called from the metrical enigma she proposed to the Thebans. For this and its solution, see the *Introduction.*

37. **καὶ ταῦτα**: sc. *ἐποίησας* (H. 508, b). — **ὑφ' ἡμῶν**: to be connected with *ἐκδιδαχθείς* alone. — **ἐξειδώς** (G. 277, 5; H. 789, f). — This word signifies information gathered casually; while *ἐκδιδαχθείς*, that given him by the Thebans with a purpose. — **οὐδὲν πλέον**, *nothing more* (than the fact that the riddle had been proposed).

38. "The priest says that the deliverance wrought by Œdipus was accomplished by the assistance of a god, while in actual fact Œdipus is an *ἐχθροδαίμων*." Schn.

39. **λέγει** (G. 114, 2, N. 1; H. 363, rem. a). — **ἡμῖν** (G. 184, 3; H. 597). Note also the accent (G. 79, N. 2, ad fin.; H. 232, ad fin.).

40. **πᾶσιν** : see 8. — **Οἰδίπου κάρα** : a poetic expression frequently occurring and equal to the simple vocative, Οἰδίπους.

42, 43. **εἴτε του, κ. τ. λ.**, *whether by having heard the voice of some one of the gods thou knowest of it, or perchance from a man.* — **του** (G. 84; H. 244, b). — After the first **εἴτε** supply *οἶσθα*, with the subject of which **ἀκούσας** will agree.

44. **καί** : the poet had in mind at first a co-ordinate relation for the substantives, which finally, as the sentence took shape in his mind, yielded to the genitive construction : *not only the plans, but also their results.*

45. **μάλιστα**, *most of all*, to be taken with the dat. *τοῖσιν ἐμπείροισι*, itself an adverbial element. — Note the position of the attributive gen.

46. *Go, O best of men, restore the state.*

47. *εὐλαβήθητι, μὴ τὴν προϋπάρχουσαν δόξαν ἐπὶ τῇ εὐποιΐᾳ ἀπολέσῃς.* Schol.

48. **προθυμίας** (G. 173, 1; H. 577, a).

49, 50. *Let not this be our recollection of thy reign, that it both led us to prosperity and saw us fall.* — **ἀρχῆς** (G. 171, 2; H. 576). — **μεμνώμεθα** (G. 253; H. 720, a, and 393, rem. a). — **στάντες** (G. 280; H. 799 and 802). The fact that *μεμνώμεθα* has the gen. *ἀρχῆς* depending on it does not invalidate this construction. — **ἐς ὀρθόν** = *ὀρθῶς*, and expresses manner.

51. **ἀσφαλείᾳ** : "Dative of the manner. The noun is used with a consciousness of the verb *σφάλλεσθαι*, referring to *πεσόντες*. 'Let your restoration of this city be without failure or falling.'" Camp. But Wund., "erige civitatem, ut firma stet," making *ἀσφαλείᾳ* a dat. of *intent* or *purpose*.

52. **ὄρνιθι αἰσίῳ** : not that Œdipus actually observed the flight of birds in his solution of the enigma. Cf. 398. The phrase conveys simply the thought that he was successful in his attempt, since in the ordinary sense to do anything *ὄρνιθι αἰσίῳ*, was to do it successfully. — **καί — καί**, *as — so.*

54. **ἄρξεις — κρατεῖς**: no difference of meaning in these words is intended. The second is used for the sake of variety. So certain of the editors. But according to Young, *ἄρχειν* means to *exercise* authority ; *κρατεῖν*, to *possess* or *be invested* with it.

55. **ξὺν ἀνδράσιν** is best considered an adjective element, corresponding to *κενῆς*.

56. **οὔτε** (G. 283, 8; H. 843).

57. *Without men dwelling together within.* There is a seeming redundancy here of the negative idea. The negative notion of **ἔρημος**, *destitute*, i. e. NOT

having, is made explicit by the apparently pleonastic **μή**. The two constructions, ἔρημος ἀνδρῶν and ἀνδρῶν μὴ ξυνοικούντων ἔσω (a gen. abs.), are united in one. — **ἀνδρῶν** (G. 180, 1; H. 584, b). — With the sentiment cf. —

> *Sicinius.* What is the city, but the people?
> *Citizens.* True,
> The people are the city.
> CORIOLANUS, Act III., Scene 1.

So Proverbs xiv., 28.

58. The fatherly address as in 1. — **γνωτά — ἄγνωτα**: "The acc. for the gen. after ἱμείρω occurs only here." Wolff.

60, 61. **νοσεῖτε**, *sick* both in body and at heart. The word evidently has a double sense. — **καὶ νοσοῦντες, κ. τ. λ.**, *and yet, although ye are sick, there is not one of you whose grief is equal to mine.* — **καί** = καίτοι — **νοσοῦντες** modifies the real subject of the sentence, but the construction is changed from the formal completion of it by οὐ νοσεῖτε ἐξ ἴσου ἐμοί to the more emphatic expression of the text. An anacoluthon (H. 886). See lexx., **ἀνακολουθία.**

62, 63. *For your distress afflicts one alone in his own person and none other.* — **οὐδένα**: governed by εἰς.

65. **ὕπνῳ γ' εὕδοντα**: the repetition is emphatic. — **ὕπνῳ** (G. 188, 1; H. 608).

66. **πολλά**: adverbial. — **δακρύσαντα**: see references on **ἰσούμενον** in 31.

67. *And have journeyed many ways in the wanderings of thought,* i. e. have much considered how we might obtain relief.

68. *But what sole cure on careful consideration I found, this I put into execution.* — **ἴασιν**: the noun thrown into the relative clause instead of the demonstrative, by which ἥν becomes adjective (G. 154; H. 809, 3 and a).

69. **παῖδα** = υἱόν.

70. **Πυθικά**: let the student here read the article DELPHI in his Dictionary of Geography.

71, 72. **πύθοιτο** (G. 216, 1; H. 739). — **δρῶν** (G. 226, 1; H. 751). — Obs. the use of ὅ τι and τί in the same sentence (G. 149, 2, top of p. 126; H. 682). — **ῥυσαίμην** (G. 224 and N.; H. 722 and c).

73. *The day being already commensurate with the* (sc. *computed*) *time* (sc. *for his absence*) *troubles me as to what he is doing.* Another construction is possible. Wolff arranges: (ὁ Κρέων) λυπεῖ με, ξυμμετρούμενον (middle voice) ἦμαρ (τόδε τῷ καθήκοντι, cf. 75) χρόνῳ.

74, 75. The use of two different expressions in **τοῦ εἰκότος πέρα** and **πλείω τοῦ καθήκοντος χρόνου** for the same idea, *longer than is necessary*, is emphatic. — **πλείω**: sc. χρόνον.

76, 77. ἵκηται (G. 232, 3; H. 758). — **τηνικαῦτα...θεός**: "Œdipus, unconscious of what he is saying, by these words imposes upon himself the necessity of investigating a matter, the discovery of which casts him into the greatest calamity." WUND. "Many cases of this sort occur in this tragedy, especially in the first part, the double meaning of which the spectators easily understand, but Œdipus, since he is conscious of no guilt, fails to discern." DIND. — **μὴ δρῶν ἂν εἴην**: the same use of the moods that occurs in 13. — **δηλοῖ**: pres. subj. We should have expected the optat. without *ἂν* here by assimilation (G. 235), since *μὴ δρῶν* = *εἰ μὴ δρῴην*. But while the optat. accurately expresses the thought of the condition, since the supposition that the speaker will *not do* must be shown by the form of expression to be as remote as possible, it would not that of the relative sentence, that the god will make manifest his wishes, being an hypothesis that under the circumstances is very likely to be realized, and so to be stated distinctly. See M. 64, 2, rem. 1. The use of *ἵκηται* in 76, which depends on *ἂν εἴην* at once, is the same. Creon's coming is a supposition to be stated distinctly and vividly.

78, 79. The young eyes of the boys have descried Creon approaching in the distance, and while Œdipus has been speaking they have informed the priest of the fact, not by words, but by pointing. This fact, joined to Œdipus' evident reliance on the oracle, which it is fair to suppose Creon is bringing, gives the priest hope of speedy deliverance. So he says, *εἰς καλὸν εἶπας* and *Κρέοντα εἰς καλὸν προσστείχοντα*. Not only has Œdipus spoken *at the right moment* (*εἰς καλόν*), but equally *at the right moment* Creon approaches.

80, 81. εἰ γάρ, κ. τ. λ., *may he come invested with some saving fortune, even as he is beaming in eye.* — **τύχῃ σωτῆρι**: a masculine substantive used adjectively with a feminine noun. To be parsed as an appositive. — **βαίη** (G. 251, 1; H. 721 and a). — **ὄμματι**: the dat. as *κάλυξιν* in 25.

82. *But, as far as we can judge, he brings good news.* — **εἰκάσαι** (G. 268, fifth ex.; H. 772). — **κάρα** (G. 160, 1; H. 549 and a).

83. πολυστεφής: as was the custom in the case of those who, having consulted the oracle, returned with a joyful answer from the god. — **ἂν εἷρπε** (G. 222; H. 746). The protasis is omitted. — **δάφνης**: the Mediterranean laurel or bay-tree. For the case, see references on *ἀνδρῶν*, in 57.

84. ξύμμετρος, κ. τ. λ., *for he is within hearing distance.* — **κλύειν** (G. 266, 2, N. 1; H. 875, f).

85–88. So anxious is Œdipus to learn what is to be done, that he calls aloud to Creon, yet at a distance, inquiring what Apollo commands. The latter, prudently thinking that the oracle should first be considered by

Œdipus alone, that the guilty one may not betake himself to flight, answers evasively, *a fair one; for I am sure that even the difficulties that beset us, if they should by chance have good issue, would turn out altogether well.* This means to Creon, that if the effort to discover and punish the murderer of Laïus, difficult because of the length of time that has elapsed since the event, should be successful, they would be freed from the plague; but to those he addresses, his answer is as unintelligible as he designed it to be. — **ἄναξ,** used in 85 in the address to Creon, is an honorable title of very extensive application. — **κήδευμα,** *relation,* for *κηδεστής, relative* (by marriage). — Creon, coming from abroad, enters the theatre through the left-hand or eastern parodos, and goes upon the stage. His coming is so timed that he begins his reply as he ascends its steps. — **λέγω** shows that Creon, and not the oracle, is the authority for the statement. — **ἐξελθόντα** (G. 279, 2; H. 801). — **εὐτυχεῖν** (G. 242, 2, and 224; H. 734, c, and 748).

89. **ἔστιν, κ. τ. λ.,** *but the oracle, the* ORACLE, *tell me what* THAT *is.*

90. **οὖν** emphasizes the antithesis between *θρασύς* and *προδείσας.* — **τῷ γε νῦν λόγῳ,** *by* YOUR *saying.* — **λόγῳ** (G. 188, 1; H. 611).

91-93. Quasi dicat — *Do you wish* ALL *to hear?* And the answer, *Yes, tell all.* — **εἰ τῶνδε... κλύειν,** *if you wish these at hand to hear.* *τῶνδε χρῄζεις κλύειν,* where in prose we probably should have had *τούσδε χρῄζεις κλύειν.*

92. **εἰπεῖν**: see references to G. and H. on *φωνεῖν* in 10. — **εἴτε... ἔσω:** there is an ellipsis: *εἴτε (μὴ τῶνδε χρῄζεις πλησιαζόντων κλύειν, ἕτοιμός εἰμι) καὶ στείχειν ἔσω*; or more simply for the first part: *εἴτε (στείχειν ἔσω χρῄζεις, ἕτοιμός εἰμι), κ. τ. λ.*

93, 94. **ἐς... αὔδα**: Œdipus by this command seals his fate. The oracle is made public, and the first step taken that leads to his eventual overthrow. — **τῶνδε, κ. τ. λ.,** *for the anxiety that I feel in behalf of these irks me more than my anxiety for my own life even.* To put his life to hazard would be less a cause of grief to him than the present misery of his subjects. And how certainly, though unconsciously, was he putting his life to hazard! — **τῶνδε**: *scilicet περί.* — **πλέον φέρω,** *feel more sensibly.* — **τὸ πένθος,** *my grief.* Note the force of the article. — **πέρι** (G. 23, 2; H. 102, b).

95. **λέγοιμ' ἄν** (G. 226, 2, ad fin.; H. 722, b). — **πάρα**: as *πέρι* in 94.

97. **χώρας**: see refs. on **βυθῶν** in 24. — **ὡς**: to express subjectivity, as in 11.

99. **ποίῳ καθαρμῷ**: sc. *ἄνωγεν ἡμᾶς ἐλαύνειν.*

100. After Œdipus' question, Creon resumes his speech, as if not yet complete. Accordingly, *ἀνδρηλατοῦντας* must be referred to *ἡμᾶς* in 96.

101. **ὡς τόδε, κ. τ. λ.,** *since this is a case of bloodshed troubling the state.* Sc. *ἐστί.* The adj. *τόδε* impugns the construction of *αἷμα* as an acc. abs.

αἷμα is now mentioned for the first time, and ought therefore to be anarthrous. — The same figure underlies *χειμάζον* (from *χεῖμα, a storm*), that occurs in 23.

102. **γάρ** expresses surprise. — **μηνύει** : sc. *ὁ θεός*.

103. **ἡμίν** (G. 184, 4; H. 598 and a).

104. **ἀπευθύνειν** (G. 274; H. 769).

107. **τοὺς αὐτοέντας τινάς,** *the murderers, whoever they may be.*

108. **οἱ δέ** (G. 143, 1, N. 2; H. 525, (γ)). — **γῆς** (G. 168, ninth ex.; H. 589, first ex.). — **τόδε,** *this,* which we must discover.

112. **ἠ 'ν** : "Sometimes in Attic poetry a weak and grammatically unimportant syllable is excluded by a preceding long vowel; this is especially the case with the augment. This omission of the vowel is called aphæresis (*ἀφαίρεσις*)." Kühner. See also H. 68, D.

113. **συμπίπτει** : historical present.

114, 115. *He went, as he said, to consult the oracle, but never returned.* Creon answers in general terms, not specifying either the place where Laius was murdered, or the occasion that he had for consulting the oracle, — not even saying what oracle it was. Here the skill of the poet is seen, for any one of these might have put Œdipus on the right track. This effect is increased by the confused account in 122, 123. — **ἀπεστάλη** (H. 706; M. 19, N. 4, (b)).

116, 117. *But was there no one to announce the deed, no fellow-traveller who saw it, whose information could have been used to advantage?* — **ἐχρήσατ' ἄν** : sc. *τῇ μαθήσει*. Note the form of this apodosis (G. 222; H. 746), and the tense of the contrary reality.

118, 119. **θνήσκουσι,** *they are dead,* being equal to *τεθνήκασι*. — **εἷς τις** : when this attendant got back to Thebes, all that he could say was that the king had been set upon by a numerous band of robbers and killed. This statement, that the robbers were many in number, which in the course of the action of the play is provèd false, for a long time delays the self-conviction of Œdipus. Undoubtedly the attendant was terrified at the cross-roads. Well might he be; but still not so badly as actually to magnify the one man, Œdipus, into a number. His aim in this falsehood was to shield himself from the charge of cowardice. — Schn. calls attention to the emphatic connection of *πλὴν εἷς—πλὴν ἕν*, meant to show how very remote the chance of discovering the murderer was. — **ὧν** (G. 153 and N. 1; H. 808, 1). — Syntax of **ἕν**?

120, 121. **τὸ ποῖον,** *what was that?* (H. 538, d). — **ἂν ἐξεύροι, εἰ λάβοιμεν** (G. 224; H. 748). — The order for the English sentence will be either *ἓν ἂν ἐξεύροι πολλὰ μαθεῖν*, or *μαθεῖν ἓν ἂν ἐξεύροι πολλά.*

123. **κτανεῖν** (G. 260, 2; H. 717, b).

124, 125. **ὁ λῃστής**: "The singular referring to the plural may only be an idiomatic way of speaking, but may also be a stroke of art in representing Œdipus as wholly careless about the number of the persons, which at a later period (842 ff.) is his only refuge." CAMP. — **τὶ**: subject of ἐπράσσετο. — **ξὺν ἀργύρῳ ἐνθένδε**, *with money from here*, i. e. bribes sent to the robbers from Thebes. — **τόλμης** (G. 168 and N. 1; H. 559, c).

126. **Λαΐου**: limit of ἀρωγός.

128. **τυραννίδος**: the use of the abstract term is emphatic.

129. M. 95, 2, (a), fourth ex.

130. **ποικιλῳδός**: cf. on 36.

132. It is not an exact expression by which the two adverbs **ἐξ ὑπαρχῆς** and **αὖθις** are connected with **φανῶ**, since **ταφανῆ** of 131 had never yet been brought to light. But the participle ὑπάρχων is sufficiently implied in the substantive ὑπαρχῆς. *But I a second time* (*αὖθις, entering upon the inquiry*) *from the beginning* (*ἐξ ὑπαρχῆς*), etc. The subjects of Laius had once begun an investigation of the causes of his death, but had been obliged to drop it. Œdipus declares that it shall not only be again begun from the very start, but that it shall be brought to a successful conclusion.

133. **σύ**: Creon.

134. *Have shown this care in behalf of the dead.* — **ἔθεσθε** (G. 199, 2; H. 689). The way in which the interest of the twofold subject in the matter is indicated by the use of the middle is very delicate.

136. **γῇ**: as ἡμῖν in 39.

137. **τῶν ἀπωτέρω φίλων**: his wife's former husband, whom he said (105) he had never seen. And yet how closely related he was to this same man!

138. **αὐτοῦ** (G. 146, N. 2; H. 672, a).

139. **τάχ' ἄν**: *perhaps* (G. 212, N.).

140. "Since Œdipus assumes as a fact the surmise expressed above (124), he is apprehensive lest the murderer, a political malcontent or one hired by political opponents, may in like manner with violent hand (107) take vengeance on him." SCHN. — **τοιαύτῃ χειρί**: "The same hand which unwittingly slew Laius did, eventually, wreak vengeance on Œdipus by tearing out his eyes." YOUNG. — **θέλοι** (G. 226, 2, and 224; H. 722).

142. **ὡς τάχιστα**: for τάχιστα ὡς (δύνασθε) (H. 664 and 821). — **βάθρων** (G. 174; H. 590, b, first ex.).

143. Cf. on 3. — **ἱκτῆρας**: cf. on σωτῆρι in 81. The two substantives here are of the same gender.

144. **ἄλλος**: one of his own attendants.

145. **ἢ γάρ, κ. τ. λ.**: to the spectators the king's words have a double

meaning. The prosperous issue at which he aims — the discovery and punishment of the murderer — will prove to him the direst ruin.

146. Œdipus and Creon go into the palace by the middle door. See *Introduction.*

147. **παῖδες** : cf. on 32. Possibly here, as being the oldest, he addresses all in general as children. — **ἱστώμεσθα** (G. 253 ; H. 720, a). For the ending see 32. — **χάριν** (G. 160, 2, sixth ex.; H. 552, tenth ex.).

148. **ἐξαγγέλλεται**: "Subjective middle. 'Which he announces as coming from himself.'" — CAMP.

149, 150. *And may Phœbus, he that sent this oracle, come at the same time both our deliverer and the stayer of the pestilence.* — Their request granted, the suppliants retire into the city by the same way by which they had entered.

151-215. The *parodos.* ANALYSIS: An eager inquiry as to the nature of the command with which Creon had returned, addressed to the Oracle itself (Θήβας); great anxiety on the part of the Chorus in regard to what it will enjoin upon the city (χρέος); it is besought to disclose itself (Φάμα); Athene, Artemis, and Phœbus severally invoked to appear in defence of the state (μοί), and to come again to her aid as they have done in times past (νῦν); the general ground of this petition given to be immediately explained at length (ἀλέξεται); namely, the fruits of the earth wither and the women perish in child-birth (γυναῖκες); the dead are speeding like well-fledged birds to the realms of night, leaving the city desolate (ὄλλυται); death-bringing corpses strew the plain (ἀνοίκτως); bereaved wives and hoary-haired mothers wail at the altar's base (ἐπιστενάχουσιν); the voice of lamentation mingles with the hymn for help (ὅμαυλος): to relieve all this woe the oracle is implored to send help (ἀλκάν), and drive the plague into the sea for his destruction (κλύδωνα), since day destroys what night spares (ἔρχεται); Jove is besought to blast him with his bolt (κεραυνῷ); glad would be the sight of Apollo's arrows showered forth to protect the city (προσταχθέντα), and of the bright torches of Artemis (διᾴσσει); Bacchus too is invoked to draw near with his train and flash death upon this god unhonored among gods (θεόν).

151 sq. *O sweetly speaking Oracle of Jove, of what purport, pray, art thou come from Pytho rich in gold to illustrious Thebes?* — The CHORUS, representing the Κάδμου λαός of 144, now enters the orchestra from the city. — For **ἁδυεπές, τᾶς, ἔβας,** and many such cases hereafter in the choric parts, G. 30, 1; H. 24, D, b. — **Φάτι**: the voice of Zeus is personified and addressed. The oracle comes through Apollo, but its original source is the father of all things, Jupiter. The Chorus has evidently heard of Creon's return. — **τίς** stands in the predicate to ἔβας. — **πολυχρύσου**: the immense riches stored away in the temple at Delphi have been the subject of remark ever since even Homer's day.

153. **ἐκτέταμαι, κ. τ. λ.**: "'I lie outstretched, my timorous heart quaking with dread.' The uses of ἐκτέταμαι favor this punctuation."— CAMP. The commoner punctuation is to put the comma after φρένα in place of ἐκτέταμαι: *I am distracted in mind, shaking with fright.* In either case φρένα is an acc. of respect. — "In dramatic poetry a CHORUS is commonly treated as an individual, the Coryphæus being regarded as speaking and acting for the whole body; so that the singular is often used in reference to it." HADLEY, 519, a. — **φοβεράν**, *timentem.* — **δείματι πάλλων**: ἀντὶ τοῦ παλλόμενος φόβῳ, ἀγωνιῶν. SCHOL.

154. Apollo is now himself addressed, but interjectionally. So the Schol.: ἐν τῷ μεταξὺ τοῦτο. — **ἰήϊε**: derived from the cry ἰή, with which the god was invoked. — **Δάλιε**: Apollo was born in Delos.

155 sqq. — **ἀμφὶ σοὶ ἁζόμενος, τί μοι ἐξανύσεις χρέος**, *in holy dread of thee as to what destined thing thou wilt accomplish for me.* — **σοί**: its antecedent is Φάτι. — **νέον** is used adjectively. On the other hand the word in corresponding relation is the adverb πάλιν, which in prose would have been connected with χρέος by means of some participle, say φαινόμενον. So that **περιτελλομέναις...πάλιν** means *again appearing in the course of time.* The Schol., however, construes differently: τί μοι ἢ νῦν ἢ μετὰ χρόνον ἀνύσεις. In accordance with this the lines have been freely translated:

> Daughter of hope, fair child of light,
> What great events in time's dark womb concealed,
> Are now emerging to our sight;
> Or wait the circling hours to be revealed?— MAURICE.

— **ὥραις** (G. 189; H. 613).

158. **τέκνον Ἐλπίδος**: because those who consulted the oracle always hoped for the best. So in 151 the oracle is called ἀδυεπές, though the Chorus as yet knows nothing at all of its import. — **ἄμβροτε**: because from Jupiter, first of the immortals. The student will notice throughout this drama, and especially in the present chorus, that the tendency to repeat a word once used, in a different connection, and even with a different meaning, a practice not allowed in modern languages, seems to have been unusually strong in Sophocles.

159. **κεκλόμενος**: cf. a corresponding irregularity in 60, 61. In regular construction with the participle one expects λίσσομαι προφανῆναί μοι in 163. In its excitement the Chorus changes the form of expression and breaks into the exclamation ἰώ, κ. τ. λ. — The three divinities here invoked,

Athene, Artemis, and Apollo, are doubtless those whose altars stood before the palace, upon the steps of which the three classes of suppliants had sat.

160. γαιάοχον = πολιοῦχον. SCHOL.

161. κυκλόεντ' ἀγορᾶς θρόνον = κυκλοέσσης ἀγορᾶς θρόνον, according to a not infrequent custom of the poets of joining the adjective belonging to one noun with another immediately connected with it. See lexx., ὑπαλλαγή, II. The forum was of circular shape. But Neue takes κυκλόεντα at once with θρόνον and interprets it πολλοὺς κυκλοὺς (choruses of dancers) ἔχοντα. — **ἀγορᾶς** (G. 179, 2; H. 590, a). — **εὐκλέα**: a shortened form for εὐκλεέα, εὐκλεᾶ. The throne or pedestal is called so because the goddess is there celebrated.

164 sqq. *If ever in the case of a former calamity also rising against the state ye put the flame of mischief out of the way, come now as well.* But in the place of ὕπερ governing the gen. ἄτας we may read ὑπέρ (adverb), or, *e conjectura Musgravii*, in one word, ὑπερορνυμένας, though this word occurs nowhere else. ἄτας then is a gen. abs., *if ever, formerly also calamity impending, to the city's weal ye extinguished*, etc., πόλει being a dat. com. with ἠνύσατ' ἐκτοπίαν. According to the first construction πόλει is a dat. incom. with ὀρνυμένας. With ἄτας ὕπερ, *because of calamity, to avert calamity*, cf. ὧν ὕπερ in 188. — **ἄτας**: the presence of ποτέ shows that a specific reference to the case of the Sphinx is not intended.

166. ἐκτοπίαν (G. 166; H. 556).

169, 170. νοσεῖ δέ μοι πρόπας στόλος, *my whole people is sick, the entire population is sick on my hands.* — **φροντίδος ἔγχος**, *weapon* (= *device*) *of thought*, i. e. a means of defence gained by a careful consideration of their present exigency.

171. ἀλέξεται: future. See 538, 539.

172–174. A third divine judgment is mentioned in 26. Cf. Deut. xxviii., 18. — **τόκοισιν**, *in the hour of birth;* cf. on τόκοισιν, κ. τ. λ., in 26. — **ἰηΐων**, *accompanied by cries, grievous*, from the noun ἰή, Ionic for 'ΙΑ', *a cry.* — **ἀνέχουσι**, *recover, find relief.*

175 sqq. *But thou couldst see one speeding close upon another as a well-winged bird more swiftly than irresistible fire to the shore of the evening god.* — **ἄλλῳ**: as βωμοῖσι in 16.

177. ἀκτάν: because the river Acheron flows around Hades.

178. ἑσπέρου θεοῦ: Pluto, whose realms according to the Homeric belief were at the western extremity of the world, where the sun sets. — **πρός** governs the accusative that precedes it, on which the adnominal genitive of possession, θεοῦ, depends.

179. *In countless numbers of whom the city is perishing.* — **ὧν** (G. 180, N. 1;

H. 584, b). — Schneid. notes the striking similarity of the first part of the strophe and antistrophe.

181. **θαναταφόρα**: rendered so by contagion and putrefaction. Such numbers die that many remain unburned.

182. **ἀνοίκτως**, *with none to pity.*

183. **ἐν**, *among them.* Used adverbially. Cf. 27. So **ἐπί** following. — **πολιαί, κ. τ. λ.**, *and hoary-headed mothers withal.*

184. **ἀκτὰν παρὰ βώμιον**, *along the altar's slope.* The altar was on raised ground, so that there would be an ascent, like that of a sea-shore, in reaching it. — **παρά**: when an oxytone preposition of two syllables stands between the noun it governs and an adj. modifying this noun, it does not suffer anastrophe.

185. **ἄλλοθεν ἄλλαι**, *some from one place, some from another.* Their lamentation rises from different places in the vicinity of the altar. — **πόνων**: to be construed with *ἐπιστενάχουσιν*. See the references on *προθυμίας* in 48.

187. **παιάν, κ. τ. λ.**, *and the pæan sounds forth clear, but blended with the voice of woe.* See 5. — **λάμπει**: the metaphor doubtless suggested by the circumstances. Cf. the note on *φλέγει* in 192 and the following: —

> "His beams shall cheer my breast; and both so twine,
> Till even his *beams sing,* and my *music shine.*"

— **γῆρυς** is in the feminine gender.

188. **ὧν** refers not to persons, but to the woes which have been detailed. — **θύγατερ**: the oracle, as in 158.

190. **Ἄρεα**: "The pestilence is called Ares because both are *βροτολοιγοί*; but to mark him as distinct from the actual god of war, the poet adds, *ἄχαλκος ἀσπίδων.*" — Schneid. The plague was less distinctly called *θεός* in 27.

191. **ἄχαλκος ἀσπίδων**, *unarmed with brazen shield.* The genitive as *ὧν* in 179.

192. **φλέγει με**: lit. *burns me.* The funeral pyres lighted by the plague burn throughout the city, and so the idea of fire, devouring and destructive, is constantly present to the mind of the speaker. Cf. the use of *φλόγα* in 166, *πυρός* in 177, and *μαλερόν*, the Homeric epithet of fire, in 190. It will be understood, however, that when the Chorus says of the plague, *φλέγει με*, it does not of course refer to any physical effect of either fire or fever on itself, but uses the word in a tropical sense, *consumes me.* See lexx., *φλέγω*, A, 2. — **περιβόατος**: having called the plague Ares, the poet is easily able to employ a term, which, although eminently fitting to the god of war as delighting in tumult and confusion and advancing against his

enemies with loud outcry, is not applicable to the pestilence itself. There is more or less reference, however, in this word to the cries and lamentations occasioned by the plague, giving the word a causative meaning, *spreading lamentation around.* — **ἀντιάζων**: in the hostile sense, *confronting.*

193 sqq. **Ἀρεά τε τὸν μαλερὸν παλίσσυτον, κ. τ. λ.**, *and force ravening War to turn back his course in backward hurrying flight from the borders of my fatherland.* The accumulation of words of the same signification is highly intensive. Cf. 430, 431. — **νωτίσαι**: governed by the notion of causing involved in *πέμψον* in 189. It is trans. with *δράμημα* as acc. obj. — **παλίσσυτον**: lit. *rushing hurriedly back* (G. 138, N. 7; H. 488, rem. c). An acc. masc.

195. **θάλαμον Ἀμφιτρίτας**: the Atlantic Ocean. The pestilence is to be driven for its destruction into the depths of the Atlantic or the Euxine.

196. **ὅρμον**: the entire land-locked sea is called a *harbor.*

198, 199. **τέλει, κ. τ. λ.**, *for if night at her close leave aught, this day assails.* — **τέλει**: poetic use of the dat. of time without *ἐν*. So the Schol., who paraphrases *ἐπὶ τῷ ἑαυτῆς τέλει*. — **εἰ** (G. 223, N. 2; H. 747, b).

200. **τόν**: the plague. The article used as the relative. — **ἀστραπᾶν** (G. 39, Gen. Plur.; H. 128, D, c). So **τᾶν** for *τῶν*.

201. **κράτη νέμων**, *who hast power over, who controllest.*

202. **ὑπό**: "Since the thunder-bolt is shot down from above. Otherwise the poet would have been able to use *ἀπό* by tmesis for *ἀπόφθισον σῷ κεραυνῷ*." — DIND.

203, 204. **Λύκει' ἄναξ**: Apollo. — **χρυσοστρόφων ἀπ' ἀγκυλᾶν**, *from thy bow-string of twisted gold.* Plural for singular as in 496, 779, 1095, and elsewhere in this play.

205. **ἀδάματα**, notwithstanding its position, which makes it emphatic, is here used attributively. — **ἐνδατεῖσθαι**: to be taken passively, *to be sent forth, to be showered* (H. 694, c). So the Schol.: *βουλοίμην δὲ καὶ τὰ σὰ βέλη, ὦ Ἄπολλον, τὰ ἀδάμαστα καταμερίζεσθαι εἰς αὐτόν, καὶ τὰς λαμπάδας Ἀρτέμιδος.*

206. **ἀρωγά**: predicate adj. to the following participle.

208. **αἴγλας**: a case of zeugma (H. 882).

209. **χρυσομίτραν**: the luxuriant locks of Bacchus were bound up in a golden head-band. — Some time in the course of this last antistrophe Œdipus appears again upon the stage through the middle door of the palace, but alone. He pauses as he comes to hear the last words of the Chorus.

210. **ἐπώνυμον γᾶς**, *named after this land.* He was called *ὁ Θηβαῖος*. — **γᾶς**: a gen. of connection (H. 587, d).

211. **οἰνῶπα**, *his face flushed with wine.*

212. **ὁμόστολον**, *accompanied by, with.*

213 sqq. **πελασθῆναι, κ. τ. λ.**, *to approach blazing with his beaming torch as our ally against the god dishonored among gods.*

215. **τὸν ἀπότιμον θεόν**: i. e. τὸν λοιμόν. — SCHOL.

216–218. **ἅ**: the antecedent of the relative is at first vague. But as the sentence proceeds the expression of the thought becomes more accurate and **ἀλκήν** and **ἀνακούφισιν** are made the objects of **λάβοις**. — **θέλῃς** (G. 227, 1; H. 750; M. 54, 1, (b)). — **ὑπηρετεῖν**, *to obey the requirements of.*

219 sq. **ἁγώ**: the antecedent of the relative is ἔπη in 216. — **ξένος μέν, κ. τ. λ.**, *ignorant formerly as well of this report of the murder of Laius as of the deed itself.* So the Schol.: οὐκ ἀκηκοὼς πρότερον περὶ τοῦ φόνου τοῦ Λαΐου, οὐδὲ μὴν καθ' ὃν χρόνον ἐπράχθη ὁ φόνος παρών. — **λόγου** (G. 180, 1, and 171, 2; H. 584, c). — The Chorus as yet being ignorant of what has been done to-day, so far, Œdipus proposes to bring the matter before them. When he speaks of himself as ξένος τοῦ λόγου and ξένος τοῦ πραχθέντος he does not mean to protest his innocence, for he had as yet not the faintest suspicion of the fact that he was the murderer. He means as he says, that until to-day he has never been made acquainted with the particulars of the murder. Cf. his inquiries in 112 sqq. Of the fact of the murder he may have known, but not its details. This certainly is improbable; but the improbability is external to the action of the play, and must be overlooked in favor of the poet. At 112 sqq. the dramatic interest demands that the particulars of the death of Laius shall be brought out before the spectators.

220, 221. **γάρ**, to be taken with **ἐξερῶ**, explains why he is so explicit with them, he needs assistance: *for, since I have no clew at all, I should not, restricted to myself* (αὐτός), *be getting far into the matter.* αὐτός here takes the place of the suppressed condition, εἰ μὴ ἐξηγόρευον ὑμῖν, and ἔχων is used as δικαιῶν in 6. The Laur. MS., however, reads here αὐτό, μὴ οὐκ, where αὐτό refers to the murder, μὴ οὐκ is used as in 13, and σύμβολον is to be referred to the oracle which Creon had brought. So the Schol. interprets: οὐ γὰρ ἂν τοσούτου ὄντος τοῦ χρόνου τοῦ μεταξὺ ἀνεζήτουν (*investigate*) τὸ πρᾶγμα, εἰ μὴ ᾔδειν καταληψόμενος. Here μὴ οὐκ ἔχων = εἰ μὴ εἶχον, and γάρ may be translated *though.*

222. **δέ**, *so then,* resumes 219 after the explanatory parenthesis. The clause beginning with ὕστερος must stand in connection with νῦν: *so then I now make proclamation, (and I do it* NOW, *for when formerly the matter of this murder was before you I had not yet been enrolled among your citizens)*, etc. — **τελῶ**: see lexx., II., 3, and cf. its use in 232.

223. **ὑμῖν πᾶσι Καδμείοις**: he addresses the Chorus.

224. **Λάϊον**: a case of *prolepsis*. The noun, which is properly the subject of *διώλετο*, has been transferred from the dependent to the principal sentence with change of case. Cf. —

> Let my intrusion here be called my duty,
> That come *to see my sovereign how he fares.*
> Old Play of Edward III., Act II., Scene 1, quoted by Boyes.

— **τόν** (G. 141, N. 4; H. 509, b, (β)).

227, 228. *And if he fears* (as is shown by his) *having withheld* (or *suppressed*) *the self-accusation*, (*nevertheless let him now declare all*). Sc. *σημαινέτω*. The eagerness of Œdipus makes the ellipsis extremely natural. *αὐτὸς καθ' αὑτοῦ* depends partly on the verbal notion implied in *ἐπίκλημα*, (though the ordinary prose construction would be *ἐπικαλεῖ αὐτὸς αὑτῷ*), and partly on *σημαινέτω* to be supplied. In the first case *αὐτὸς καθ' αὑτοῦ* is a compound adjective phrase modifying the noun *ἐπίκλημα*. Cf. the English translation. In the second it is to be divided, *αὐτός* being construed with the subject of *σημαινέτω*, and the adverbial phrase *καθ' αὑτοῦ* modifying that verb itself. These verses have been variously interpreted.

230. **ἐξ ἄλλης χθονός** is to be taken in connection both with **τὶς** and **ἄλλον**. That the murderer was a foreigner is possible, since Laius was killed beyond the borders. In this case the partaker of his secret would in all likelihood also be a foreigner.

232. **τελῶ**: Attic future. In 222 it is a present.

233. Antithesis to 224 sqq. — **φίλου**: as *προθυμίας* in 48.

234. **ἀπώσει τοὔπος**, *shall refuse to give information*, *τοὔπος* itself being the *edict* of the king. — **φίλου** — **αὑτοῦ**: the cases are here cited in inverse order. Cf. 228 and 230.

235. **ἐκ τῶνδε**, *postea*. — **ἐμοῦ** (G. 171, N. 1; H. 576, a). — Profound silence and feeling throughout the theatre as the ill-fated king in the following verses lays his commands, so dire to himself, in solemn tones upon his people.

236. **τὸν ἄνδρα τοῦτον**: the murderer. — **γῆς** depends on *τινά* by the principle which governs *ἀνδρῶν* in 33. **τινά** is the subject of the infinitives, **ἄνδρα** their object.

238. **μήτε** (G. 283, 6; H. 838). — **ἐσδέχεσθαι**: supply *εἰς οἴκους* from 241.

240. **κοινὸν ποιεῖσθαι**, *to make him an associate*. — **χέρνιβος νέμειν** (G. 170, 2; H. 574, a). Those who were to take part in sacrifice were beforehand sprinkled with consecrated water. Here equivalent to admitting one into the religious fellowship of the family.

241. **ὠθεῖν**: dependent on *αὐδῶ* understood from *ἀπαυδῶ* in 236. — **μιάσματος**: cf. 97.

244. **μέν**: its correlative is in 252. — **τῷ δαίμονι**: Apollo. Cf. 136 and 253.

246. **τὸν δεδρακότα** is the subject of *ἐκτρῖψαι*. The subject is resumed for the sake of precision after the two interposed clauses in the pronoun *νιν*.

249. **ἐπεύχομαι**: sc. *ἐμαυτῷ*. This imprecation shows how terribly in earnest he is.

250. **εἰ γένοιτο** (M. 54, 2, (a)). This protasis depends on the infinitive *παθεῖν*, which would naturally have had *ἐὰν γένηται* for its apodosis.

251. **παθεῖν**: sc. *ἐμέ*. — **τοῖσδε**: the guilty ones, the murderers. We must look for the antecedent in 246, 247, where it is evident that Œdipus had not yet determined whether the murder had been done by one man or by a number, as he was told in 107 and 122. For the time being the latter seemed the more probable, and so the pronoun is in the plural. In like manner when *ἅπερ* is put in the plural the reference is not alone to the single curse in 248, but also to the terrible consequences which would follow obedience on the part of his people to the commands laid on them by the king in 238 - 241. If Œdipus consciously concealed the murderer, well might he imprecate on himself just the curses he had imprecated on him, for in that case he becomes his abettor. The apparently careless way in which the murderer is mentioned, sometimes as one person and again as a number, greatly enhances the effect hereafter when just this point becomes to Œdipus one of vital importance. See 842 sqq., and the note on 124.

253. **ὑπὲρ ἐμαυτοῦ**: cf. 137 - 141.

254. "Ruined with sterility and the frown of Heaven." — Camp. With *ἀκάρπως*, cf. 25 and 171, 172.

255, 256. *For not even if the inquisition were not ordered by Apollo, was it right that you should have let this murder go thus unpunished* (G. 222 and N. 2; H. 746 and b). The protasis refers to present time, the apodosis to past. See here M. 49, 2, rem., (a).

257 - 269. "Every line calls attention to the real position of Œdipus, of which he is profoundly unconscious. Note esp. (1) *ὁμόσπορον*, cf. l. 460; (2) *κοινῶν παίδων*; (3) *εἰ κείνῳ γένος μὴ 'δυστύχησεν* (Œdipus says this in ignorance of Laius having had a child, but he unwittingly expresses the fact of his own misfortune); (4) l. 263, which points to the curse pursuing Laius and his offspring; (5) the words *ὡσπερεὶ τοὐμοῦ πατρός*. The effect of all this on the spectators may be imagined. Yet every word is suitable to the apparent situation and to the generous character of Œdipus." — Camp.

258. Note the anacoluthon found in 258 sqq., by which the subordinate sentence **ἐπεὶ... ὁμόσπορον,** after the two declarative sentences in 261-263, suggested by *ὁμόσπορον*, have been thrown in parenthetically, is made dependent not on an independent member, as would be legitimate, but on the relative sentence, **ἀνθ' ὧν, κ. τ. λ.**

258, 259. **κυρῶ ἔχων** (H. 801; M. 112, 2).

260. **γυναῖχ' ὁμόσπορον**: sensation throughout the theatre. — **ὁμόσπορον** = *ὑπ' ἀμφοῖν σπειρομένην.*

261, 262. There is a vagueness of expression here which is increased by the tautology, **κοινῶν — κοινά.** The meaning, however, is clear: *there would be a family of common children,* i. e. his children and mine would now be associating as half brothers and sisters. *κοινά* is a singular use of the neuter plural to express the same idea that is conveyed by *κοινῶν παίδων.* Literally: *and (his) children, kindred to (my) kindred children, would have been born from her* (**ἐκ**). *κοινός, kindred, having a common mother,* followed by a genitive of connection. More precisely: *and, had not offspring failed him, children would have been born to him from her akin to my children, akin to his.*

263. **κρᾶτα**: acc. See lexx. — **ἐνήλατο**: fr. *ἐνάλλομαι.*

264, 265. **ἐγὼ τάδε ὑπερμαχοῦμαι,** *I will fight this battle for him.* — **ἀνθ' ὧν,** *for which things' sake.* — **τάδε** (G. 159, N. 2; H. 547, c). — **πατρός** (G. 177; H. 583). He says, *as* IF for his own father! — **ἐπὶ πάντ' ἀφίξομαι,** *will resort to every expedient, will use all possible means.*

266. **τὸν αὐτόχειρα,** *the perpetrator.*

267. **Λαβδακείῳ**: the adj. is logically equivalent to the following genitives. — **παιδί**: as *ἡμῖν* in 39.

268. For the pedigree of Laius see note on 1. Agenor was the father of Cadmus. — **πρόσθε — πάλαι**: cf. *πάλαι* in 1.

269, 270. **τοῖς μὴ δρῶσιν**: those not willing to aid him in his search (*ζητῶν*, 266). The words stand grammatically in connection with *ἀνιέναι.* — **θεούς** would properly be *θεοῖς* after *εὔχομαι* (G. 184, 2; H. 595, b), but is made the subject of *ἀνιέναι.* — **ἄροτον**: note the accent and see lexx. — **αὐτοῖς** as *νιν* in 248. See note on 246.

271. **οὖν** is continuative. For the sentiment cf. note on 172-174.

272. **φθερεῖσθαι** (M. 27, note 2 and (a)).

273. Cf. on 223.

276. *As thou hast bound me by a curse.*

278, 279. Order: *εἰπεῖν δὲ τόδε τὸ ζήτημα (this question), ὅστις εἴργασταί ποτε, ἦν Φοίβου, τοῦ πέμψαντος (τὴν φήμην, 86).* — **Φοίβου** (G. 169, 1; H. 572, e).

280. **ἔλεξας**: "Interlocutors, in referring to the words of the last speaker, use the aorist, where in English the present would be used." Jones. — **ἀλλά, κ. τ. λ.**: he speaks from experience. Cf. 789.

281. **θέλωσιν** (G. 232, 3; H. 757). The apod. is **ἀναγκάσαι**, *to compel the gods to what they may not wish* (= *ἐὰν μὴ θέλωσιν*). — **οὐδ' ἂν εἷς ἀνήρ**, NO *man* (G. 77, 1, N. 2; H. 255). — **ἂν δύναιτο** (G. 226, 2; H. 722, a).

283. **καί** emphasizes **τρίτα**. — The text, **ἔστι**, makes *τρίτα* subject, *if there is even a third point.* The accent **ἐστί**, the common reading, makes *τρίτα* a predicate, *if the things you have in mind are even less important, third in rank.* — **παρῇς**: from *παρίημι*. — **τὸ μὴ οὐ φράσαι** (G. 263, 2, and ad fin.; H. 847, a, second ex.; M. 95, 3, next to last ex.).

284-286. Notice the triple application of **ἄναξ**. — **ἄνακτι** (G. 186; H. 603). — **ὁρῶντα** (G. 280; H. 799). — **μάλιστα**: modifies *ὁρῶντα*. — **σκοπῶν**: conditional. See lexx., *σκοπέω*, I., 4.

287. **ἐν ἀργοῖς** = *ἀργῶς*. Schol. Min. — Note the force of the mid. voice.

288. **Κρέοντος εἰπόντος**: see 555. Creon gave Œdipus this advice after they entered the palace together at 146. — **διπλοῦς**: Œdipus first sent one attendant after Tiresias, and then in his impatience a second.

289. **μὴ παρών** = *εἰ μὴ πάρεστι*, the regular construction with *θαυμάζω* (G. 228). See also lexx., *θαυμάζω*, I., 6, a, and II., 1: A, IV., and B. This justifies the use of *μή*.

290-292. While they wait for Tiresias the Chorus, emboldened by Œdipus' injunction in 283, says that there is another matter which occurs to it (*τὰ τρίτα*), namely, reports abroad immediately after the death of Laius that he had been killed by robbers, which reports, however, it supposes now to have been forgotten. Line 290 is spoken meditatively. The Chorus is acquainted with the action of the play only from 151 on, and does not know that this same old (*παλαιά*) report was revived by Creon in 122, 123. — **θανεῖν** (G. 260, 2; H. 717, b). The form of the verb in the orat. rect. was *ἔθανεν*. — **ὁδοιπόρων**: Creon called them (122) *λῃσταί*. So Jocasta in 716.

293. Œdipus refers to what he had learned from Creon. He adds that the only eye-witness of the deed (the servant that escaped, 118) is not immediately at hand (*ὁρᾷ*). He does not send for this servant at this point because of his momentary expectation of Tiresias, by whom he hopes the whole matter will be cleared up. When he consulted with Creon within the palace, doubtless the plan of summoning the servant suggested itself, but was abandoned for the better one of sending for Tiresias.

294. **μὲν δή**: see lexx., *μέν*, B, I., 3; II., 4. — **ἔχει**: not the servant, but the murderer. Note the number.

295. The Chorus expects a confession. — **μενεῖ** : ὑπομενεῖ.

296. **ᾧ μή 'στι** (G. 231 and 232, 1; H. 761). The antecedent of ᾧ is the object of φοβεῖ.

297. **οὐξελέγχων** : the present tense expresses certainly, *he is as good as discovered, for the seer is here.* Literally: *there is one who convicts him.* οὐξελέγχων is the reading of Cod. Laur. The future οὐξελέγξων occurs. — **οἵδε** : the two attendants whom Œdipus had sent after Tiresias (288), and the boy that was the blind seer's ordinary guide (444).

300 sqq. "The eloquent description of the high endowments with which Tiresias as a seer is gifted makes the ensuing disunion and altercation stand out in more startling contrast, where Œdipus is led to doubt first the good-will, then the power of the seer to help." SCHN. — **νωμῶν** : see lexx., νωμάω, II., 3. — **διδακτά,** *what may be learned, knowledge.* — **ἄρρητα,** *mysteries.* — Led by the hand of his boy-attendant, the white-haired and blind old prophet here slowly ascends the stage.

302. **πόλιν** : as Λαΐου in 224. — **εἰ καί,** *although* (H. 874, 1, ex. and 874, 2, a). — **δέ** (G. 227, 2; H. 862, b).

303. **ἧς** : its antecedent is πόλιν.

304. **μοῦνον** : Ionic form. See lexx., μόνος.

305. **καί** gives a slight emphasis to the following words, *indeed.* — **κλύεις** (H. 698; M. 10, N. 5).

307 sqq. **ἂν ἐλθεῖν — εἰ κτείναιμεν ἢ ἐκπεμψαίμεθα** (G. 224 and 246 with N.; H. 748 and 734, c). — **μόνην** : this is the only method of deliverance.

308, 309. Cf. 101.

310. **δέ** slightly contrasts **σύ** with **Φοῖβος** ; **οὖν** draws the inference that since the god has done so much, the seer, as his ally, should also aid the distressed about himself. — **φθονήσας** : see lexx., φθονέω, II., 2 : 3. — **ἀπ' οἰωνῶν** : see on 55.

311. **ὁδόν** : see lexx., III., 1.

313. The construction of the two clauses in 312 is carried on into this, where we should have expected τοῦ μιάσματος. The use of ῥύομαι here is parallel to that of ἐκλύω in 35.

314, 315. **ἐσμέν** : as the verb subs. εἰμί retains its accent in all persons. — **ἄνδρα** has here a pronominal use. The infinitive of which it is the subject is itself the subject of the copula that is to be supplied, of which the predicate is κάλλιστος (πόνος). — **ἀφ' ὧν ἔχοι, κ. τ. λ.** : we should expect ἀφ' ὧν ἂν ἔχῃ τε καὶ δύνηται κάλλιστος πόνων (ἐστίν). See H. 760, d; M. 63, 4, (b). — "**ἔχοι** refers to outward means, **δύναιτο** to inward, mental resources." — SCHN.

316. Tiresias says this rather to himself, in a low, distressed voice, and with his head partly averted. — **τέλη λύῃ** = λυσιτελῇ. SCHOL.

317. **λύῃ** (G. 234 and 225, ad fin.; H. 759). Cf. *ἀφῇ* in 198. — **ταῦτα**: its antecedent is the preceding sentence. The prophet came, not knowing the recent course of events at the palace, and not stopping to consider for what purpose his king had summoned him.

318. **διώλεσα,** *I altogether forgot it.* — **οὐκ ἂν ἱκόμην**: sc. *εἰ μὴ διώλεσα.*

319. **τί δ' ἔστιν,** *what ails thee?* Note the accent of *ἔστιν.* The interrogation-point might be carried to the end of the line: *what is the matter, why is it, how comes it, that thou hast come despondent?*

320. Note the inversion, **τὸ σόν — σύ** : **ἐγώ — τοὐμόν.** — **τό** : sc. λάχος.

321. **διοίσω** (G. 135, N. 1; H. 511, h). From *διαφέρω.* — **πίθῃ** : referring to *ἄφες*, 320.

322. **εἶπας** : cf. note on 280.

323. **φάτιν** : see 310.

324. With reference to what Œdipus had said in 305–315, as well as to his last words.

325. **ταὐτόν** (G. 79, 2, N.; H. 234). — **πάθω** (G. 216, 1; H. 739). — The seer half turns to leave.

326, 327. Œdipus excitedly interrupts him: *in the name of heaven, when thou knowest (the truth), turn not thyself away from us, seeing we all as suppliants here beseech thee!* — **φρονῶν γε** : the participle could be made conditional, *if at least you understand the matter.*

327, 328. Note the emphatic place of **πάντες** in each verse.

328, 329. *But I will never reveal what I know,* (and this is my motive), *that I may not tell the evil plight in which thou art.* The order is: *ἐγὼ δ' οὐ μή ποτε ἐκφήνω τἄμ', ὡς ἂν εἴπω μὴ τὰ σὰ κακά.* — **οὐ μὴ ἐκφήνω** (G. 257; H. 845; M. 89, 1). — **ἂν εἴπω** (G. 216, N. 2; H. 741).

330, 331. Œdipus questions with surprise and rising indignation.

332. **ταῦτα** : see references on *τάδε*, 264.

333. **τί...ἐλέγχεις** : "The seer pauses and then speaks with compassionate earnestness." MITCH. — **ἄλλως,** *to no purpose.* — **ἂν πύθοιο** : see the references on *λέγοιμ' ἂν* in 95.

334. He faces the prophet in a passion.

334, 335. **ἂν πέτρου φύσιν σύ γ' ὀργάνειας** : compare —

> And put a tongue
> In every wound of Cæsar, that *should move*
> *The stones of Rome to rise and mutiny.*
> JULIUS CÆSAR, Act III., Scene 2.

— **ὀργάνειας** (G. 116, N. 1; H. 349, rem. b).

336. **ἄτεγκτος κἀτελεύτητος,** *hard-hearted and impracticable.* — **φανεῖ** (G. 114, 2, N. 1; H. 363, rem. a).

337. **ὀργήν** : see lexx., the two meanings. — **ἐμέμψω** : cf. on 280. — **τὴν σήν** : referring in fact to *ὀργήν*, but capable of being interpreted of Jocasta, in which case the added words *ὁμοῦ ναίουσαν* are especially significant. Œdipus of course does not see this covert reference.

338. **ἀλλ' ἐμὲ ψέγεις** : emphatically repeating the first part of the preceding line.

339. **ἄν — ἄν** (G. 212, 2 ; H. 873, a).

340. **ἅ** (G. 159, N. 4 ; H. 555). This is not the proper correlative of *τοιαῦτα*, which would be *οἷα*. There is an ellipsis: *hearing such words* (as these are), *which thou speakest in dishonor of the city.*

341. *For these things will of themselves* (**αὐτά** = *αὐτόματα* : SCHOL.) *meet their accomplishment.*

342. That we may arrive at a definite settlement of the matter with as little delay as possible. — **καί** : construe with *λέγειν*. — The reading **οὔκουν** ...**ἐμοί**; is perhaps preferable.

343. **ἂν φράσαιμι** : cf. with *ἂν πύθοιο* in 333. — **πρός** : see lexx., C, III., 2; C, III., 3.

344. **ἥτις ἀγριωτάτη** (**ἐστίν**) = *ἀγριωτάτης*.

345, 346. *And indeed I will in my anger pass over nothing of what I know.* When Œdipus declares in great passion that he knows that the prophet was accessory to Laius' death, his complete and lamentable ignorance is brought into bold relief. — **ὡς ὀργῆς ἔχω** : literally, *as* (not *thus*) *of anger I have* (*myself*), i. e. *in the condition of anger in which I am* (G. 168, N. 3 ; H. 589, fifth ex. fr. the last). — **δοκῶν** : as *ὁρῶντα* in 284.

347, 348. **καί**, *even*, throws its force on both infinitives. Schn., among others, says, "not in correlation with **τέ**." — **ξυμφυτεῦσαι** : see 124. — **ὅσον, κ. τ. λ.**, *except so far as killing him with your own hand.*

350. Terribly angered at the charge made against him, the prophet loses self-control and speaks the awful truth. — **ἄληθες**, *indeed?* Note the accent and see lexx., III., 2. — **κηρύγματι** : see 224–275. It was only by his more than human power that Tiresias had any knowledge of this proclamation. And yet Œdipus, in his passion, quite overlooks this so significant fact.

351. **ᾧπερ** (G. 153 ; H. 808, 2). — **ἐμμένειν**, *abide by.*

352. Cf. 238.

353. **ὄντι** agrees with *σοί* understood, the object of *ἐννέπω*. — **μιάστορι** : cf. 241.

355. **ποῦ** : see lexx., II. : I., 2. — **τοῦτο** : i. e. *τόδε τὸ ῥῆμα*, the charge itself, though the punishment for it is meant. — **φεύξεσθαι**, *thou wilt escape.*

356. **τἀληθές, κ. τ. λ.,** *for I have in my bosom truth in its might,* i. e. what I have affirmed is true.

357. *By whom hast thou been taught truth? Thou certainly didst never learn it from thine art.*

358. **πρὸς σοῦ**: sc. τἀληθὲς διδαχθείς. When the sentence is completed in this way from what precedes, as if it is completed must evidently be done, the statement is not correct in fact, since the prophet was far from having been taught the particular truth in question by the king. Aside from the purposes of grammar, however, it is not necessary to press the sentence too closely, uttered as it was in the heat of altercation. In the mind of the speaker the instigation to speak is the chief idea, and what he means by these two words is explained by what immediately follows.

359. **λόγον**: observe that a pronoun referring to this word is to be supplied as the direct object of each of the verbs in this and the two following lines, with the exception of ἐκπειρᾷ.

360. **ἢ 'κπειρᾷ λόγῳ,** *or are you trying me in talk?*

361. The answer is to the former question. — **εἰπεῖν** (G. 266, 1; H. 770).

362. **Ordo**: φημί σε κυρεῖν (ὄντα) φονέα τἀνδρὸς οὗ (φονέα) ζητεῖς. See references on 258, 259, and lexx., κυρέω, II., 3. Or φονέα predicate to εἶναι understood and κυρεῖν transitive, its object being φονέα to be supplied, of which οὗ will be the limit.

363. **πημονάς** = λοιδορίας. — **χαίρων,** *with impunity.*

364. **εἴπω** (G. 256; H. 720, c). — **ὀργίζῃ**: with reference to 335 and 345. The human side of the prophet is coming out strongly.

365. Spoken with assumed indifference. — **γέ**: see lexx., II., 2; A, I., 4, ad fin. — **μάτην,** *in vain, without effect.* — **εἰρήσεται**: fut. perf. of ἐρῶ.

366, 367. **λεληθέναι ὁμιλοῦντα,** *hast unwittingly associated* (G. 279, 2; H. 801). — **φιλτάτοις**: the reference is to his wife. The use of the mas. plur. designedly obscures the relationship. Œdipus had as yet no thought that his wife was also his mother. — **κακοῦ**: as γῆς in 108.

368. **γεγηθώς**: cf. the use of χαίρων in 363.

369. *Yes, at least if there is any power in truth.* Cf. 356.

371. Notice the remarkable assonance of letters and syllables in this line, and cf. 425. There is a line in Cicero quoted from the Annals of Ennius:

> O Tite, tute, Tati, tibi tanta, tyranne, tulisti.

— **ὦτα** (G. 160, 1; H. 549, a, third ex.).

372, 373. **ἃ**: obj. of ὀνειδιεῖ. Eng. order: ἃ (ἔστιν) οὐδεὶς τῶνδε ὃς οὐχὶ τάχα ὀνειδιεῖ σοί.

374. *You live in perpetual night*, referring to his blindness.

375. **βλάψαι ἄν**: if the metre and negative had allowed, we might have had here the opt. mood, βλάψειας ἄν. See M. 41, N. 4.

376. **ἐμοῦ**: emphatic, contrasted with Ἀπόλλων.

377. **τάδε**: i. e. τό σε πεσεῖν.

378. When the prophet openly accused Œdipus of being the murderer of Laius, the king could come to but one conclusion, that the seer, for purposes of his own, was deliberately falsifying. And how certain he must have felt of this! His active mind immediately jumps to the idea of a conspiracy. But it was not until the name of Apollo was mentioned, that he suspected Creon as the seer's accomplice. He rapidly establishes a chain of evidence sufficient for himself: it was Creon who brought back the answer from Delphi, and he it was who advised to send for the prophet. Yea, this man and the blind seer have taken this time, when the city is in such dire distress, to endeavor to deprive me of my kingdom!

380, 381. **τέχνη, κ. τ. λ.**: "*Art surpassing every art in the life of man, which is so full of emulous endeavors.* Œdipus is thinking of the proof which his solution of the enigma has given of his mental acumen, which he here calls τέχνη (in 398 γνώμη), not without sarcastic allusion to Tiresias' τέχνη, 389. Cf. the counter-taunt of the seer, 440." SCHN.

382. **φυλάσσεται**, *abides, is in store.*

383. **οὕνεκα** (οὗ and ἕνεκα) as a preposition is exactly equivalent to ἕνεκα, οὗ having lost all significance.

384. **δωρητόν** modifies ἥν (G. 63, N.; H. 209, rem. a). So **αἰτητόν.**

385. **ταύτης** repeats τῆσδέ γ' ἀρχῆς after the relative sentence.

386. **ὑπελθών**: see lexx., ὑπέρχομαι, III., 2; III.

388. **ὅστις, κ. τ. λ.**, *who has an eye for his gains only.*

391. **πῶς οὐχ**, *how does it come that thou wast not*, etc. — **ὅτε** (G. 12, N. 2, and 17, 1; H. 70, D and 72). — **ῥαψῳδός**: cf. on 36.

393. **αἴνιγμα**: obj. of διειπεῖν. — **τοὐπιόντος** = τοῦ τυχόντος, *of the chance-comer* (G. 169, 1; H. 572, c).

394. **μαντείας ἔδει**, *divinatione opus erat.* — **μαντείας**, *real inspiration.*

395, 396. *Which it was plainly manifest* THOU *neither hadst from birds nor hadst learned from any one of the gods.* — **ἔχων** (G. 280; H. 797). — **γνωτόν** (G. 166, N. 2; H. 556). See also on 384. — **μολών**: cf. 35.

397. **ὁ μηδὲν εἰδὼς Οἰδίπους**: εἰδώς, notwithstanding its position, expresses condition (G. 277, 4; H. 789, e), and so its negative is μή, not οὐ (G. 283, 4; H. 839). *But I having come, Œdipus, even if* (as was said, cf. verse 37) *I did know nothing, put an end to her.* — **νίν**: the Sphinx.

398. **γνώμη**: said in depreciation of the seer's "art." — **κυρήσας**: see lexx., κυρέω, II., 2.

401. **κλαίων**, *to thine own hurt.* — **καὶ σὺ χῷ, κ. τ. λ.** : cf. 378.

402. **ἀγηλατήσειν** : cf. 100 and 309.

403. *Punishment would have taught thee what sort of things thou art plotting,* i. e. well punished once thou wouldst have begun to appreciate how dangerous a thing it is to attack the king.

404. The Chorus interposes. — **εἰκάζουσι**, *comparing* (the impressions your words have made upon us).

406. **ὅπως, κ. τ. λ.** : the indirect question is in apposition with *τόδε*.

407. **ἄριστα** : adverbially. — **λύσομεν**, *shall fulfil.* See lex., III., 1. — **σκοπεῖν** : sc. *δεῖ* from the preceding line : *but it behooves us to consider this,* etc. (G. 259 and 134, N. 2). H. makes this the obj. rather than the subj. of **δεῖ** (764, b, ad fin.).

408. Paying no attention to what the Chorus has interposed, Tiresias addresses the king. — **ἐξισωτέον** (G. 281 ; H. 804).

409. **τοῦδε, κ. τ. λ.** : as a prophet under the protection of Apollo, his words would be held in reverence.

410, 411. Tiresias proudly declares the god his sole master. In consequence, he needs not the patronage of Creon, for Apollo's protection is enough. — **Κρέοντος** : as *ἐπιόντος* in 393. — **γεγράψομαι** : see lexx., *γράφω*, A, II., 3 ; A, III., 3.

412 sqq. Three sentences constitute the obj. of **λέγω** : first, *σὺ καὶ...μέτα* ; secondly, *καὶ λέληθας...ἄνω*, and thirdly, *σ' ἀμφιπλὴξ...σκότον.* — The question, **ἆρ' οἶσθα, κ. τ. λ.**, in 415, is thrown in skilfully. The seer knew how the matter of his parentage had once distressed Œdipus, and how calculated it was now again to cause him pain. — **ἐπειδή, κ. τ. λ.**, *since indeed thou reproachest me even with being blind.* Cf. 371. — Syntax of **μέ** ?

413. **ἵν' εἶ κακοῦ** : cf. 367.

414. **ἔνθα** : i. e. in thine own father's house. — For a similar change of verb, see 54. — **ὅτων** : see on 366, 367.

416. **αὐτοῦ** (G. 137, N. 1 ; H. 675, b, and 676, ad fin.). — The reference is to Laius and Jocasta.

417. **μητρός τε καὶ τοῦ σοῦ πατρός** : epexegetic of **ἀμφιπλήξ**.

418. **δεινόπους** : cf.—

> And long upon my startled ear
> Rang his dark courser's *hoofs of fear.*
>
> BYRON, The Giour, 206, 207.

419. **βλέποντα σκότον**, *seeing darkness,* i. e. *being blind.* Cf.—

> Looking on *darkness, which the blind do see.*
>
> SHAKS., Sonnets, xxvii.

420. **βοῆς τῆς σῆς σύμφωνος**, *echoing to thy cry.* "Particularly do verbs and adjectives compounded with σύν or ὁμοῦ often take the gen. in place of the dat." MATTHIÆ, Griech. Gram., § 379.

421. **ποῖος Κιθαιρών** = *ποῖον ὄρος*, with reference to the exposure of the infant Œdipus. "Perhaps to the route which he would take on quitting Thebes." JONES.

422, 423. *When thou shalt have come to understand aright thy marriage, that inhospitable haven* (inhospitable because eventually he is driven out from it upon a stormy sea), *into which with favoring gale* (his solution of the enigma) *thou didst sail in the palace halls.* Perhaps *δόμοις* is governed by *ἄνορμον* (= *ἄνολβον*), *inhospitable*, i. e. *destructive*. — **λιμήν**, in 420, doubtless suggested the figure which appears in *ἄνορμον*, *εἰσέπλευσας* and *εὐπλοίας*. The appropriateness of such frequent use of the nautical metaphor as occurs in the Greek tragic poets will be allowed, if the student will but call to mind that the theatre at Athens, in which their dramas were presented, afforded from its 30,000 to 40,000 unroofed seats a wide prospect of the expanse of the Ægean Sea.

425. I. e. *which will show thee what thou art, and that thou art thine own children's brother.* — Note the sigmatismus.

426. **πρός** : see on 343. — **τοὐμὸν στόμα** = *τοὺς ἐμοὺς λόγους*.

427, 428. Eng. order : *ἔστιν γὰρ οὔ (τις) βροτῶν ὅστις ἐκτριβήσεταί ποτε κάκιον σοῦ.* Cf. the similar expression in 248.

429. Œdipus in this line turns to the Chorus. In his anger it is difficult to say what he might have done to Tiresias, if he had not known and remembered the great reverence of the people for their prophet. This same fear of incensing them was doubtless what stayed his hand in 402 and 403, rather than that which he asserted, — the seer's advanced years. — **κλύειν** (G. 261, 1 ; H. 767).

430, 431. He turns again to Tiresias. — **θᾶσσον** (H. 662). — **οὐ πάλιν, κ. τ. λ.**, *wilt thou not turn from these halls and get thee back?* Notice the variety of ways in which in his heat the idea of *departure* is expressed.

433. (True, I did so,) *for*, etc.

434. **σχολῇ** : cf.—

> I 'll trust *by leisure* him that mocks me once.
> TITUS ANDRON., Act I., Scene 2.

— **ἂν ἐστειλάμην**, *would I have had thee fetched.*

435, 436. Uttered with the intention of again calling the attention of Œdipus to the question of his parentage. — **τοιοίδε** (G. 148, N. 1 ; H. 679). — **μῶροι** : calling up *μῶρα* in 433. — **γονεῦσι δ', οἵ σ' ἔφυσαν**, *thy* REAL *parents.*

437. **μεῖνον** : Tiresias had turned to leave. — **ἐκφύει** : note the historical present.

438. Enigmatically: *to-day will declare thy birth, and overwhelm thee with calamity.*

440. Tauntingly. Cf. note on 380, 381.

441. **οἷς**: see on 340.

442. **τύχῃ**: the seer virtually denies that Œdipus had done what he had done *τέχνῃ* (380). He solved the enigma by a lucky hit, which the prophet here ominously says *σὲ διώλεσεν.*

443. **οὔ μοι μέλει,** *I care not.*

444. **τοίνυν**: in connection with *οὔ μοι μέλει.* Œdipus, in the preceding line, not deigning to ask what ruin the prophet means, has just declared that it is a matter of no concern to him. — **παῖ**: Tiresias' page. The Sophoclean drama had three characters (*πρόσωπα*) only at one time on the stage, but these might be attended by any number of mutes.

445. **κομιζέτω δῆτα,** *ay, let him,* spoken with bitterness.

446. **συθείς**: fr. *σεύω.* — Note that **ἄν** occurs twice in this line. Cf. on 339.

447. **ὧν οὕνεκ' ἦλθον,** *to tell which you summoned me.* Tiresias did not come with the deliberate intention of revealing what he knew, and was at first most unwilling to do so. See 317, 318, and 320, 321. There is a bitter reference here to the fact that Œdipus has forced from him this revelation of his own pollution. — **οὕνεκα**: see 383.

448. **δείσας**: depends on **ἄπειμι,** and expresses cause. — **ἔσθ' ὅπου,** *in any way.* See lexx., *ὅπου,* III., 2; I., 2. — **πρόσωπον**: *thy threatening front.* Cf.—

> —his *look*
> *Haughty* as is his pile high-built and proud.
> SAMSON AGONISTES, 1069.

449. **ἄνδρα** (G. 153, N. 4; H. 817).

451. For the repetition of **οὗτος** cf. 383-385.

452. **λόγῳ,** *in name.* — **εἶτα,** *soon.*

454. **τυφλὸς γὰρ ἐκ δεδορκότος**: cf.—

> How cam'st thou *speakable of mute.*
> PARADISE LOST, IX., 563.

455. **ἔπι**: notice the anastrophe.

456. **γαῖαν**: Attica. The self-exiled king wanders to Colonus, where he meets his death. This forms the subject of the "Œdipus Colóneus."

460. **ὁμόσπορος** = *τὴν αὐτὴν σπείρων γυναῖκα.* SCHOL. Cf. the passive use of the word in 260.

462. Spoken bitterly with reference to 390. — **φάσκειν** (G. 269; H. 784). — Tiresias, led by his boy attendant, returns to the city. Œdipus retires within the palace. The Chorus begins to sing the first stasimon.

463–512. The *first stasimon.* Analysis: the first strophe and antistrophe refer to the oracle sent by Apollo in itself considered, the second to the dread declaration of Tiresias that Œdipus himself was the murderer. More at length: —Who, pray, is the accursed one? (χερσίν); now should he fly on the wings of the wind (νωμᾶν), for the armed son of Zeus assails (γενέτας), and the dread, unerring fates pursue him (ἀναπλάκητοι); from Parnassus comes the command to track the murderer by every means (ἰχνεύειν); for outcast and forlorn he wanders wide (χηρεύων), striving in vain to escape the oracles from the central spot of earth (περιποτᾶται). Dread are the words of the seer, and unable I to answer (ἀπορῶ); I hover in uncertainty, seeing neither what is nor will be (ὀπίσω); I know of no quarrel between the Labdacid and the son of Polybus, by which my King shall be convicted of this deed (θανάτων); Jupiter and Apollo are my stay (εἰδότες); a seer is but a man (ἀληθής), and in wisdom one man may surpass his fellow (ἀνήρ); I would never assent to this charge against Œdipus until fully proved (καταφαίην); for how wise and good to our state has he been shown (ἁδύπολις); I will not then believe him base (κακίαν).

463 sqq. *Who is he whom the fatidic Delphic mount* (Parnassus) *declared to have done with bloody hands the most horrible of deeds?* — **ἃ**: see second note on 151.

464. **Δελφίς**: see lexx., Δελφοί, II., ad fin. The oracle of Delphi lay under a lofty wall of rocks at the foot of Mt. Parnassus. Cf. 473–475.

465. **τελέσαντα**: an extended use of the supplementary participle (G. 280; H. 799).

467, 468. *'T is time for him to ply in flight a foot mightier than storm-swift steeds.* — **ἵππων**: obs. that the sentence is condensed. — **σθεναρώτερον**: an adj. in agreement with **πόδα**. Lit. *stronger*, but here of speed, *swifter*. So κρεῖσσον in 177, from ΚΡΑ'ΤΟΣ.

469. **ἐπενθρώσκει**, *is leaping forth.* Cf. 263.

470. **πυρὶ καὶ στεροπαῖς**: as in 151 Apollo was endowed with the prophetic power of his father Jove, so he appears here as an avenger, to pursue the murderer of Laius with his sire's lightnings. The two words by hendiadys. Connect them with **ἔνοπλος**. — **γενέτας**: generally *father*, but here *son*. Apollo is meant.

472. **Κῆρες**: according to Hesiod, avenging deities, daughters of Night, and sisters of the Mœræ. See Dict. of Biog. and Mythol., CER. — **ἀναπλάκητοι** = ἀναμπλάκητοι, *whom there is no escaping*, from α privitive, and ἀμπλακεῖν, *to miss*, akin to ΠΛΑ'ΖΩ, *to make to wander*, the α being euphonic, and the μ inserted.

473 sqq. *For the command flashed forth, just now having come to light from* *snow-clad Parnassus, to track the hidden man by every means.* — **ἔλαμψε φάμα**: cf. *παιὰν λάμπει* in 187. The oracle brought by Creon is aptly compared to a beacon set on the summit of the Delphic mount, to lead to the discovery of the concealed murderer. — **νιφόεντος**: cf. —

> O thou Parnassus! whom I now survey,
> Not in the frenzy of a dreamer's eye,
> Nor in the fabled landscape of a lay,
> But soaring *snow-clad* through thy native sky,
> In the wild pomp of mountain majesty!
>
> CHILDE HAROLD, I., lx.

476. Schn. says, **τὸν ἄδηλον**, obj.; **ἄνδρα πάντα**, subj.

478. **πετραῖος**, *among rocks.* This word corresponds to the two adverbial elements, **ὑπ' ἀγρίαν ὕλαν** and **ἀνὰ ἄντρα.** — **ὁ ταῦρος** (G. 137; H. 500, c).

479. **ποδί**: modifies **φοιτᾷ.** — **χηρεύων**, *outcast, living in solitude*, referring to the curse under which the murderer lay. See 236 sqq. — The figure in these verses is suggested by *ἰχνεύειν* in 476. As a bull escaped from the herd roams alone through the wild, rocky, cavernous woodlands, and is not easily caught, so the murderer wanders, harassed and wretched, an outcast from society, making every effort to escape detection.

480. **μεσόμφαλα**: Delphi was considered by the ancient Greeks to be the centre of the earth. Cf. 898. — **γᾶς**: the gen. is partitive and depends on the included substantive, as if we had, *τὰ τοῦ μέσου τῆς γῆς ὀμφαλοῦ* (H. 587, e). — **ἀπονοσφίζων**, *shunning.* — How entirely contrary to what the Chorus pictures are the actions of the actual murderer! He is present among them enjoying the association of friends, and using his every effort to obey the commands of the oracle!

483 sqq. *Fearfully then, fearfully does the wise seer trouble me, neither assenting nor denying. For I am at a loss what to say. But I hover in uncertain expectation, seeing neither what is nor will be.* The participles modify *μέ* understood, the object of **ταράσσει.** A second interpretation, but not so good, makes **δεινά** the object of *ταράσσει*, and the participles agree with it in the sense, as explained by the Schol., of *οὔτε πιστὰ οὔτε ἄπιστα.* — Obs. the delicate use of **μέν** and **οὖν** difficult to express in translation. *μέν* in connection with **δέ** in 487 contrasts the terrors caused by the seer's words with the uncertain expectation of the Chorus (**ἐλπίσιν**), inclining, however, toward hope. **δέ** in 486 is causal, and almost equals *γάρ*. *οὖν* is continuative, joining the thought that precedes, the miserable state of the accursed and the certainty of his punishment, to the allied but more definite one that follows, — the accusation of Œdipus by the seer as himself the murderer.

487. **πέτομαι δ' ἐλπίσιν**: as we should say, *to be suspended between hope and fear.*

488. **οὔτ' ἐνθάδε — οὔτ' ὀπίσω**, *neither the present nor future*, i. e. neither whether Œdipus or the seer is right, nor who will be shown the murderer. — **ὀπίσω** : lit. *behind*. So our own poet —

> We were, fair queen,
> Two lads that thought there was no more *behind*
> But such a day to-morrow as to-day,
> And to be boy eternal. — WINTER'S TALE, Act I., Scene 2.

489, 490. *For what quarrel existed either between the house of Labdacus* (and the son of Polybus), *or between the son of Polybus* (and the Labdacidæ), etc. So explained by the Schol. The disjunctive form of the expression makes the name of the aggressor in the quarrel prominent, each in turn being put first. — **Λαβδακίδαις** : Laius. Poetic use of plural for singular. — **τῷ Πολύβου** : Œdipus, the supposed son of Polybus (G. 141, N. 4; H. 509, (β)).

492. **τανῦν**, *in the present case*. — **ἔμαθον** : with **πάροιθεν** translate as an aorist, with **πώ** as a perfect. — The antecedent of **ὅτου** is *τινός* understood to be taken with **ἔμαθον**, *at whose word I assail with proof the popular renown of Œdipus*. Or the antecedent, as often construed, may be **νεῖκος**, *from which*, as a starting-point.

495. **Οἰδιπόδα** : gen. See lexx., *Οἰδίπους* and *Οἰδιπόδης*, and H. 191, D.

496. **Λαβδακίδαις** : the number as in 489. So also **θανάτων**, limiting gen. of **ἐπίκουρος**.

497. **ἀδήλων**, *mysterious*. — **θανάτων** : an objective genitive.

500 sqq. *But that a prophet among men surpasses me in wisdom, there is no sure way of judging; but a man might surpass wisdom by wisdom.* Cf. with the last sentiment 380. He is thinking of the success of Œdipus, and how signally superior he was even to this same seer, Tiresias. Cf. 390 – 398.

505. **ἴδοιμι** (G. 240; H. 760, d; M. 67, 1, ninth ex.).

506. **ὀρθόν** : predicate adjective, *before I should see their charge proved*.— **μεμφομένων** : sc. *ἄλλων* (G. 278, 1; H. 790, a, and 791, a).

507. **ἂν καταφαίην**, *would assent*. — **φανερά** : in opposition to *ἀδήλων* in 497. Nom. sing. fem.

508. **αὐτῷ** : Œdipus, who is prominently in mind.

510. **βασάνῳ**, *by actual test*.

511. **τῷ**, *therefore*. — **ἀπ' ἐμᾶς φρενός**, *by my mind*.

512. **ὀφλήσει** : from *ὀφλισκάνω*, *to incur a charge of*.

513. Creon, who left the stage at 146 on the best of terms with Œdipus, having heard with astonishment of the charge made against him by the king, here hurriedly returns. He enters from the city through the western parodos, and during his dialogue with the Chorus stands in the orchestra. — **δείν' ἔπη** : see 378 – 389, and sqq.

514. **τύραννον** : not our *tyrant*, but rather *monarch*, possessed however of absolute power.

515. **ἀτλητῶν**, *ill brooking it.* — **ἐν ταῖς ξυμφοραῖς ταῖς νῦν**, *in the existing crisis.*

517. The first εἴτε is omitted. — **εἰς βλάβην φέρον**, *tending to injury.* Sc. τί.

518. **τοῦ** : the article points out a *long life* as an unusual gift of the gods, and one generally desired by men.

519. **ἁπλοῦν** does not mean *slight, small* (μικρόν), but *single.* He means the injury done him will be manifold.

520. *This charge damages me.* — φέρω occurs three times in four lines. See on 158.

521. **ἐν πόλει** : i. e. by those in the city, by the citizens in general.

522. **κεκλήσομαι** : fut. perf. as simple future (H. 712 and a ; M. 29, N. 5).

523, 524. The Chorus says, in a conciliatory way, *to be sure* (μὲν δή, like μέντοι : see lex., μέν, B, I., 3) *this charge was made, but perhaps rather in the violence of anger than by a deliberate judgment of his mind.* — **τάχ' ἂν** : Wunder says that ἂν does not here belong to **ἦλθε**, but to the participle **βιασθέν**. He has thus explained its force by a periphrasis : ἀλλὰ τοῦτο, τὸ ὄνειδος, ὃ ἦλθε, τάχ' ἂν ὀργῇ βεβιασμένον ἂν εἴη μᾶλλον, κ. τ. λ.

525, 526. *From what was it shown that the seer spoke his words falsely persuaded by* MY *counsels?* The singular inversion in **τοῦ πρός**, and the position of **ταῖς ἐμαῖς γνώμαις** before **ὅτι**, express the excitement under which the speaker was laboring. — **λέγοι** (G. 243 ; H. 736, 1).

527. *Such was the report, but I know not with what proof.* Sc. ηὐδᾶτο ὅτι ταῖς σαῖς γνώμαις πεισθεὶς ὁ μάντις τοὺς λόγους λέγοι. — **γνώμῃ**, *a ground for judgment, a proof.*

528. Creon wishes to learn from the outward bearing of Œdipus, at the time he made the charge, whether he was honest in what he was doing, and sane, or not. — **ἐξ**, *with.*

529. *Was this charge brought against me?*

530. The Chorus will not commit itself.

531. **δ' ὅδε**, *but see.*

532. Creon turns toward the king, who is entering from the palace. — **οὗτος** (G. 148, N. 2 ; H. 680, a). Emphasis on **σύ**.

534. **ἵκου** (G. 237 ; H. 771). — **τοῦδε τἀνδρός** = ἐμοῦ. Œdipus declares Creon to be to him, in intention at least, **φονεύς** and **λῃστής**.

535. **λῃστὴς τῆς ἐμῆς τυραννίδος** : cf. —

> — the attempter of thy Father's throne,
> And *thief of Paradise.*
>
> PARADISE REGAINED, IV., 603, 604.

538. ὡς οὐ, κ. τ. λ. : dependent on some such word as *νομίσας*, implied in *ἰδών*. — **ὡς οὐ γνωρίσοιμι,** *that I should not detect.*

540. ἆρ' οὐχί (G. 282, 2; H. 829). — **μῶρον** : with reference to *μωρίαν* in 536.

542. ὅ, (a thing) *which,* etc. Cf. the similar use of the predicate adj. (G. 138, N. 2, (c); H. 522, fifth ex.).

543. Creon, who during the preceding violent charge of Œdipus had been in mute protest unconsciously approaching the steps of the stage, here rapidly ascends them, and addresses his king face to face. — **οἶσθ' ὡς ποίησον** : Sophocles here in place of saying *οἶσθ' ὡς* (for *ὅπως*) *ποιῆσαι δεῖ*; or *ποίησον ὡς κελεύω*, combines the two, and that not into *ποίησον, οἶσθ' ὡς*; but the more remarkable expression of the text (G. 252, N.; M. 84, N. 3).

545. *Thou art a sharp talker, but I am slow to learn from thee.*

547. *First hear now this very point* (whether I am hostile to thee) *from me, how* I *shall tell it.* — **πρῶτα,** *before thou condemnest me finally.* — Creon concluded that he had been maligned to the king by his enemies, and believed that he could clear up the matter if given a chance to explain. *νῦν* indicates his desire that this should be done at once.

548. τοῦτ' αὐτό : here and in the ff. ll. Œdipus repeats Creon's words sneeringly. — **ὅπως** : the declarative conjunction (G. 249, 1, ex.).

550. αὐθαδίαν χωρὶς τοῦ νοῦ : see on 55.

552. οὐχ, κ. τ. λ., *thou wilt not pay the penalty.* — 551, 552, are spoken with bitter contempt.

554. πάθημα : cf. on *Λαΐου* in 224.

555. See 288.

556. σεμνόμαντιν : Œdipus is now far from believing Tiresias such, and uses the word ironically.

557. *And I still think that was good advice.* — **βουλεύματι** : as *ἄνακτι* in 284. Like the phrase *ὁ αὐτὸς ἐμαυτῷ.*

558. πόσον τιν' ἤδη χρόνον, *how long a* (*τινά*) *time ago* —

559. Creon, whose mind is on Tiresias, breaks in on the question of Œdipus.

560. ἄφαντος ἔρρει, *did* (i. e. Laius, occurring above) *disappear and perish.* — It will be noted that *ἔρρει* (lit. *is clean gone*) has the force of a perfect. (M. 10, 1, N. 4.) The perfect (**δέδρακε,** *has been doing*) is the tense Creon employed in the preceding line. This enables us to see the pertinence of the acc. of duration of time, *χρόνον*, in 558.

561. I. e. *μακροὶ παλαιοί τ' ἂν εἴησαν οἱ χρόνοι, εἰ μετρηθεῖεν.*

563. γέ : cf. *γέ* in 365.

564. ἐμνήσατο : see lexx., *μιμνήσκω*, B, 2. — **ἐμοῦ** : as *ἀρχῆς* in 49.

565. **οὐδαμοῦ** is the antecedent of the subordinate conjunction of time implied in **ἑστῶτος** (G. 278, 1, and 277, 1; H. 790, a), and is incorporated into the relative sentence (H. 811, a). Observe that it is transferred from the signification of *place* to that of *time*, — *at no time when I was standing by.*

566. **τοῦ θανόντος** (G. 167, 3; H. 565).

567. *Of course we made inquiry, but we learned nothing.* The parenthetic question, **πῶς δ᾽ οὐχί**, strengthens **παρέσχομεν**, which in itself is stronger than the word used by Œdipus (*ἔσχετε*) in his question just asked. Creon would show the earnestness that the people manifested. They began a vigorous inquiry, but the overwhelming calamity of the Sphinx (130, 131) paralyzed their effort. Œdipus refers to this partial and abortive effort in the compound verbs in 129 and 258.

568. **οὗτος ὁ σοφός**: contemptuously repeating the appellation Creon had given Tiresias in 563.

569. **ἐφ᾽ οἷς** (G. 153 and N. 1; H. 810).

570. Œdipus echoes Creon's words, *οἶδα* and *φρονῶ*. So Creon in the next line repeats *οἶδα*. — Œdipus thinks that Creon, in the maxim he has just uttered, *it is well for one to be silent concerning the things he understands not*, is talking at him, and answers scornfully. — **εὖ φρονῶν** expresses manner, *couldst say understandingly*, and is retorted with a sneer upon the *μὴ φρονῶ* of the last speaker.

572, 573. The sentence depends on the verbs *οἶσθα* and *λέγοις ἄν*, supplied from 570. — **ὁθούνεκα**, *that*, equalling *ὡς* or *ὅτι* (M. 78, N.). — **τὰς ἐμάς**: "'He would not have spoken, as he did (362), of my being Laius' murderer.'" Camp. The student will easily see the double meaning possible in the words, 'he would not have spoken of *my murder of Laius*.'

574. Creon was not present during the altercation between Œdipus and Tiresias. Somewhat angered, he repeats *οἶσθα* sarcastically. He now endeavors to show Œdipus how unlikely a thing it is that he (Creon) would wish to exchange his present honorable position for one bringing but little more honor and much more anxiety.

575. **ταὔθ᾽ ἅπερ**, *just as*. That is, just as thou hast tried by interrogating me to prove that I suborned Tiresias, in the same way do I wish to show that that is impossible.

576. **ἐκμάνθανε**: defiantly. — **οὐ γάρ, κ. τ. λ.**: Œdipus suspiciously thinks that Creon is aiming to convict him of the murder.

577. **γῆμας ἔχεις**: periphrastic perfect (M. 112, N. 7).

578. Œdipus was not expecting this sort of a question. So in place of the flat denial he was ready to make, he answers ironically, *there is no denying* THAT.

579. **δέ**: as if *μέν* occurred in 577, and there had been no interruption. — **ταὐτά**: cogn. acc., being equal to *τὴν αὐτὴν ἀρχήν*, i. e. *conjointly.* Cf. the lexx. for the cases allowed with *ἄρχω* in its second signification. — **ἴσον**: sc. *μέρος*, with which connect **γῆς**. Jocasta was queen in her own right, and so she and Œdipus were joint rulers of Thebes. But he, like a man, arrogates dominion to himself. See not only his answer in the next line, but also 237. — Possibly *γῆς* is the object of **ἄρχεις**.

580. He seems to evade the question. — **θέλουσα** (M. 108, 2, N. 6, first ex.). This construction is quite common in this drama.

581. **ἰσοῦμαι**, *am on an equal footing.*

582. (Undoubtedly, and that is what astonishes me), *for in this very thing thou showest thyself even a bad friend.*

583. **οὔκ**: sc. *ἂν φαινοίμην*. — **εἰ διδοίης γε σαυτῷ λογον**, *if thou wouldst only render an account to thyself.* — **ὡς ἐγώ**: sc. *σοὶ δίδωμι λόγον.*

584. **πρῶτον**: adverbially. So in the thought *ἔπειτα* occurs in 603. — — **εἰ** (G. 282, 4; H. 733). — **ἄν**: to be taken with *ἑλέσθαι.*

585. **ἄρχειν ξὺν φόβοισι**: with Creon's general sentiment, cf. —

> *Uneasy lies the head that wears a crown.*
> Henry IV., Part II., Act III., Scene 1.

586. The circumstantial participle **εὕδοντα** expresses manner, just as the adverbial phrase *ξὺν φόβοισι* in 585. Cf. the use of **ἄτρεστον** with that of *ὕπνῳ* in 65. — **ἕξει**: a case where protasis and apodosis belong to different forms. For *ἕξει* see G. 221, N. Then the whole expression comes under G. 227, 1. See here M. 49, 1, N. 3, and 54, 1.

587. **ἐγώ**: emphatic. — **μὲν οὖν**: a strengthened form of *οὖν*, *so then.* See lex., *μέν*, B, II., 2. — **ἱμείρων ἔφυν**, *am of a nature to desire.*

588. **τύραννα**: adj. use of *τύραννος.*

589. **οὔτ' ἄλλος**: evidently with reference to Tiresias, with whom Œdipus had affirmed he was in collusion. — **ἐπίσταμαι**, like *οἶδα*, takes either the participle or infinitive, but with a difference of meaning (G. 280, N. 3; H. 802). Cf. the construction in 284.

590. **ἄνευ φόβου**: contrasted with *ξὺν φόβοισι* in 585. — **φέρω**, *I obtain.*

592. **ἔχειν**: as *κλύειν* in 429.

594. *Not yet am I so misled.* — **ἠπατημένος κυρῶ**: cf. 258, 259.

595. **τὰ σὺν κέρδει καλά**, *honor accompanied with profit.*

596. **νῦν πᾶσι χαίρω**, *now I am on good terms with all.*

597. **σέθεν** (G. 79, 1, N. 2; H. 233, D).

598. Make **πᾶν** the subject of **τυχεῖν**, and consult lexx., *τυγχάνω*, B, 2. Or it may be taken adverbially with what follows, *rests wholly here.*

599. **κεῖνα**: i. e. *τὸ αὐτὸς ἄρχειν*, while **τάδε** is *τύραννα δρᾶν.*

600. *No mind that judges rightly* (sees things as they are) *could turn to evil.*

601. **τῆσδε τῆς γνώμης**, *this way of thinking.*

602. **μετ' ἄλλου**: see on 589. — **τλαίην**: sc. δρᾶν from the preceding **δρῶντος.**

603. In the second part of his address, 603 - 615, Creon exhorts Œdipus to look at the facts and not rush into hasty judgment. — **ἔλεγχον**: in apposition with the following sentence as a whole. The correlatives, **τοῦτο μέν** and **τοῦτ' ἄλλο**, are distributively in similar construction before the two imperative sentences. — **Πυθώδε** — **πεύθου**: no intentional play on the similar syllables; nor in 70, 71, Πυθικά — πύθοιτο. That is, not cases of *paronomasia.* See lexx., παρονομασία, II.

604. **τὰ χρησθέντα**: a case of prolepsis.

605. **τερασκόπῳ**: Creon calls Tiresias so, says Schn., with reference to the meaning of his name, ὁ τὰ τείρεα σκοπῶν.

606, 607. **κτάνῃς λαβών**, *take and slay me* (G. 254; H. 723, a).

608. **γνώμῃ ἀδήλῳ**: lit. *on the ground of an uncertain opinion*, i. e. an opinion concerning the soundness of which not even thou canst be certain. Better, *on a vague surmise.* — **χωρίς** is used absolutely, *without evidence.*

609. **μάτην**, *without cause.*

612. **καί** (H. 856, c). — **ἐμβαλεῖν** is to be repeated before **βίοτον.** — **τὸν παρ' αὑτῷ βίοτον**, *one's own life.*

614, 615. "Because the bad but too easily betray their worthlessness, while the good are often modestly retiring, and the recognition of their worth is a work of time." Schn.

616. *A cautious man would judge he had counselled well.* — **εὐλαβουμένῳ**: as πᾶσι in 8. — **πεσεῖν** depends on εὐλαβουμένῳ.

617. Connect **φρονεῖν** with both **ταχεῖς** and **ἀσφαλεῖς**, *a hasty judgment is unreliable.* Colloquially in Eng., "slow and sure." — Note how appropriate ἀσφαλεῖς (α priv. and ΣΦΑΛ'ΛΟΜΑΙ) is to the figure employed in πεσεῖν.

618. "'When my secret enemy is swift in his advance.'" Camp. — Œdipus will hear no arguments. — **ταχύς τις** is predicate to **χωρῇ.** τίς with adjectives indicates that the epithet must be taken in a restricted sense. See lexx., A, 8: ΤΙΣ, IV., 1.

618, 619. Cf. with this —

> We must be brief when traitors take the field.
>
> Richard III., Act IV., Scene 3.

620. **τοῦδε**: referring to οὑπιβουλεύων in 618, but at the same time meaning Creon.

621. *Will have been accomplished,* etc.

623. **θνήσκειν — φυγεῖν** (G. 202, 1, ad fin.; H. 716, a, ad fin.).

624. Sc. ἑτοῖμος θνήσκειν before **ὅταν, κ. τ. λ. — τὸ φθονεῖν** = ὁ ἐμὸς πρὸς σὲ φθόνος. See 382.

625. *Dost thou speak as determined neither to yield nor obey?* The king demands unconditional obedience. — The altercation has now reached its highest point, and finds expression only in short, condensed sentences, which the speakers deal at one another like blows.

626. **τὸ γοῦν ἐμόν** : sc. εὖ φρονοῦντά με βλέπεις. So in the first half of the next line; sc. εὖ φρονεῖν σε.

628. **εἰ δέ,** *but what if,* etc. — **ξυνίῃς** : pres., not imperf., indic. — **ἀρκτέον (ἐμοὶ σοῦ) γ' ὅμως,** *ay, I must maintain my authority even then* (G. 281, 2; H. 804, b). Or ἀρκτέον passively, *thou must obey.*

629. *Never, if thou rulest unjustly.* — **ἄρχοντος** : sc. σοῦ. A gen. absol. — **πόλις** (G. 157, N.; H. 541, ad fin.).

630. **πόλεως** (G. 184, 2, N. 1; H. 571). — Creon would have a claim upon the state, not only as a citizen, but also as brother of the queen.

632. **τῆνδε** : use in English an adverb (H. 678, a, sec. ex.). Or δεικτικῶς, cf. 811.

633. **εὖ θέσθαι,** *to settle.*

634, 635. Jocasta enters from the palace. As she comes, the two men pause in the midst of their altercation, at the words of the Chorus, and turn to meet her. — **στάσιν γλώσσης,** *strife of tongues.* — **ἐπήρασθε** : see lex., ἐπαίρω, I., 4. The force of the middle can be expressed by, *against one another.*

636. **ἴδια κινοῦντες κακά,** *to stir up private quarrels.* Cf. —

> What! in a town of war,
> To manage private and domestic quarrel!
> 'T is monstrous. OTHELLO, Act II., Scene 3.

637, 638. A fine example of the different uses of **οὐ** and **μή** in interrogative sentences (G. 282, 2; H. 829; M. 89, 2, N. 2). — **σύ τε** : Joc. addresses her husband imperiously. — **οἴκους** : the place *whither.* It is fanciful to draw a distinction of meaning here between **οἴκους** and **στέγας.** A variation in the verb similar to this in 414. — **εἶ** = πορεύσῃ.

639 sqq. Creon seizes the first opportunity to address her: *O my sister, thy husband designs a terrible deed, of these two evils, either to banish me or to take and kill me, having determined upon — Yea, I* HAVE, *for,* etc. Notice the great excitement under which the speakers labor. Before Creon can complete his sentence, Œdipus breaks in on him. See 325. Jocasta would easily gather from the connection which punishment Creon meant.

643. **τοὐμὸν σῶμα,** *my person, me.*

644. **ὀναίμην** : the mood as in 81.

645. **ὧν** : attracted.

646. **τάδε** (G. 160, 1; H. 549, c). Sc. αὐτῷ with the verb.

647. **μάλιστα μέν,** *first and above all.* — **τόνδ' ὅρκον θεῶν,** *this oath sworn by the gods.* Objective gen. The reference is to ἀραῖος in 644.

648. **καί,** *also.*

649 sqq. "Sophocles has here employed the Chorus with great skill. Without any pause in the action, which must be continued until the colloquy between Jocasta and Œdipus has taken place, the short musical strains which allay the exasperation of Œdipus, and assure him of his people's loyalty, also relieve the mind of the spectator from the tension caused by the preceding dialogue, and prepare him to give undivided attention to the central scene, — in which the first doubt is suggested to the mind of Œdipus, while the impious confidence of Jocasta is revealed." CAMP. — The Oxford trans.: "*Be prevailed on willingly and sensibly.*" Campbell translates better: "*We pray thee, bend to our request thy will and mind.*" The Chorus, believing that Œdipus, in his accusation of Creon, is in the wrong, entreats him to be differently minded (φρονήσας), yield his hitherto, in this matter, stubborn will (θελήσας), and be prevailed upon (πιθοῦ) by their united request. Jocasta had just besought him to believe Creon.

651. *In what wilt thou, then, that I give way to thee?* — **εἰκάθω** (G. 256; H. 720, c).

654. **καταίδεσαι** : first aorist imperative middle.

655. **φράζε, κ. τ. λ.**: he speaks impatiently.

656, 657. *That thou accuse* (**ἐν αἰτίᾳ βαλεῖν**) *not nor dishonor with an obscure suspicion the friend that has bound himself by an oath.* Sc. χρήζω. — The adverbial phrase **σὺν ἀφανεῖ λόγῳ,** (with which cf. γνώμῃ ἀδήλῳ, 608) modifies **ἄτιμον.**

658, 659. Œdipus still believes it was Creon who had charged him with the murder of Laius. Cf. 703. If Creon should be let off, then he would press his charge and bring Œdipus, innocent though he should be, to punishment. — **ἐπίστω** : imperative. — **ζητῶν** : cf. the use of ὁρῶντα in 284.

660 sqq. "This solemn adjuration, made by the whole choral body with uplifted hands and while a vernal sun, it may be, was shining brightly over their heads, must have produced no small effect in the theatre." MITCHELL.

661. **θεόν** (G. 163, N.; H. 545). — **πρόμον** : seeing, but not understanding, the existing confusion, and much desiring that Œdipus and Creon may be illuminated and brought to understand one another, the Chorus swears

by the sun as *foremost of the gods*, which, as the god who brings all things to light, in their present exigency he is to them.

662. **ἄθεος**: cf. ἀθέως in 254.

663. **ὅ τι πύματον** sustains (the antecedent being incorporated) the relation of cognate accusative to **ὀλοίμαν**, as if the poet had said, τὴν πυμάτην ἀπώλειαν. — **πύματον**: predicate to ἐστί understood.

665 sqq. *But the wasting* (φθινάς, see lexx.) *land consumes my wretched soul, if she is to add to her other evils these which arise from you two.* But see lexx., προσάπτω, II. — **προσάψει** (G. 221, N.).

666. **φθινάς**: cf. 25–27.

669. **ὁ δέ**: cf. οἱ δέ in 108. — **δ' οὖν**, *well then.*

671. **στόμα**: see on 426.

673, 674. *It is evident that thou yieldest* (**εἴκων** as ἔχων in 395) *sullenly, but weighed down by remorse wilt thou be whenever thou shalt have passed from thy anger.* Cf. the Schol.: δῆλος εἶ ἀηδῶς εἴκων, ὅταν δὲ ἐπὶ τὸ πέρας ἔλθῃς τῆς ὀργῆς, τότε βαρέως οἴσεις τὸ πράγμα. οἷον, μετανοήσεις καὶ ἄδικα ἐνθυμηθήσῃ. — **θυμοῦ**: a poetic gen. of separation, or the gen., says Dind., *quod* **περάσῃς** *idem est, quod* **πέραν ᾖς**. — Schn., taking **στυγνός** actively, translates differently: *plainly thou art full of hatred toward me, though thou yieldest,* etc.

677. **ἀγνῶτος**, *without discernment.* — **ἐν δέ, κ. τ. λ.**, *but in the estimation of these the same as ever.* But perhaps **ἴσος** = δίκαιος. Schol. Min., followed by some of the commentators. — *Creon exit.*

678 sqq. The Chorus addresses Jocasta apart, and entreats her to conduct Œdipus immediately into the palace. The king stands at one side wrapped in moody thought. The queen, though she was herself desirous at 637 that Œdipus should at once go within, now refuses to comply with the request of the Chorus until she learn the occasion of the quarrel. This very natural action on her part leads skillfully to the unravelling of the plot.

680. Sc. κομιῶ αὐτόν. — **ἥτις ἡ τύχη**, *what has happened.*

681-683. *An unfounded suspicion found vent in words, and words even when unfounded sting.* The Chorus speaks with designed ambiguity. What it says may refer either to the accusation of Tiresias and the consequent anger of Œdipus, or the charge that the latter himself made against Creon, and the distress with which he thereby afflicted him. — **λόγων** is a vague gen. depending on **δόκησις**.

684. **ἀμφοῖν ἀπ' αὐτοῖν**: sc. ἦλθε. Jocasta has in mind Œdipus and Creon. — **ναίχι**: compelled to answer the question as to these two, the Chorus says *yes*, though it evidently shrinks from giving Œdipus pain. Its good-will to him is so extreme as to make it unjust; for it says this *unfounded suspicion* was mutual, which was not the fact.

685. **προπονουμένας**: see lexx., *προπονέω*, II., 2; II. Stronger than the simple verb.

686. **ἔληξεν**: sc. ὁ λόγος.

687, 688. Œdipus, who has heard the last words of the Chorus, loses his temper, and says, *dost thou see to what thou art come, honest man though thou art at heart, leaving my interests out of view, and trying to blunt my wrath?* He means that, if it had not been for the Chorus, he would have punished Creon. **καταμβλύνων** (G. 200, N. 2; H. 702, ad fin.). The principle extends to the participle. Cf. *ἐκτρέποντα* in 806.

689 sqq. The Chorus again (see 660–664) protests its loyalty: *Prince, I have said it not once alone, but know that I should be proved beside myself, destitute of sense, to abandon thee,* etc. — **πεφάνθαι ἄν**: in the orat. rect. *πεφασμένος ἂν εἴην*. — **νοσφίζομαι** (G. 227, 1; H. 750).

694. On the correlation of **τέ — τέ** here, cf. on 35, where an exactly parallel case occurs. Similarly *καί — καί* in 52, 53.

695, 696. **σαλεύουσαν**: the image is continued in **οὔρισας**, *didst speed on her course,* from *οὖρος*, *a fair wind* directly astern. — **κατ᾽ ὀρθόν**: the same phrase in 88.

697. **γένοιο** (G. 251, N. 2; H. 721, a).

699. *Thou hast conceived so great wrath.* — **πράγματος**: see refs. on 48. — **ἔχεις**: see lexx., B, IV., 1: A, IV., 7. Cf. the use of *ἔχειν* with the perfect participle in 701.

700. *For I respect thee more than these do.* The Chorus, 685, had refused to explain the matter to the queen. Or, *I respect thee more than I do these,* i. e. am more willing to comply with thy request than with the desire of the Chorus, who want the matter dropped. The latter interpretation accords better with the emphatic **σέ**. — "As he turned from Creon to the Chorus, 671, so now, being angry with them, he turns gladly to Jocasta. With similar impetuosity he breaks away from her, *infra* 1078." CAMP.

701. **Κρέοντος**: answering to *πράγματος* in 699. Sc. *μῆνιν τοσήνδε στήσας ἔχω*. — **οἷα, κ. τ. λ.**, *in respect to what he has plotted against me.* Epexegetic. — The whole line can be expressed by *τῶν Κρέοντος βουλευμάτων*, where the second word answers to *πράγματος*.

702. *Speak, if, though charging the quarrel on him, thou art willing to speak plainly.* Jocasta has heard enough ambiguous statements, and demands impatiently the cause of the quarrel.

703. Creon had said nothing of the sort. What Œdipus means can be gathered from 705, 706.

704. *On his own knowledge, or by report?*

705. *Nay, rather* (see lexx., *μέν*, B, II., 2; II., 6) *by introducing,* etc.

706. Explained by Triclinius: *αὐτὸς γὰρ περὶ τούτου καθάπαξ σιγᾷ.*— **ἐλευθεροῦν στόμα** is literally *to free one's mouth* of a subject. Œdipus means that Creon himself has never directly made the charge, but always through Tiresias as a mouth-piece.

707 sqq. "The catastrophe hangs upon this speech. Jocasta, in endeavoring to direct the attention of Œdipus from the charge of Tiresias, incidentally mentions a circumstance which confirms the charge. The contempt here thrown upon the oracles by Jocasta, is the sin which justifies the catastrophe as far as she is concerned. It is also a sin which is ingeniously made to be the occasion of its own punishment." JONES. — **σύ νυν, κ. τ. λ.**, *letting then these things go of which thou speakest, hearken thou to me*, etc. With *ἀφεὶς σεαυτόν* sc. *τούτων*.

708. **σοί** (G. 184, 3, N. 5; H. 599). So sometimes in English. Cf. —

> Here's a scull now hath lain *you* i' th' earth three-and-twenty years.
>
> HAMLET, Act V., Scene 1.

So, TAMING OF THE SHREW, Act I., Scene 2.

709. **ἔχον** is here used as the middle *ἐχόμενον*, *depending on, having to do with* (G. 171, 1; H. 574, b). Jocasta does not mean to say that mortals have no share in the art of prophecy, the sentiment toward which the Chorus inclined in 500, but that absolutely no dependence is to be placed upon it, and that men in consequence should pay no attention to it.

710. **σύντομα**, *briefly*.

711, 712. **οὐκ ἐρῶ, κ. τ. λ.**, *I won't say it came from Phœbus himself.* Spoken with more or less contempt. As much as to say, although I believe it, I won't say so, in order that I may not seem to blaspheme the god. In 720 she says, without qualification, that Apollo did falsify himself.

713. **ἥξοι**: the mood as in 526.

714. **ὅστις γένοιτο**, *who should be born.* The original prophecy was— *αὐτὸν ἥξει μοῖρα πρὸς παιδὸς θανεῖν, ὅστις ἂν γένηται, κ. τ. λ.*

715. **καί** = *καίτοι*. — **τὸν μέν**: i. e. Laius. Contrasted with *παιδὸς δέ* in 717. — **γέ** strengthens **πέρ**, which means *at all events, at least.* — **ξένοι**: says Jocasta, not only did not his own son kill him, but also even those who did were foreigners!

716. **τριπλαῖς ἁμαξιτοῖς**: these words give Œdipus the first suspicion of the truth. See 730.

717. Literally, *but as to the birth of the child, three days had not intervened, when*, etc., i. e. *the child had not been born three days, when*, etc.

718. **καί**: temporal. — **ἄρθρα**: in partitive apposition with **νίν**, which is the object of the participle. — For the manner in which Œdipus was exposed, see the *Introduction;* also 1032, with the note on 1034.

719. **ὄρος**: Cithæron.

720. **ἐνταῦθα**, *herein*, as in 582.

721, 722. **οὔτε Λάϊον, κ. τ. λ.**: a repetition in a new form of the preceding thought, *οὔτ' ἐκεῖνον, κ. τ. λ.* — **τὸ δεινόν** (G. 137, N. 3; H. 502, a and b).

723. Not spoken with much reverence.

724, 725. **ὧν** (G. 171, 2; H. 576). — **ὧν γάρ, κ. τ. λ.**, *for whatever things God seeks as necessary, these unaided will he easily bring to light.* *ἤγουν ἃ γὰρ ἂν ὁ θεὸς ζητῇ, πρέποντα κρίνας ζητεῖσθαι, ῥᾳδίως, ἤγουν εὐκόλως, αὐτὸς δείξει.* Schol. Min. Necessitatem sive utilitatem rei dixit pro re qua opus est. HERMANN. This apparently devout sentiment, coming on the heels of her blasphemy, cannot be supposed to mean much to Jocasta. She speaks in too vague a way, the anarthrous *θεός* referring neither to Apollo nor to any particular deity, but meaning *god* in a general sense. But to the pious spectator her words mean that whatever the god determines to do, he easily accomplishes of himself, and they find a startling verification in the impending catastrophe. That is, Apollo commands the discovery of the murderer, and discovered will he be before the day's close. — **αὐτός** = *ἄνευ μαντείων.*

726, 727. An exclamatory sentence.

728. **μερίμνης**: a causal gen.

730. **πρὸς τριπλαῖς ἁμαξιτοῖς**: see 716.

731. **λήξαντ' ἔχει**: cf. *στήσας ἔχεις* in 699.

732. **οὗ**: relative adv. of place.

734. **ἐς ταὐτό**: not meaning *to Phocis*, but *to the same place in Phocis*, for both Delphi and Daulia were in this country. The third road, starting from the point where they all met, led to Thebes. — Cf. the similar omission of the preposition with one of the nouns in 637.

735. *And what length of time has elapsed since this event?* — **τοῖσδε** (G. 184, 3, N. 1). And supplying *ποιηθεῖσι* (H. 601, a).

736, 737. **σχεδόν**: see lexx., IV., ad fin.; II., ad fin. — **ἔχων ἐφαίνου**, *didst appear as ruler of this land.*

738. Spoken half aside.

739. *But why is this a cause of alarm to thee? Why dost thou take this to heart?*

741. **τίνα δέ, κ. τ. λ.**: literally, *but what point of life (he was) having*, i. e. how far advanced he was in years. — **ἥβης**: properly *youth*, the time when the beard begins to grow, but here used as applicable to any period of life. Perhaps the speaker has in mind the unexpected strength and vigor (characteristics of youth) which Laius displayed in attempting to force him from the road.

742. *He was a man of large stature and just turning gray.* — **χνοάζων**: literally, *getting downy*, generally applied to the first appearance of the beard in youth, but here to the first gray hairs as the sign of coming age.

743. Jocasta does not know what a startling comparison she is making, and that the likeness between the old king and the new is that between father and son.

744, 745. **οἴμοι τάλας**: Œdipus is terribly affected by what he hears. Jocasta looking upon him says in 746, **ὀκνῶ τοι, κ. τ. λ.** — **ἔοικ' ἐμαυτόν, κ. τ. λ.**, *I seem to have unwittingly exposed myself just now to terrible curses.* — **εἰδέναι** (G. 203, N. 1).

747. **μὴ βλέπων, κ. τ. λ.**, *lest after all the prophet see only too well.* With reference, doubtless, to the reproach he had cast on the seer in 371.

749. **μαθοῦσα**, *if I have learned,* i. e. *know, them.*

750. **βαιός**, *thinly attended.*

751. **ἄνδρας**: see lexx., VI., 1. — **οἷα**, *as.*

752. *They were five all together.*

753. **ἀπήνη μία**, *a single chariot.* Laius was travelling unostentatiously.

754. The five men and the single chariot are so exactly what Œdipus remembers, that the terrors of conviction seize him.

755. **ὑμῖν**: with reference not only to Jocasta but also the other Thebans.

756. Cf. 118.

758. **ἀφ' οὗ** = *ἀπ' ἐκείνου τοῦ χρόνου ἐν ᾧ* (G. 153, N. 2; H. 808, a, and 810).

760. **ἐξικέτευσε**: the *οἰκεύς* recognized Œdipus as the man who had done the bloody work at the triple ways. His earnestness and desire to get away from Thebes would be explained to Jocasta, who, of course, did not know the real motive, by his love for the murdered king.

761. **ἀγρούς**: as *ἄστυ* in 35. With **νομάς, ἐπί** is expressed for the sake of variety. Or *ἐπί* can be supplied with *ἀγρούς* from *νομάς.* So in 637. — **σφέ** (G. 79, 1, N. 2; H. 233, D).

762. **ἄστεως** (G. 180, 1, and 174; H. 584, f).

763. **ὥς γ' ἀνήρ, κ. τ. λ.**: Jocasta means this man had done more for her than might have been expected from a mere slave. This remark would recall to the spectators the fact that this same servant was he who exposed the infant Œdipus on Mt. Cithæron.

765. The form of the question implies an earnest wish on the part of the interrogator (obs. *ἐφίεσαι* in 766), and to this the answer is made in the next line, **πάρεστιν**, *it can be done* (M. 82, N. 5). The sentence is exclamatory rather than interrogative.

767, 768. *I fear me, O wife, lest I have said too much; it is on account of this I wish to see him.* — **πόλλ' ἄγαν**: in particular what is given in 236 – 243. Cf. 816 – 820. — **μοί** (G. 188, 3; H. 600).

770. **κἀγώ,** *I too,* as well as thou.

771. **στερηθῇς**: sc. *τοῦ ταῦτα μαθεῖν.* For the mood see *ἐκφήνω,* 329. — **γέ,** (*now*) *at least, when,* etc. — **ἐλπίδων**: *ἐλπίς* is here the *expectation* of something bad.

772. **τῷ** (G. 84; H. 244, b). — **καί,** *besides this.* — **μείζονι,** *more worthy.* Schol. Cf. 769.

773. **διὰ...ἰών,** *when at such a crisis in my life.*

777. **τοιάδε,** *such* as I shall relate to thee. — **μοὶ ἐπέστη,** *befell me.* — **θαυμάσαι** (G. 261, 1; H. 767).

778. *Not however worthy at least of the earnest heed that I gave it.* — **σπουδῆς** (G. 178, N.; H. 584, e).

779, 780. *For at a banquet a man overcharged with wine brands me, as we are drinking, with being a supposititious son of my father.* We should have expected, in place of the dependent clause, the adj. in the acc. as predicate modifier of **μέ,** *καλεῖ με πλαστόν.*

781. **βαρυνθείς**: sc. *χόλῳ.*

782. **κατέσχον**: sc. *ἐμαυτόν.* — **θατέρᾳ** (G. 11, N. 2; H. 68, rem. c).

783. **μητρός** (G. 182, 2; H. 589). — **δυσφόρως ἦγον,** *they were regarding with anger.*

784. **τῷ μεθέντι**: the adverb *δυσφόρως,* denoting disposition toward an object, is followed by the dat. just as the verbs *δυσφορέω, χαλεπαίνω,* etc. (G. 185; H. 595, b).

785. I. e., I was pleased at seeing how grievously they bore the insult that had been offered me. Of course Polybus and Merope, from the start, treated the man's charge as a foul slander, never giving Œdipus the slightest ground to believe it was true. But he was a man of sensitive mind and could not forget it, slander though it was. It kept creeping upon him as time passed on until it got full possession of him, so that there was finally but one thing for him to do, — consult the oracle, and be forever freed from his trouble by its holy utterance.

786. **ὑφεῖρπε**: sc. *ἐμέ.* Literally, *to creep under,* or, as we should say of an involuntary (expressed by *ὑπό* in composition) feeling, *to creep upon, to get possession of.*

787. *Unknown to my parents.* — **λάθρα** (G. 182, 2, ad fin.; H. 589, last ex.).

788. **ὧν**: as *οὗ* in 758. For the case of the relative required by its own sentence, see G. 188, 1; H. 611. For the case of the antecedent, see G. 180, 2, N.; H. 584, b.

789. **ἄτιμον**: the oracle refused to enlighten him on the subject of his parentage.

790. **ἄθλια καὶ δεινὰ καὶ δύστηνα**: just as the oracle that follows is threefold. — **προυφάνη λέγων**, *he clearly uttered.*

791. **ὡς χρείη**, *that I was doomed.*

792. *And that I should make manifest a race unendurable to the eyes of men.* — **ὁρᾶν**: parallel in syntax to *κλύειν* in 429.

794, 795. Cf. —

> Save back to England, all the world 's my way.
>
> Richard II., Act I., Scene 3.

795. That is, judging where Corinth lay by means of the stars, and so keeping clear of it. — **τὸ λοιπόν** (G. 160, 2, ninth ex.; H. 552, a, eighth ex.).

796, 797. *Where I should never see come to pass the disgrace predicted by those evil prophecies concerning me.* — **ἔνθα**: i. e. *ἐκεῖσε ἔνθα.* — **ὀψοίμην** (M. 65, N. 1, (a), first ex.).

799. **ὄλλυσθαι** (G. 203, N. 1).

800. **καί σοι, κ. τ. λ.**: these words give him pause to collect himself as he approaches the critical point of his story. — **τριπλῆς**: the all-important word (cf. 716 and 730), and so, emphatic, not only from its isolated position at the end of the line, but also since it begins the sentence.

801. **ὅτε**: see on 391. — **ἦ**: imperfect of *εἰμί.* — **ὁδοιπορῶν**, *journeying, on my journey.*

802. **κῆρυξ**: cf. 753. — **πωλικῆς**, *drawn by young horses.* Because they were travelling through a rough, hilly country.

803. **ἀπήνης**: cf. 753. — **οἷον σὺ φῄς**: cf. 742, 743.

804. **ὅ θ' ἡγεμών**: there were five persons in the company. See 752. The herald with his staff preceded. Then followed the driver, who, at the time Œdipus met them, was leading the horses over the hilly road. With reference to this Œdipus calls him *ἡγεμών.* Then Laius in the chariot, and behind two attendant servants, one of whom was the *οἰκεύς* mentioned by Jocasta in 756.

805. **ἠλαυνέτην** (G. 200, N. 2; H. 702).

806. **ἐκτρέποντα**: cf. on *καταμβλύνων* in 688. — **τροχηλάτην**: the *ἡγεμών* of 804.

807. **δι' ὀργῆς**: the same expression in 344. — **ὡς ὁρᾷ με**: sc. *παίοντα τὸν τροχηλάτην.*

808, 809. Construe **ὄχου**, denoting the origin of motion, with **καθίκετο** in the next line, and cf. *βάθρων* in 142. — **μέσον κάρα μου**, *the middle of my* *head.* — **διπλοῖς κέντροισι**: a goad with two prongs, used to urge on the horses.

810. **ἴσην**: sc. *τίσιν*. — **συντόμως**, *instantly*.

811. **ἐκ τῆσδε χειρός**: with appropriate gesture. "The son shows his mother the very hand with which he slew his father. There is an unconsciousness in the expression which calls forth at once horror and pity. For Œdipus, though beginning to be doubtfully aware that he has slain Laius, has as yet no idea of his relation to him." CAMP.

813. **ξύμπαντας**: there seems to be a discrepancy between the statement of Œdipus, when he says that he killed them all, and the declaration of Jocasta in 756 that one attendant escaped. Wolff explains, that the attendant in question, struck by the hand of Œdipus, fell to the ground and either pretended death or was actually so stunned as to be senseless. After the latter left, he rose and fled back to Thebes with the report of the death of Laius.

813, 814. **εἰ δὲ τῷ, κ. τ. λ.**, *but if this stranger I have mentioned had any connection with Laius*, etc. Œdipus tries to fight off the conviction that is coming home to him, that the man he had killed was Laius himself. — **ξένῳ** depends on **προσήκει** and is parallel in syntax to *βωμοῖσι* in 16. — **Λαΐῳ** stands with **συγγενές** (G. 186; H. 602).

815. **τοῦδέ γ᾽ ἀνδρός**: i. e. *myself*. So in 534. He strikes his breast with his hand.

817. *To whom it is not allowed any one of the aliens or native citizens to receive him in their homes*, etc. — **ξένων**: aliens dwelling in Thebes. These are a part of the class represented by *γῆς τῆσδέ τινα* in 238, on whom the commands of the king were laid in 236 – 243.

819. **ὠθεῖν**: change of dependence from upon a negative clause to an implied positive, as in 241. Sc. *χρὴ πάντας*. — **τάδε**, the object of **προστιθείς**, is repeated in the more specific expression, **τάσδ᾽ ἀράς**. "Note the growth of the idea in the mind of Œdipus. He now imagines as certain what he at first treated only as a supposition." CAMP.

821. By the words, **λέχη...χραίνω**, the spectator is led to remember how much more terrible his pollution is than Œdipus himself knows. And yet how terrible even to him. As he pauses and looks at Jocasta, once the wife of the man his own hands murdered, how horrible must seem to him the truth he utters! — **ἐν** has here an instrumental force.

822. **ὧνπερ**: obs. the lack of agreement in number between the pronoun and its antecedent.

823 sqq. **εἴ με χρή, κ. τ. λ.**: the three conditional sentences of co-ordinate value of which this is the first, whose verbs are **χρή**, **ἐστί**, and **δεῖ**,

depend as subordinate members of the complex sentence on the principal member, **ἆρ' οὐχὶ πᾶς ἄναγνος.** The first and second are united copulatively by **καί**, the second and third disjunctively by **ἤ**; the third, that is, cannot be realized unless the second fail.

824. **μήστι**: a crasis.

825, 826. **πατρίδος**: as he supposes, Corinth. The case as that of ἀγορᾶς in 161. — **γάμοις μητρός**, *in marriage with my mother.* μητρός depending on γάμοις is at the same time a subjective and an objective gen., since marriage is a reciprocal act.

828. **ἀπ' ὠμοῦ δαίμονος** is a predicate adj. phrase denoting source and modifying **ταῦτα**, and is used after **κρίνων** just as πρῶτον in 33 is used after κρίνοντες.

829. **ὀρθοίη λόγον**, *would guide his speech aright*, i. e. *speak the truth?*

831. **ταύτην ἡμέραν**: when the conditions beginning with ἢ γάμοις in 825 would be fulfilled.

832. **βαίην ἄφαντος**: as in 560. — **ἰδεῖν** (G. 274, N.; H. 768).

835. **ἐκμάθῃς** (G. 239, 2; H. 758 and 760, a).

837. The infin. phrase, **τὸν...προσμεῖναι**, is in apposition with **τοσοῦτον** and is modified by μόνον. — **τὸν βοτῆρα**: cf. as to syntax τὸν τροχηλάτην in 806.

838. *And what, pray, dost thou expect after he shall come?* — **πεφασμένου**: sc. αὐτοῦ.

839, 840. **ἦν γάρ, κ. τ. λ.**: the moods as in 216 and 218.

841. **περισσόν**, *remarkable.*

842. Cf. 716. — **λῃστάς**: emphatic by its position. In construction as Λάϊον in 224. — **ἐννέπειν**: representing the imperfect indicative.

843. **κατακτείναιεν** (G. 203; H. 717, b; M. 21, 2, a).

844. **ἐγώ**: emphatic. — Cf. note on 124, 125.

845. **τοῖς**: the restrictive article distinguishing **πολλοῖς** as before mentioned.

846. **οἰόζωνον** (ΟΙ'ΟΣ and ζώννυμι), *girt up alone*, i. e. *travelling alone*, since to gird one's self was a necessary preparation for a journey.

847. **ῥέπον**: as the heavier side of the scale.

848. **φανέν**, *uttered.* Note the change of meaning from the root signification of φαίνω, and cf. the example given in the note on 187. — **ὡς φανέν** (M. 113, N. 10, b). Jocasta speaks with all possible emphasis.

849. **ἐκβαλεῖν**, *to retract.* — **πάλιν**: not of time, but strengthening ἐκβαλεῖν, as in the English phrase, "to take a thing *back.*"

851. **δ' οὖν**, *so then.* — **τί**, *in any respect.*

852. "*Will never show the murder of Laius to be in true accordance with the*

prophecy." CAMP. — Jocasta's attempt to show that the oracle concerning Laius had totally miscarried, although made with the intent of calming the mind of Œdipus, was irrelevant, for entirely disregarding everything else he was now all concerned to know what were the facts of the triple cross-roads. And so, while assenting in 859 to what she had said, he persisted in demanding that the *οἰκεύς* (756) should be brought at once.

853. **ὀρθόν** : predicative, as in 506. — **ὅν γε, κ. τ. λ.** : a causal sentence (G. 238).

854. **διεῖπε** : *διά* in composition here means *expressly* or *distinctly*.

855. Cf. 720 sqq. — **νιν** : Laius.

857, 858. **μαντείας** : governed by *οὕνεκα*. — **οὔτε τῇδε — οὔτε τῇδε**, *neither this way nor that.* *τῇδε — τῇδε* are used without particular reference. The design is to show her utter contempt for all oracles.

859. **ἐργάτην** : the *οἰκεύς* of 756.

862. **γάρ** : giving a reason for *πέμψω ταχύνασα* in 861. — **ἃ** (for *ὧν*, which gets its case by attraction) *οὐ σοὶ φίλον* (*ἐστὶ ἐμὲ πρᾶξαι*). — Œdipus and Jocasta retire into the palace.

863 sqq. The following ode, although far from being unintelligible at any point, is nevertheless throughout designedly obscure. Serving as it does to give pause to the action of the play, it is immediately called forth by the daring impiety of the queen. And yet, though she has outraged the religious sentiments of the Chorus, it dares not express its censure openly, since she is its queen, but to a greater or less degree veils its reproof. In the first strophe it prays that as it ever has lived obedient to the laws that the gods have laid on mankind, so it may ever continue to live thus. The hearer could not but contrast this pious prayer with the irreverent sentiments of Jocasta in 851 – 858.

863 – 865. *May it be my lot ever to be characterized by reverential purity in all my words and deeds; for these* (the words and deeds of men), *laws have been ordained on high,* etc. "In place of the infinitive *φέρειν* attaching itself to *μοὶ ξυνείη μοῖρα* and completing the notion *μοῖρα*, the participle is immediately joined on to *ξυνείη μοι*, so that from it the infinitive is to be understood. In the participle is implied the consciousness of having thus far lived purely; hence, also, **τὰν** *εὔσεπτον ἁγνείαν*." SCHN. — **εἰ** : as in 697. — **εὔσεπτον** : actively, as if *εὐσεβῆ*. — **πρόκεινται**, *have been set forth.*

866. **αἰθέρι** (G. 190 ; H. 612).

867. **Ὄλυμπος** : the seat of the gods. Used as we do the word "Heaven," meaning thereby the sovereign of heaven, the Omnipotent.

868. **νιν**, *them*, i. e. the *νόμοι* of 865.

870. *Nor will they ever sleep or be forgot.* The same figure of a *sleeping* (unenforced) *law* in —

The law hath not been dead, though it *hath slept:*
. . . . . now, '*t is awake.*
MEASURE FOR MEASURE, Act II., Scene 2.

871, 872. *Great is the divine power in these, and it grows not old.*

873 sqq. In the antistrophe the Chorus indulges in reflections upon the direful consequences of a spirit of lawlessness, when developed in the ruler of a state, and calls to mind, in contrast, the patriot, who strives only for his country's weal; it prays God never to suffer this spirit of patriotism to be lessened, and professes an unshaken confidence in Him.

873. ὕβρις φυτεύει τύραννον, *a spirit of lawless violence begets the tyrant.* Note *τύραννον.* — In the following verses **ὕβρις** personified, presumptuous and insolent and for the time successful, is represented as mounting to the topmost height, and in her mad course suddenly precipitated headlong over the precipice into the dark abyss below, where she finds her foot of no use to save her. *ὕβρις* is the opposite of the *εὔσεπτον ἁγνείαν λόγων ἔργων τε πάντων* already mentioned. There is a concealed reference to Jocasta, who has insolently avowed her utter lack of faith in oracles and her determination, hereafter, to give them no heed. In like manner, in the general case cited in 879, the Chorus cannot but remember the earnest, patriotic zeal of its now deeply involved king, manifested not in the case of the Sphinx alone, but throughout his entire reign.

874 sqq. *If she be idly glutted with much that is neither seasonable nor profitable, having mounted to the topmost height rushes into rugged doom, where she uses her foot to no purpose.* — **εἰ ὑπερπλησθῇ** : the particle as in 198. — **μάταν,** *idly, to no purpose, without satisfying her appetite for more.*

876. ἀπότομον : to be taken with **ἀνάγκαν.**

877. ὤρουσεν (G. 205, 2, and 225, ad fin.; H. 707).

878. χρῆται : indicative (G. 123, N. 2; H. 371, c).

880. θεόν : "Here generalized more completely than elsewhere in Sophocles." CAMP.

883 sqq. In the second strophe the Chorus imprecates an evil fate on him who transgresses the ordinances of Heaven, at the same time expressing its confidence that his punishment is certain and sure. In the antistrophe it becomes far more specific in its references than at any time before, and declares that if the ancient oracle concerning Laius shall not be exactly fulfilled, then the honor of the gods is at an end. The Chorus is not to be regarded as doubting the ultimate triumph of right and the overthrow of presumptuous wickedness, but only impatient and more or less bewildered, that the vindication of the infallibility of the sacred oracle is so long delayed.

883, 884. **ὑπέροπτα**: adverbially, *disdainfully, haughtily.* — **χερσὶν ἢ λόγῳ**: cf. λόγων ἔργων τε in 864, 865. The character here drawn (883–891) is in marked contrast to that to which the Chorus piously aspires in 863–865.

885. **Δίκας**: as ἀσπίδων in 191.

886. **δαιμόνων ἕδη**, *the sanctuaries of the gods.* Jocasta had cast open insult upon the oracle at Delphi.

887. **ἕλοιτο**, *may claim him for her own!*

889. The condition begun in 883 is resumed with emphasis. — **μή** modifies **κερδανεῖ** and **ἔρξεται**, but not **ἕξεται.**

890. **τῶν ἀσέπτων**, *from unholy deeds,* the opposite of εὔσεπτον in 864. — **ἔρξεται**: from ἔργω (εἴργω).

891. *Or shall wantonly lay hold on things sacred.* — **τῶν ἀθίκτων**: cf. the gen. in 709.

892 sqq. In its excitement the Chorus has highly wrought its description of the sins of the offender. The vivid portrayal of his offences seals its conviction, so consonant with its wish, that he cannot escape punishment, and it breaks forth, *what man, pray, in such circumstances, shall longer boast that he wards off from his soul the arrows of wrath?*

893. **θυμῶν**, *the wrath of the gods.* Lexx., II., 4 : II., 2. Intensive plural.

895. It is the fate of the Chorus to be subject to conflicting and rapidly changing opinions. For the moment doubt takes hold on it. Notice the form of hypothesis (G. 221 ; H. 745).

896. **τί δεῖ με χορεύειν**: "These words are to be understood of the sacred dances common at the festivals of the gods, and so of their worship." WUNDER. The other interpretation of χορεύειν, *to perform the part of the chorus,* necessarily supposes that the Chorus has forgotten its historic character.

897. The apodosis in 897–900 finds its protasis in 901, 902.

898. **ὀμφαλόν**: cf. 480. — **σέβων**, *with reverential soul.*

899. **Ἄβαισι**: Abae, an ancient town of Phocis. Near it was a celebrated temple and oracle of Apollo.

900. **Ὀλυμπίαν**: the temple and sacred grove of Zeus Olympius, situated somewhat west of Pisa in Elis. An oracle of the Olympian god existed on this spot from the most ancient times.

901, 902. **τάδε**: the oracle of Apollo given to Laius on the one hand, and the actual facts connected with his death at the cross-roads on the other. — **χειρόδεικτα, κ. τ. λ.**, *shall manifestly coincide in the sight of all men.*

903. **ἀκούεις**: see lexx., III., 1.

904. **πάντ᾽ ἀνάσσων**, *all-ruling, the all-ruler,* predicate to ἀκούεις. — **λάθοι**: an impers. verb, whose subject is the thought in 906–910.

908. ἐξαιροῦσιν, *they set aside.* The plural in a general way, though the reference evidently is to Jocasta.

909. *And nowhere is Apollo in manifest honor.*

911. Jocasta here enters from the palace with attendants. How little true piety she has, is seen from her language: *I have taken the fancy into my head to go to the temples of the gods.* See *Introduction.* — **χώρας ἄνακτες,** *ye nobles of the land.* Cf. the terms used in addressing them by the *ἐξάγγελος* in 1223.

913. στέφη, *suppliant boughs.* In v. 3 the poet calls them *κλάδοι ἱκτήριοι.*

914. *For the soul of Œdipus is sorely tossed on high by all sorts of griefs.* **αἴρει θυμὸν Οἰδίπους,** where we should have expected rather *αἴρεται ὁ Οἰδίπου θυμός.* The Schol. enumerates as the causes of his disquietude, *αὐτὸν τὸν φόνον· τὸ τὴν γυναῖκα ἔχειν τοῦ ἀνῃρημένου· τὴν προσδοκωμένην φυγήν· τὸ μὴ δύνασθαι ἀνατρέψαι πρὸς τοὺς οἰκείους· τὸ δέος τῶν χρησμῶν.*

915. ὁποῖα, *as.*

916. τὰ καινά: the words of Tiresias, who had declared Œdipus the murderer. **τοῖς πάλαι:** the oracle that Laius should perish by the hands of his own son, concerning the miscarriage of which Jocasta has not the shadow of a doubt. And she thinks that, since the god has been shown in fault in this oracle, no reliance should be placed on the words of his prophet, Tiresias. It will be observed that she fails to remember that the cause of the fears of Œdipus is not nearly so much the assertions, in themselves considered, of the seer, as the fearful coincidence in time and place of his own bloody slaughter, in a moment of uncontrollable anger, of five travellers, with the death of Laius and his party. Indeed, it may be said that, for the time, Œdipus lets oracles and seers pass from his mind. Much nearer home to him are facts too terrible to contemplate. No wonder his soul sits on the borders of distraction!

917. ἔστι (G. 28, N. 1, (3)). — **εἰ:** as in 198. — **φόβους:** i. e. *φοβερά.*

918. *Since then I effect nothing.*

919. In place of going to the temples (912), she contents herself with making her prayer before the first (*ἄγχιστος*) image of a god that presents itself as she comes from the palace, which happens to be that of Apollo. This is in keeping with the want of piety that she has before shown.

920. κατεύγμασιν: see lexx.

921. εὐαγῆ, *that shall free* (*εὖ*) *us of our guilt* (ἌΓΟΣ).

923. *ὡς* (*ἂν ὀκνοῖεν ναῦται ἐκπεπληγμένον*) *κυβερνήτην νεὼς* (*βλέποντες*). The simile is condensed.

924 sqq. The entrance of the messenger interrupts the worship of Jocasta, who, when he comes in and begins to speak, turns and listens. He enters through the eastern parodos, and, while questioning the Chorus, stands in the orchestra. But for this man's coming, the facts of the birth of Œdipus would not have been brought to light. For the herd, for whom they had sent, though he had recognized in Œdipus the murderer of Laius, had no thought that he was the child whom he had been commissioned to expose to death on Cithæron. The messenger from Corinth supplies the missing link, though himself unacquainted with the fact that the child, whom he had received from the herd's hands years ago, was the son of Laius.

925. **ἐστίν** (G. 28, N. 1, (2); H. 111, c).

926. I. e., *μάλιστα δ' εἴπαθ' ὅπου αὐτός ἐστιν, εἰ κάτιστε.*

927. The chorāgus points with his right hand first to the palace before which they stand, and then, lowering his arm somewhat, with respectful gesture to the queen.

928. *And this lady is the mother of his children.* — **γυνὴ δὲ μήτηρ ἥδε**: the Schol. says that there is a studied ambiguity in the arrangement of these words, suggestive to the spectator of the terrible fact soon to be revealed, that Jocasta, namely, is the *wife-mother* of Œdipus.

929. He bows low to the queen as he speaks.

929–932. So Jessica and Portia exchange fair wishes with one another in the *Merchant of Venice,* Act III., Scene 4.

930. **ἐκείνου παντελὴς δάμαρ,** *his perfect wife,* said, says the Schol., with reference to *τῶν τέκνων* in 928, children being the object of wedlock. "Here seems to be a masterly allusion to the real state of things. The very messenger, whose intelligence leads to the fatal discovery, lays emphatic stress upon the *married* felicity of Jocasta." BUCKLEY.

931. **αὔτως,** *hoc ipso modo.* It is worthy of note that the Laur. MS. writes this word here with the rough breathing.

932. With natural (feminine?) curiosity Jocasta does not stop to send for Œdipus, but at once asks the man what his business is.

934. The messenger ascends its steps and stands upon the stage. — Sc. *σημῆναι θέλω.* So in the next line, *σημῆναι θέλεις.*

936. As he was not officially sent, but had undertaken the journey on his own responsibility and for his own advantage (1005, 1006), he replies in general terms, *from Corinth.* — **ἔπος**: the antecedent is assimilated to the case of the relative immediately following it. *ἥδομαι* governs the dative.

937. From **πῶς δ' οὐκ ἄν,** *ἄν* must be supplied with **ἥδοιο** and **ἀσχάλλοις.** — **ἥδοιο**: because the kingdom of Corinth would now fall to her husband. **ἀσχάλλοις**: because her (supposed) father-in-law had died. The Schol. says, *διὰ τὸ ἀπιέναι Οἰδίπουν ἐπὶ τὰ οἰκεῖα.*

939, 940. *πιθανῶς ὁ ἄγγελος τὰ ἡδέα πρῶτον ἀπαγγέλλει, πρὶν εἰπεῖν τὰ περὶ θανάτου.* SCHOL. — **Ἰσθμίας**, *Corinthian.*

943. We can well believe the cold-hearted Jocasta to be overjoyed at what she hears.

945. She despatches an attendant to tell Œdipus. *θεραπαινίδι κελεύει.* SCHOL. — **ὡς τάχος**: i. e. *ὡς τάχιστα.*

947. **ἵν' ἐστέ**: more an exclamation than interrogation, *see where ye are!* So the Schol., *ὅπου* (not *ποῦ*) *ἐστέ.*

949. **πρὸς τῆς τύχης**, *by course of nature, by a natural death.*

950. Œdipus hurriedly enters through the central door of the palace and at once addresses Jocasta, not regarding the messenger.

951. **ἐξεπέμψω**: causative middle, *why hast thou had me called out?*

952. For the change of the verb, cf. 54 and 414.

953. **σεμνά**: contemptuously, as *σεμνόμαντιν*, 556.

954. He turns and scans the man standing by, but still questions Jocasta.

955. **ἀγγελῶν** (G. 277, 3; H. 789. d).

956. **ὡς οὐκέτι ὄντα** (G. 280 and N. 4; H. 797 and 795, e). Cf. 959 below, where, since the messenger himself speaks, the *ὡς* does not occur.

957. To the messenger himself. — **σημήνας γενοῦ**: for *σήμηνον.* — **σημήνας** (M. 108, 2, N. 6).

958. The messenger would prefer to tell his good news first. Cf. the Schol. on 939, 940.

959. **θανάσιμον βεβηκότα**: lit. *has gone dead.* Similarly in German, *mit dem Tode abgegangen ist.*

960. *By treachery or visitation of disease?*

963. Strictly literally, *and by the long too being-measured-with* (*it*, sc. **αὐτῷ** referring to *χρόνῳ*) *time;* i. e. *yea, and by the years too, whose long course he had measured.* Possibly **συμμετρούμενος** expresses manner (see lex.), the dative not being causal, as in the first interpretation, but depending on the participle.

964. **φεῦ φεῦ**: expressing not so much grief as wonder passing into momentary exultation, which, however, quickly subsides when he thinks of his still living mother (976).

965. *The prophetic shrine at Pytho.*

966. **ὄρνις**: acc. plur. — **ὧν ὑφηγητῶν**: gen. abs.

967. *Was to kill my father.* — **ἔμελλον** (G. 98, 3, and 202, 3, N.; H. 711).

968. **κεύθει**: intransitively. See lexx.

969. **ἄψαυστος** (α priv. and *ψαύω*, ΨΑΎΩ, *to touch*) is used actively. Cf. *εὔσεπτον* in 864. Sc. *εἰμί.* — **ἐμῷ** = *ἐμοῦ* used objectively.

970. **οὕτω** (G. 226, 1, last ex.; H. 751).

971. **δ' οὖν**, *however that may be* (*δέ*), *true it is that* (*οὖν*).

972. **ἄξι' οὐδενός**, *so that they are worth nothing*. Note the position of these words. Œdipus does not speak them with bold confidence, but is in the anomalous position of a man saying what he wishes above all else to say believingly and what the facts seem to render an inevitable conclusion, and yet speaking with no great assurance.

975. **ἐς θυμὸν βάλῃς**, *take to heart*.

976. Immediately after saying in 972 that the oracles (791–793) were worth nothing (and that conclusion was seemingly unavoidable), he here is terrified at the thought of the possibility of their being in part, at least, fulfilled. This corresponds well with what Jocasta declares concerning him in 914 sqq.

977. Notice that **ᾧ** of this verse stands syntactically in the second relative sentence also, after **ἐστίν**. — The form of the question **τί...ἄνθρωπος**, implies the negative affirmation, *οὐ δ' ἂν φοβοῖτ' ἄνθρωπος*, *man should not fear*. The idea of propriety or obligation, however, conveyed by the word *should* does not come from the optative, *φοβοῖτο*, (the optative mood never has this force in Greek), but from the suppressed protasis, which supplied, the sentence would be, *man* WOULD *not fear, if he should do as he ought*. **ἂν φοβοῖτο** is the ordinary potential optative. — **τὰ τῆς τύχης** (G. 141, N. 4).

979. **ὅπως, κ. τ. λ.**, *as one best can*. For the mood cf. 315.

980. **εἰς μὴ φόβου**, *have no fear of*.

982. **ταῦτα**: oracles, dreams, and the like.

983. **παρ' οὐδέν**, *for nothing, as nothing*.

985. **ἐκύρει ζῶσα**: see 258, 259.

987. **καὶ μήν**, *and yet*. The words both introduce another statement to be added to what has been said in 977–983, and in particular express opposition to what Œdipus has just said.

988. **τῆς ζώσης**: objective gen. depending on *φόβος*. The thought is *ἡ ζῶσα φοβεῖ με*.

989. *But say further, on account of what woman feel ye so great fear?* The messenger has been listening to what has been said with great interest. See lex., *καί*, B, II., 2.

991. *But what is there that leads you to fear her?* — **ἐκείνης**: as *τῆς ζώσης* above.

992. **θεήλατον**: the same word in 255.

994. **μάλιστά γε**, *most certainly it is*. Sc. *ῥητόν*. *γέ* strengthens *μάλιστα*. Cf. *ἥκιστά γε* in 1386. — For the oracle see 791–793.

997. **ἡ Κόρινθος, κ. τ. λ.**: lit. *Corinth was long ago emigrated from by me a long way*, i. e. *for many years I have had my home far from Corinth*, *ἐξ ἐμοῦ*

occurring for ὑπ' ἐμοῦ. πάλαι μακρὰν ἀπῴκουν (first pers. sing.) τῆς Κορίνθου, would be the more common way of expressing the thought; but the case is quite parallel to the not unusual, though inelegant, construction in our own language of an intransitive verb in the passive voice with a preposition, the object of the preposition when the verb is in the active voice becoming its subject when changed to the passive. Cf.—

> There are more things in heaven and earth, Horatio,
> Than *are dream'd of* in your philosophy.
>
> HAMLET, Act I., Scene 5.

998. **εὐτυχῶς**: referring to his overthrow of the Sphinx, marriage, and sovereignty.

999. And all these years one of his parents at least had been ever by his side!

1000. The messenger is somewhat taken aback at what Œdipus has said. He came to announce good news, but had no idea that he would be able to do the king so great a benefit as he now sees it lies in his power to do him, namely, by a word (the announcement that Polybus and Merope are not his parents) release him from a great fear. — In **τάδε** the messenger refers to both parts of the oracle. But in the next line, 1001, Œdipus in his overpowering horror of τὸ μιγῆναι μητρί thinks that in τάδε he has referred to this part of the oracle alone, and so answers, πατρός τε, κ. τ. λ. — **κεῖθεν, κ. τ. λ.**, *hast thou been self-banished from there?*

1002, 1003. **τί δῆτ' ἐγώ, κ. τ. λ.**, *for what reason then do I not free thee from this fear?* The question, although addressed to Œdipus, is really propounded to himself, *why do I delay to end his fear?* For this use of the aorist see M. 19, N. 6, ad fin. — **ἐξελυσάμην** (G. 199, 2; H. 689). Even now, as the voice of the verb shows, the thought of personal advantage is present to him. Cf. 1005, 1006.

1004. The messenger had virtually said, *I will free thee*, and so Œdipus replies, **καὶ μήν, κ. τ. λ.** — Sc. εἰ τοῦδε τοῦ φόβου μ' ἐκλύσειας.

1005. The word **χάριν** suggests anew to this man what a hold for gratitude he has on the king, and so, easily forgetting the feeling that prompted him in 1002 to instant revelation, he keeps delaying the vital statement down to 1016, thinking that his reward will be greater in direct ratio to the strength of the reaction in the mind of the king. — **τοῦτο** = διὰ τοῦτο.

1006. **πρὸς δόμους**: i. e. to Corinth. — **εὖ πράξαιμι** (G. 165, N. 2).

1007. **ὁμοῦ**, *together with.* — **τοῖς φυτεύσασιν** = τῇ μητρί. Œdipus accepted the fact that Polybus was dead.

1008. **ὦ παῖ**, *my son.* An address warranted by the old man's years.

Œdipus calls him γέρον in 943, and again in the line following the present one, γεραιέ.

1011. **ἐξέλθῃ σαφής,** *may turn out true.* Cf. σαφής in 390.

1012. Sc. ταρβεῖς. — **φυτευσάντων**: as in 1007.

1014. **πρὸς δίκης οὐδέν,** *from no just cause.* — **τρέμων** (G. 280; H. 799).

1016. **ὁθούνεκα,** *because.* — **σοὶ οὐδὲν ἐν γένει,** *of no kin to thee,* ἐν γένει being equal to ἐγγενής. οὐδέν is used adverbially.

1018. **τοῦδε τἀνδρός**: as in 815. — Says the messenger, *he was no more thy father than I am.*

1019. *And how can my father be my father no more than he who is nothing of the kind?* Sc. ἐξέφυσέ με from 1017. — **τῷ μηδενί**: Sch. explains by completing, τῷ μηδενὶ (ὄντι κατά γε τὸ φῦσαι ἐμέ), i. e., τῷ μηδὲν φύσαντι.

1021. **ὠνομάζετο**: the middle conveys less forcibly the idea that σόν with παῖδα would have done.

1022. **λαβών**: causal. — By taking and adopting the child, Polybus bound himself to raise him as his own son.

1023. Sc. λαβών, *though he had taken me,* from 1022.

1029. **ἐπὶ θητείᾳ πλάνης**: μίσθιος καὶ ἐπὶ μισθῷ πλάνης. SCHOL. — **πλάνης**: the man took his flocks in the summer from Corinth to Mount Cithæron for pasturage.

1030. **ὦ τέκνον**: cf. on 1008. The address further comes appropriately from the man who had for a time exercised a father's care for the foundling.

1031. "The question is supposed to be suggested by the word **σωτήρ**; i. e. 'From what pain that I was suffering in my misfortunes did you rescue me?' but is introduced, as the Scholiast properly observes, in order to lead to the mention of the personal mark by which Jocasta's conviction is brought home. In his eagerness to 'delve to the root" the mystery of his birth, Œdipus is wholly unconscious of the effect which fact after fact he elicits has upon the mind of the queen — the horror of whose discovery is the chief interest of this part of the play, and who may be supposed to remain immovable until her outbreak in l. 1056. The same explanation applies to l. 1037, which adds poignancy to the stroke." CAMP.

1032. **ἄρθρον** ('ΑΡ-, *to join*), the part of the limb where the foot is *ar*ticulated to the ankle. See 718.

1034. **διατόρους**: see lexx., II. — **ποδοῖν ἀκμάς** ('ΑΚΗ', *a point*), *the extremities of thy feet,* meaning exactly what is expressed by ἄρθρα above. When the child was exposed on the mountain, thongs were passed through his limbs between the so-called *tendo Achillis* and the bones of the ankle, and his feet were thus bound together.

1035. **σπαργάνων,** *from my swaddling-bands.* See, however, the lexx., *sub voce,* for another interpretation.

1036. **ὃς εἶ**: i. e. **Οἰδίπους**, from *οἰδέω*, *to swell*, from ΟΙ'ΔΟΣ, *a swelling*, and ΠΟΥ'Σ, *a foot*.

1037. Not to be taken with *ὠνομάσθης* in the preceding verse, but rather, *was the cruel deed done by my mother or my father?* It is evident that he was named *Οἰδίπους* by neither mother nor father. — **πρός**: in two different significations with the same case.

1040. **οὔκ**: sc. *αὐτὸς τυχὼν ἔλαβον*, *οὐκ* negativing *τυχών*.

1042. **δήπου**, *I am quite sure.* — **ὠνομάζετο**: here *passive*. Cf. 1021.

1043. The prose order and expression would be, probably: *ἦ τοῦ τῆσδε τῆς γῆς πάλαι ποτὲ τυράννου*;

1044. **μάλιστα**, *yes*.

1045. **ἐμέ** is the subject of the infinitive.

1046. **εἰδεῖτε**: for the longer form, *εἰδείητε*.

1047. Œdipus addresses the citizens immediately at hand, the old men who compose the Chorus.

1050. **εὑρῆσθαι** (G. 202, N. 2, second ex.). The tense is emphatic, *the time for full discovery.*

1051. **μέν** is correlative to **ἀτάρ** in the next line. — **οὐδέν' ἄλλον**: sc. *αὐτὸν ἐννέπειν*.

1053. **οὐχ ἥκιστα** = *ἄριστα*. — For the repeated **ἄν**, see on 339.

1054. **νοεῖς**, *hast thou in mind.*

1055. **ἐφιέμεσθα**: imperf. mid. from *ἐφίημι*. — **τόνδε, κ. τ. λ.**: lit. *does this man* (*οὗτος*, i. e. *ὁ ἄγγελος*, in speaking of the man who gave him the child) *speak of that one* (*τόνδε*, i. e. *ὅντινα ἀρτίως, κ. τ. λ.*)? — i. e. *is he the man of whom he speaks?*

1056. **τί, κ. τ. λ.**, *but why ask of whom he spoke?* The fatal truth has at length dawned on Jocasta. So overcome as not to see that her effort to conceal will only the more excite Œdipus to investigation, as it does, she wildly and unsuccessfully endeavors to dissuade him from further inquiry. — **μηδέν, κ. τ. λ.**: note the asyndeton.

1057. **μάτην**: to be taken with **ῥηθέντα**.

1058. **ὅπως** is the declarative conjunction, equalling *ὅτι*, and the clause it introduces is in apposition with **τοῦτο**. See 548.

1061. **ἅλις νοσοῦσ' ἐγώ**: lit. I *suffering* (*am*) *enough*, i. e. it is enough that *I* should be tormented. This construction of an adverb in the predicate modifying the subject is unusual.

1062, 1063. Œdipus thinks Jocasta is horrified at the thought that he may be of plebeian birth. — **οὐδ' ἐὰν τρίτης, κ. τ. λ.**, *not even if my mother and hers and hers be thrice proved slaves.* — **κακή**, *of low birth.*

1065. **μὴ οὐ** (G. 283, 7; H. 847).

1066. **καὶ μήν**, *and yet.*

1067. **τοίνυν**, *why now.* — **πάλαι** (G. 200, N. 4).

1068. **ὅς**: the simple relative in indirect question.

1069. Both the personal attendants of Œdipus here leave the stage through the side door in the eastern parascenium to execute his command.

1070. Said with a touch of irony. He still supposes that all her efforts to dissuade him from following up the clew of his birth are prompted by her fear that he will be proved plebeian. — **ταύτην**: emphatic.

1072. Impious woman though she was, the wretchedness of the doomed queen could not but move the spectators to pity. With this wild wail upon her lips, she rushes into the palace through the middle door, bent on suicide.

1074. **ὅπως μή** (G. 218, N. 1; H. 743, a).

1075. **ἀναρρήξει** is used intransitively with **κακά** as subject. So **ῥηγνύτω** in the next line.

1076. **χρῄζει**: sc. ἡ Ἰοκάστη.

1077. *But I will choose to see my origin, even if it is mean.*

1078. **φρονεῖ ὡς γυνὴ μέγα**, *is high-minded for a woman.*

1080. He calls himself the son of Fortune, proverbially fickle, but to him, in the main, heretofore beneficent, **τῆς εὖ διδούσης**.

1082. **τῆς**: used demonstratively (G. 140 and N. 4, ad fin.; H. 524 and a). "The article as a demonstrative is generally accompanied, in Sophocles, by γάρ or δέ." CAMP. — **συγγενεῖς**, *connate.* Sc. ἐμοί.

1083. **μικρὸν καὶ μέγαν**: referring to the fact that, though once a foundling, he was afterwards a king's adopted son; and that though once a self-exiled wanderer, he is now himself a king. — **διώρισαν**: διά in composition here means *by turns, at one time —, at another time —.*

1084, 1085. Being the child of Fortune and having experienced many changes of life, I could never hereafter turn out other than that which I have been (whatever, that is, be the result of the present investigation it will leave me only what I have been before); so that I have no sufficient motive for refusing to learn my race. After such vicissitudes of fortune mere fear of changing my estate cannot deter me from the investigation of my birth.

1086-1109. *Hyporchema.* TRANSLATION: —

STROPHE.

If my prophetic soul doth well divine,
Ere on thy brow to-morrow's sun shall shine,
  Cithæron! thou the mystery shalt unfold:
The doubtful Œdipus, no longer blind,
Shall soon his country and his father find,
  And all the story of his birth be told:

Then shall we in grateful lays,
Celebrate our monarch's praise,
And in the sprightly dance our songs triumphant raise.

ANTISTROPHE.

What heavenly power gave birth to thee, O king?
From Pan, the god of mountains, didst thou spring,
With some fair daughter of Apollo joined?
Art thou from him who o'er Cyllene reigns,
Swift Hermes, sporting in Arcadia's plains?
Some nymph of Helicon did Bacchus find;—
Bacchus, who delights to rove
Through the forest, hill, and grove,
And art thou, prince, the offspring of their love?

FRANCKLIN.

1086 sqq. Œdipus remains on the stage anxiously awaiting the coming of the herdsman. Taking up the thought to which the king has given utterance, the Chorus sings a joyful ode, whose confident tone serves to give greater emphasis to the coming catastrophe.

1087. **κατὰ γνώμαν ἴδρις**: this explains what the Chorus means when it calls itself **μάντις**. It is not in any strict sense a prophet, but thinks it sees with prophetic eye the facts that the day will bring to light. Cf. the remarkably similar language of Milton:—

If there be aught of presage in the mind,
This day will be remarkable, etc.

SAMSON AGONISTES, 1387, 1388.

1088. **Ὄλυμπον**: see *θεόν* in 661.

1089. **Κιθαιρών**: cf. 1026.

1090. **τὰν αὔριον πανσέληνον**: sc. *ἡμέραν*, *on the full-mooned morrow.* The use of the acc. without a preposition to express the time "in which" is poetic. — *οὐκ ἔσῃ εἰς τὴν αὔριον ἀπείρατος τοῦ ἡμᾶς αὔξειν σε, ὡς τροφὸν καὶ μητέρα τοῦ Οἰδίποδος.* SCHOL.

1091 sq. *Of our celebrating thee as not only compatriot of Œdipus, but also nurse and mother.* Wunder, following Elmsley, makes the *καί* before *πατριώταν* correlative with the *καί* before *χορεύεσθαι*. He also construes *Οἰδίπου* with *τροφόν* and *μητέρα*, the predicate objects of *αὔξειν*; thus—*πατριώτης τροφὸς καὶ μήτηρ Οἰδίπου.* Elmsley gives the following as the order: *μὴ οὐ καὶ τροφὸν καὶ μητέρα* (Corinthum scilicet et Thebas) *αὔξειν σε* (*ὡς ὄντα*) *πατριώταν Οἰδίπου.* — *μὴ οὐ* (G. 283, 7 and 6; H. 847 and a).

1094. **ὡς ἐπίηρα, κ. τ. λ.**, *as one who was doing* (*φέροντα* (G. 204, N. 1; M. 16, 2)) *offices of kindness to my king.* — **φέροντα** modifies the subject (*σέ* understood) of *χορεύεσθαι*, which is passive.

1096. ἰήϊε: see on 154.

1098–1102. Order: *τίς (ἔτικτέ) σε, τέκνον, τίς τᾶν μακραιώνων κορᾶν πελασθεῖσ' ὀρεσσιβάτα πατρὸς Πανὸς ἔτικτέ σε, ἤ τις εὐνάτειρα Λοξίου (ἔτικτέ) σέ γε;*

1099. κορᾶν: in the same case as *ἀστραπᾶν* in 200. The nymphs are meant.

1100. Πανός (G. 176, 2; H. 582, a).—**ὀρεσσιβάτα** (G. 39, Gen. Sing.; H. 136, rem. d).

1101. σέ γε, THEE, i. e. seeing thou art who thou art, seeing thou art so sapient as thou art.—L. reads, *ἤ σέ γε θυγάτηρ Λοξίου.* Cf. Franklin's translation.

1102. τῷ: i. e. Loxias. As *τῆς* in 1082, on which see the note.

1104. εἴθ' (*εἴτε*), not to be mistaken for *εἴθε*. Before the indirect disjunctive question sc. *μήνυσον* or an equivalent word.—**ὁ Κυλλάνας ἀνάσσων**: Hermes (Mercury), born in a cave of Mount Cyllene in Arcadia. Sc. *ἔτικτέ σε.*

1105 sqq. *Or the god Bacchus, whose home is on the tops of the mountains, received thee, foundling that thou wast, from some one of the Heliconian Nymphs, with whom he ofttimes sports.*—**συμπαίζει**: euphemistic.

1107. εὕρημα: said with reference to verse 1026, where note particularly *εὑρών*.—The thought of the antistrophe is:—Surely, Œdipus, thou art of no human stock. What nymph-mother bore thee to Pan, or to Apollo, or to Hermes, or to Bacchus?

1108. Νυμφᾶν: as in 1099.

1110, 1111. Œdipus sees the herd approaching at a distance.—*If it at all befits me too, who have never* (**μή**, H. 841) *before met with him, to conjecture,* etc.—**πρέσβεις**: he addresses the Chorus.—"The unconsciousness of Œdipus is specially marked at the beginning of the scene in which he is to learn all (also in 1115, 1116)." CAMP.

1112, 1113. ἔν τε γάρ, κ. τ. λ., *for both in respect to his advanced years does he exactly accord with this man,* etc.—**τῷδε τἀνδρί**: he indicates by a slight gesture the messenger from Corinth.

1114, 1115. ἄλλως, κ. τ. λ., *and besides, I recognize those who are conducting him as domestics of my own.*—**ἔγνωκα**: *to have distinguished* by some mark or other, so *to recognize.*—**ἐπιστήμη,** *actual knowledge* of the man. Contrasted with the preceding *σταθμᾶσθαι.*—**σύ**: he addresses the leader of the Chorus.

1117, 1118. *Yes* (sc. *προὔχοιμ' ἂν σου*), *for I recognize him, know it of a surety. For he was the herdsman of Laius, and for his degree faithful, if ever any one was.*—**ὡς νομεὺς ἀνήρ**: cf. *ὥς γ' ἀνὴρ δοῦλος* in 763.

1120. ἢ τόνδε φράζεις : cf. *τόνδ' οὗτος λέγει* in 1055.

1121. The old man, who is now ascending the stage, avoids meeting the eye of the king for fear he will recognize him as one of the five present when Laius was slain. Cf. 758 sqq. — **οὗτος σύ** : see 532.

1123. ἦ : as in 801.

1126. *Staying with* (sc. *thy flocks*) *in what places most?* — Obs. the unusual position of the interrogative.

1129. The herdsman had not as yet distinguished the Corinthian messenger from the other attendants present. In the preceding line Œdipus had made but a slight, hurried gesture in referring to him. — **ποῖον, κ. τ. λ.,** *what man too dost thou mean?*

1130. He now points him out distinctly. — **ἦ, κ. τ. λ.,** *hast thou ever yet had anything to do with him?* (H. 706; M. 19, N. 4, (a)).

1131. *No, at least I cannot say so at once* (i. e. I must have time to think), *and by the mere aid of my memory.*

1132. κοὐδέν, κ. τ. λ., *yes, and no wonder.*

1133. ἀγνῶτα : Schol. Min., *ἐπιλαθόμενον, since he has forgotten.* Actively, as in 677.

1134. ἦμος: poetic adverb of time used to introduce the indirect question, where *ὁπῆμος* would have been more regular (H. 825, b). — **τόπον** : an acc. dependent on the verb (participle) which must be supplied to express the motion necessarily antecedent to the state expressed by **ἐπλησίαζον,** say *ἐλθών.*

1135, 1136. The verb with its immediate modifiers is adapted in construction to **ἐγώ.** A similar adaptation must be made to **ὁ μέν.** — **τρεῖς, κ. τ. λ.,** *three entire periods of six months each, from spring until early autumn.*

1137. ἀρκτοῦρον : about the middle of September.

1138, 1139. χειμῶνα, *when winter came.* An acc. of specification involving the idea of time. — **ἔπαυλα** and **σταθμά** mean here just the same thing, *folds.*

1140. *Do I relate any one of these things as it happened, or not?* **πεπραγμένον** expresses the manner of the action.

1141. When the herdsman was brought into the presence of the king, his fear was that he would be forced to reveal what he knew of the murder of Laius. The fact that long years ago, by the order of the king and queen, he had exposed their child to death on Mount Cithæron, and then, moved by compassion, had given it to another shepherd, was not now present to his mind. When that time is suddenly and harshly called up, and he sees, in the man before him, him to whom he had given the infant son (of whose fate, after the transaction, he probably knew nothing at all), his fear is doubled. Jocasta, from whom he had carefully kept the fact, may now learn that her son had never perished! See the dramatic power of the poet. This man, acquainted with these two facts known to no other mortal, still does not see the terrible connection between them!

1144. Not knowing just what to say to avoid committing himself, the herdsman halts in his answer. A slight pause after **ἐστί** and a resumption of the question in another form. — **τοῦτο τοὔπος**, *this question*, acc. cogn.

1145. **ὦ τᾶν**, *O friend.*

1146. For the first time the terrible truth flashes in on him! For a moment he gazes at the messenger from Corinth in dumb amazement. Then terror at the revelation, and instantaneous and overpowering anger at the man who had made it, overwhelm him, and he raises his hand for a blow. — **οὐκ εἶς, κ. τ. λ.**: cf. 430. — **σιωπήσας**: cf. 580.

1147, 1148. The man had given slow and unsatisfactory answers, which added to his present action might well exasperate Œdipus, impatient to learn all. — **κόλαζε**: sc. πληγῇ, *strike him not.* Much the more vivid interpretation, and better suited to the following **κολαστοῦ.**

1150. See lexx., uses of **ἱστορέω.**

1151. "'He is speaking in ignorance, and laboring in vain;' i. e. He is seeking your favor, but the tendency of his speech is the very opposite, though he knows it not." Camp.

1152. *Thou wilt not speak to oblige me, but shalt be compelled to do so.*

1153. **τὸν γέροντά με**, *me, old man that I am.*

1154. Œdipus *will* have the truth. — **ὡς τάχος**: cf. on 945.

1155. **δύστηνος**: sc. ἐγώ (G. 157, n.; H. 541).

1156. **ὃν οὗτος ἱστορεῖ**, *about whom he inquires of thee?*

1157. **ὤφελον** (G. 251, n. 1; H. 721, b, ad fin.). — **τῇδ' ἡμέρᾳ**: when I gave him to him.

1158. **μή, κ. τ. λ.**, *that is, if thou dost not say what is right.* — **τοὔνδικον**, *what thou shouldst.* Not *the truth,* since the man's refusal to speak, not his want of truthfulness, was the trouble.

1159. **πολλῷ γε**, *even much*, etc. — **διόλλυμαι** (G. 200, n. 7; H. 699, a). Cf. ὄλωλας in 1166.

1160. **ἐς, κ. τ. λ.**, *will drive at delays.*

1161. **πάλαι** modifies **εἶπον.** — **δοίην**: see first part of 1157.

1162. **οἰκεῖον**, *of thine own house, thine own son?*

1164. **ποίας στέγης**, *a house of what rank.*

1165. The repetition of **μή** is emphatic.

1166. *Thou art a dead man, if I ask thee this again.*

1167. "'Well then, the child was born of the house of Laius.' The expression is purposely ambiguous. As *οἱ Λαΐου* are 'Laius' people,' so *τὰ Λαΐου γεννήματα* include their offspring." CAMP. — Note the lack of agreement in gender between *τὶς* and *γέννημα*.

1168. **κείνου**: a gen. of connection after **ἐγγενής** (H. 587, d).

1169. *Woe me! I am on the verge of the very horror itself.*—**λέγειν** does not limit *δεινῷ*, but seems to be added to the sentence epexegetically as an after-thought, where the full expression would have been, *πρὸς τῷ αὐτὸ* (i. e. *τὸ δεινὸν*) *λέγειν*.

1170. **κἄγωγ' ἀκούειν**: spoken pitiably. The man that at 1166 sternly threatened the herd's life, is for the moment overwhelmed and broken by the horror of what he sees coming. But he nerves himself again and questions till he learns the uttermost.

1171, 1172. **γέ τοι δή**: see lex., *γέ*, I., 5.—**ἡ δ' ἔσω σὴ γυνή**, *but she within, thy wife.*

1173. **μάλιστα,** *she and none else, O prince.*

1174. **ὡς πρὸς τί χρείας**: an emphatic *to what end? for what purpose?*—**ἀναλώσαιμι**: dependent on the historical present *δίδωσιν* above.

1176. **τοὺς τεκόντας**: i. e. *τὸν πατέρα.* Cf. 1007.

1181. The herdsman has not been asked to give the information for which he was summoned!

1182. During the preceding dialogue Œdipus, though with terrible effort, had kept his eyes and mind intent on the herd. But now knowing all the fearful truth, in utter despair, his hands thrown wildly over his head and his pitiable face turned upward toward the light, he cries **ἰοὺ ἰού** in a tone that fairly paralyzes the whole theatre. Cf. the cry of Jocasta as she left the stage at 1071. — **ἂν ἐξήκοι**: Camp. translates, *it would seem that all is come out clear*, and calls it a use of *ἄν* with the optative to express certain inference in present time. The Oxford pocket edition of this play makes it parallel to *λέγοιμ' ἄν* in 95. — With **ἐξήκοι σαφῆ** cf. *ἐξέλθῃ σαφής* in 1011.

1183. **ὦ φῶς, κ. τ. λ.**: suggesting the motive of his terrible act hereafter. See 1271-1274.

1184, 1185. **ὅστις** (G. 238). — **ὧν** — **οἷς** — **οὕς**: plural for singular in each of the three cases, as *φυτεύσασιν* in 1007. — The stricken king rushes into the palace. The messenger from Corinth, who had come for gain but had unwittingly led to the revelation of such fearful facts, hurries from the stage looking back fearfully over his right shoulder toward the palace, and is followed by the herd, a broken man, whose head hangs heavily on his breast. They leave through the eastern parodos. The stage is empty. After a pause the Chorus begins its dirge-like lament, so different from the hyporchema that precedes.

1186–1222. *Third stasimon.* ANALYSIS: Men are but nothing (ἐναριθμῶ); what man more than lays his hand on happiness, only to have it slip from him? (ἀποκλῖναι); with thine example and fate, O wretched Œdipus, before me, I deem naught that is mortal happy (μακαρίζω); who didst attain prosperity by overthrowing the Sphinx (χρησμῳδόν), and wast a bulwark to my land (ἀνέστας); therefore we called thee King (ἀνάσσων). But now, who more wretched, who more acquaint with woe? (βίου); O Œdipus, married to thine own mother (πεσεῖν), how rested so long the spirit of thy father in his grave at such dishonor? (τοσόνδε); omniscient time discovered thee (χρόνος), and condemns this unholy marriage (τεκνούμενον). Would I had never seen thee! (εἰδόμαν); for I bewail thee (στομάτων); yet thou wast he who gave me succor and repose (ὄμμα).

1187, 1188. *How I deem you while in life the same as nothing!* — **ἴσα καί** (H. 856, c). In actual fact **ὑμᾶς** and **τὸ μηδέν** are co-ordinate, being connected by καί, and are the direct objects of **ἐναριθμῶ,** whose predicate object is ἴσα (sc. πράγματα). Cf. ἴσον καί in 611, 612. — **ζώσας,** *while in life.* None are to be called happy till after death. Cf. 1528–1530. But Mitch. translates, *in your most flourishing condition*, and compares 45 and 482. The position of ζώσας immediately after τὸ μηδέν gives weight to this interpretation, since the two expressions are then in abrupt contrast.

1190. **φέρει**: cf. 590.

1191. **τοσοῦτον ὅσον,** *enough* (M. 93, 1, N. 1; H. 814). — **δοκεῖν**: sc. εὐδαίμων εἶναι.

1189–1192. **τίς γάρ,...ἀποκλῖναι**: with the thought cf. —

> Nativity, once in the main of light,
> Crawls to maturity, wherewith being crowned,
> Crooked eclipses 'gainst his glory fight,
> And Time that gave doth now his gift confound.
>
> SHAKS., *Sonnet* 60.

1195. **Οἰδιπόδα**: vocative from Οἰδιπόδης for Οἰδίπους. Cf. the gen. in 495, from the same form. — **βροτῶν οὐδέν,** *nothing mortal.*

1196. **ὅστις**: its antecedent is Οἰδιπόδα. — **τοξεύσας**: the figure is that of an archer who has shot with exceeding skill (**καθ' ὑπερβολάν**), and hit the exact mark, here the solution of the Sphinx's riddle.

1197. **ἐκράτησας, κ. τ. λ.,** *didst become master of that all-blissful fortune.* — **τοῦ**: the prosperity of Œdipus was well known.

1198. **ὦ Ζεῦ**: the recollection of his glory then is crossed by the involuntary thought of his misery now, and for the moment the pious Chorus apostrophizes the god, whose oracles they are that have been fulfilled. — Note the unusual position of **μέν.** — **καταφθίσας**: a case of tmesis. — **τὰν**

γαμψώνυχα: ἤ τοι τὴν Σφίγγα· ἰστέον δέ, ὅτι ἡ Σφὶγξ εἶχε πρόσωπον καὶ κεφαλὴν κόρης, σῶμα κυνός, πτέρα ὄρνιθος, φωνὴν ἀνθρώπου, ὄνυχας λέοντος.

1200. **θανάτων πύργος**, *a tower of defence from death.* The plural, since the victims of the Sphinx were many.

1204. *But now who is more wretched to hear than thou?* The reference is to 1182 sqq. But **ἀκούειν** has been construed parenthetically by some of the editors and not made dependent on **ἀθλιώτερος**, — *so far as I hear.* Cf. εἰκάσαι in 82. Perhaps, without reference to 1182 sqq., *to hear of, to be heard of.* Cf. 1224.

1205, 1206. **ἄταις ἐν, ἐν πόνοις ξύνοικος**, *a dweller among calamities and troubles.* ἆται and πόνοι are personified, and Œdipus is said to dwell with and among them. — Order: τίς (ἐστι μᾶλλον) ξύνοικος ἐν ἀγρίαις ἄταις, τίς (ἐστι μᾶλλον ξύνοικος) ἐν πόνοις (ἢ σὺ εἶ) ἀλλαγᾷ βίου; — **ἀλλαγᾷ βίου**, *through thy reverse of life.* The Schol., however, takes ξύνοικος with ἀλλαγᾷ, thus: **ξύνοικος ἀλλαγᾷ βίου** · συνοικῶν τῇ τοῦ βίου μεταβολῇ.

1208, 1209. The Schol. gives two explanations. The first is, ᾧ ὑποδοχὴ εἰς τὸ ἄμφω δέξασθαι, σὲ καὶ τὸν πατέρα, where αὐτή (with ὑποδοχή) and ἤρκεσεν must be supplied from the text. According to this interpretation Camp. translates the two lines, *in whose case the same wide harbor served for son and father to come chambering within.* The two datives, **ᾧ** and **πατρί**, stand after **ἤρκεσεν**, and **θαλαμηπόλῳ** is in apposition with them. **παιδί** is in apposition with **ᾧ**. The second interpretation of the Schol. is, ἢ ὅτι μήτηρ ἦν καὶ γυνὴ ἡ Ἰοκάστη, ἣν λέγει λιμένα: here παιδί and πατρί both refer to Œdipus, and are both in apposition with ᾧ. θαλαμηπόλῳ then stands with πατρί. In either case πεσεῖν is the object infinitive of ἤρκεσεν. — **θαλαμηπόλῳ**: one to whom the θάλαμος was open.

1210, 1211. **πατρῷαι ἄλοκες**, *the furrows that thy father ploughed.* The same figure is used in 1497, 1498 in ἤροσεν and ἐσπάρη.

1212. **ἐς τοσόνδε**: sc. χρόνον.

1213. **ἄκοντα**, *unwitting, unconscious.*

1214, 1215. *Long has it* (i. e. *time*) *been judging* (i. e. *condemning*) *this unholy* (lit. *marriageless*) *marriage, long thee, the father and son,* supplying σέ from 1213. Or throwing out the comma after **πάλαι** the two participles may modify **γάμον**, — *this unholy marriage, begetting and begotten,* a marriage by which children are brought forth whence the sire himself is born, what is strictly true in regard to Œdipus being affirmed of his marriage with his mother. — **ἄγαμον γάμον**: an oxymōron.

1217. **εἰδόμαν** (G. 251, 2; H. 721, b).

1218. **ὡς περίαλλα**: a case of incorporation, for (ὧδε) περίαλλα ὡς (δύναμαι). Like the constantly recurring phrase, ὡς τάχιστα. See 142 and the note there.

1219. **ἰακχίων ἐκ στομάτων,** *from wailing lips.* — **ἰάκχιος,** *wailing,* = ἰακχαῖος, from ἰάχω, *to cry,* through Ἴακχος.

1220. **εἰπεῖν**: as εἰκάσαι in 82.

1221, 1222. *By thy help I recovered, and lulled mine eye to rest.* Œdipus overthrew the Sphinx, and gave the people repose after their long trouble.

1223. A servant of the palace enters through one of the side doors and addresses the Chorus. For the difference between the **ἄγγελος** and the **ἐξάγγελος** on the Greek stage, see the lexx. on the latter word.

1224. The acc. with **ἀκούω** in the sense of *to hear of,* where in prose we should have had περί with the gen. The sentence is exclamatory. — **οἷ' ἔργα, κ. τ. λ.**: the suicide of Jocasta. — **οἷα δέ, κ. τ. λ.**: the blindness of the king.

1225. **ἐγγενῶς,** *with the feeling of kinsmen.* The Theban elders were closely allied by blood to the royal house. See the address in 911.

1226. **δωμάτων**: as ὧν in 724.

1227 sqq. For the sentiment cf. —

> Will all great Neptune's ocean wash this blood
> Clean from my hand? No, this my hand will rather
> The multitudinous seas incarnadine,
> Making the green — one red.
>
> MACBETH, Act II., Scene 2.

— **Φᾶσιν**: the Phasis, flowing into the Euxine from the east. From its remoteness from Greece its size was often overestimated, as here.

1228. **καθαρμῷ**: dat. of manner and equal to ὥστε καθαρὰν εἶναι. The reference in that part of the sentence ending with **κεύθει** is general and includes all the horrors of the royal house yet known to the Chorus from the exposure of the child on the mountain till now. But in **τὰ δ' αὐτίκα, κ. τ. λ.,** he speaks of the suicide of Jocasta and the self-inflicted blindness of Œdipus.

1229. **τὰ δέ,** *but other evils.* Observe that a preceding τὰ μέν fails here.

1230. **ἑκόντα, κ. τ. λ.**: the incest of Œdipus e. g. was unwitting, but these two acts (see on 1228, ad fin.) were *voluntary.*

1231. **φανῶσι**: for the omission of ἄν, see G. 234; H. 759.

1232, 1233. **λείπει οὐδὲ τὸ μὴ οὐ, κ. τ. λ.,** *fail not indeed of being grievous.* — **μὴ οὐ**: as in 283.

1234. **ὁ τάχιστος τῶν λόγων** (G. 137, N. 3; H. 501).

1236. *By what means, pray?*

1239. **γέ** helps to introduce the clause that limits the statement that they shall learn the sufferings of Jocasta, — *so much, at least, as I can recall.*

1241. **ὀργῇ**, *passionate despair.* — **χρωμένη** : see lexx., ΧΡΑ'Ω (C), C, II., 1 ; ΧΡΑ'Ω (B), C, II., 1. — Cf. —

> "I have a heart as little apt as yours
> To brook control without the *use of anger.*"

1242. **θυρῶνος** : in the Greek house this was the passage leading from the street door (*ἡ αὔλεια θύρα*) to the court (*αὐλή*). After Jocasta left the stage (1072) by the central palace door, she passed through this and across the court into her chamber. The house was of simpler construction than ordinary, having but a single court, at the farther end of which was the chamber mentioned, secured by folding doors. See Dict. Antiq., DOMUS.

1243. **ἀμφιδεξίοις ἀκμαῖς**, *with both hands.*

1244. **πύλας** : properly the gate (double) of a town or rampart, and so differing from *θύρα*. Here, however, the double-door of the chamber. The Schol. interprets the line, *ὅπως εἰσῆλθεν ἔσω, ἐπιρρήξασα τὰς πύλας, τουτέστι, κλείσασα.* Musgrave, however, takes *ἔσω* with *ἐπιρρήξασα* and translates, *vi et impetu ab interna parte occludens.*

1246. **σπερμάτων** : *συνουσιῶν, coituum.* Or perhaps *offspring*, meaning Œdipus. The plural in that case for the singular as *οἷσιν* (1248) and *τέκνων* (1250). *παλαιῶν* would then show that the mind of Jocasta was dwelling first on the early years of the child.

1247. **θάνοι, λίποι** : "If the relative clause contained merely the idea of the speaker, *ἔθανε* and *ἔλιπε* would be used." GOODWIN. See G. 248, 4; H. 755 and 736 ; M. 77, 1, (e), examples.

1249. **γοᾶτο** : without augment.

1250. **τέκοι** : as in 1247.

1251. "*And after this she perishes, in what way indeed I cannot further tell.*" CAMP.

1253. **ἐκθεάσασθαι** : note the force of *ἐκ* in composition.

1256, 1257. **ὅπου** : the indirect interrogative within the sentence in place of beginning it. — **ὅπου κίχοι** : dependent on *ἐξαιτῶν* (G. 241, 3, and 244 ; H. 733 and 737).

1260. **ὡς ὑφηγητοῦ τινος** (**ὄντος**) = *ὥσπερ ἂν ἐνήλατο, εἴ τις ὑφηγητὴς ἦν.* On the force of the conclusion in this sentence consult M. 49, 2, rem. (a), p. 95.

1261. The double-door (*πύλαι*) opened inward. When closed the outer edge of each half rested against an upright post. These valves were secured each by a bolt (properly *κλῇθρον*) which was slipped into a socket (*πυθμήν*) in the sill. There were other fastenings, but these are all Jocasta had secured after entering the chamber. See Dict. Antiq., JANUA.

1262. *But from their sockets he was bending the yielding* (**κοῖλα**) *doors.* — **κλῇθρα** : here the doors themselves. See lex., *κλεῖθρον*.

1264. **αἰώραισιν,** *nooses,* from 'ΑΕΙ'ΡΩ, *to raise.* — **ἐμπεπληγμένην** : literally, *having struck herself into,* i. e. *having leaped into.* This is the reading of the chief MS. (Laur., XXXII., 9), and a much better word than *ἐμπεπλεγμένην,* because expressing violence of action.

1266. **γῇ** : as *αἰθέρι* in 866.

1267. **δέ,** *then.* See lexx., II., 1 : 4.

1270. **ἄρθρον,** first *a joint* (from *"ΑΡΩ), then more specifically *the socket of the joint,* then *the ball* as opposed to the socket. So here *ἄρθρα τῶν κύκλων, the balls of his eyes.*

1271 sqq. **ὁθούνεκα** : the declarative conjunction *that.* — **νίν,** *him,* i. e. Œdipus. A case of prolepsis. Translate it as the subject of the two finite verbs in 1272. The original language of Œdipus was, *οὐκ ὄψεσθε ἐμέ, οὔθ' οἷ' ἔπασχον οὔθ' ὁποῖ' ἔδρων κακά, ἀλλ' ἐν σκότῳ τὸ λοιπὸν οὓς μὲν οὐκ ἔδει ὄψεσθε, οὓς δ' ἔχρῃζον οὐ γνώσεσθε.*

1272. **οἷ' ἔπασχεν,** *what he had suffered,* all the misfortunes of his life, viewed from the stand-point of their effect on himself. — **ὁποῖ' ἔδρα κακά,** *what evil deeds he had done,* the murder of his father and the incest with his mother.

1273. **οὓς μὲν οὐκ ἔδει,** *whom they should never have seen,* his children. — **ἐν σκότῳ,** *in darkness,* i. e. not at all. Cf. 419.

1274. **οὓς δέ** : his parents. The desire to know who were his father and mother had been the one great unsatisfied wish of his life. For though he fled from Corinth, he never fully believed that its king and queen were his father and mother. By putting out his eyes he prevented the possibility of his seeing and recognizing Laius and Jocasta when he came to Hades. See 1371 - 1374. — **ὀψοίατο** (G. 122, 2, fourth paragraph ; H. 357, D).

1276. **ὁμοῦ** : to be taken in the thought with **γλῆναι,** — *the pupils together,* i. e. *both pupils.*

1277. **οὐδέ, κ. τ. λ.,** *nor did they emit* (*merely*) *oozing drops of gore.* But Camp., *nor ceased from pouring the wet drops of gore.* Consult the lexx., *ἀνίημι.*

1278. **ὁμοῦ** : i. e. as above, (*φοινίων*) *ὁμοῦ* (*γληνῶν*) *ἐτέγγετο, was falling from both at once.*

1279. **αἱματοῦς** : i. e. *αἱματόεις.*

1284, 1285. **κακῶν...ὀνόματα,** *whatever evil has a name.* An inversion for *κακὰ ὅσων ἐστὶν ὀνόματα.* The five nouns preceding *οὐδέν* are to be explained by anacoluthon.

1288. **τὸν πατροκτόνον, κ. τ. λ.,** *his father's murderer, his mother's — saying unholy things and not to be repeated by me.*

1292. *However* (though he is strong in his resolution), *he lacks at least strength and some one to guide him.*

1293. **φέρειν** (G. 265, N., second ex.; H. 768, first ex.).

1294. **καὶ σοί** : as contrasted with *ἐμοί*. — **κλῇθρα, κ. τ. λ.,** *for see* (**τάδε**) *the doors are opening.* The messenger points at the central palace door with his right hand, inside of which is heard the noise of the slipping bolts.

1296. Either, *(σὲ) καὶ στυγοῦντα (αὐτὸ,* i. e. *τὸ θέαμα) ἐποικτίσαι*; or, *(τινὰ) καὶ στυγοῦντα (αὐτὸν,* i. e. *Οἰδίποδα) ἐποικτίσαι.* — **τοιοῦτον οἷον** : see 1191.

1297. His eyes mangled and bloody, Œdipus enters from the central door of the palace, and gropes his way slowly to the front of the stage. He yet holds in his hand the blood-stained brooches. The exangelus remains upon the stage, but steps back looking with dumb horror and pity on the king. — **πάθος** : as *πόλις* in 629.

1299. Only Sophocles uses **προσκυρῶ** with the acc.

1300 sqq. Order: *τίς (ἦν) ὁ δαίμων πηδήσας μείζονα (πηδήματα) τῶν μακίστων πρὸς σῇ δυσδαίμονι μοίρᾳ;* The immediate reference is to the destruction of his eyes, and the figure is of one cruelly leaping upon the man already down and trampling him into the dust. The same less vividly in 263.

1303. As Œdipus comes nearer, the Chorus is unable to bear the sight and turns away.

1307. In utter misery, seeing no one, bewildered at the sound of his own voice, the wretched and fallen king presents indeed a *θέαμα τοιοῦτον οἷον καὶ στυγοῦντ' ἐποικτίσαι.*

1307-1311. *Woe, woe! woe, woe! wretched man that I am, to what spot of earth am I, unfortunate, borne? Which way hurriedly flies my wandering voice? O fate, whither hast thou leaped!*

1310. **δι' ἄλας** : *wanderingly,* an adverbial phrase of manner, as *δι' ὀργῆς* in 807. See lexx., *διά,* A, III., c; A, III., 2. — **πέταται** : from *πέταμαι,* a form of *πέτομαι,* which see.

1311. Not the same figure as above. The man's Fate leaps violently away bearing him along without power of resistance. — **ἵν' ἐξήλλου**: see on 947.

1312. *Into a calamity too horrible either for hearing or sight.*

1313 sqq. *O horrible cloud of darkness, pressing awfully upon me,* etc. By **νέφος** he means his blindness. — The participle **ἐπιπλόμενον,** *having come upon,* and so as the result, *being upon,* must be given its proper force as an aorist, since his blindness was already an accomplished fact. — Observe the mingling of figures : first a cloud of perfect blackness surrounding the man from which it is impossible for him to free himself (**ἀδάματον**) ; then the thought of how this came about suggesting the idea of a ship driven by fair winds (his former prosperity), but *fatally fair,* since his prosperity has been followed by such complete wretchedness.

1315, 1316. The lines were begun as an epexegesis of *ἄφατον*, but the epexegesis extends only through *ἀδάματόν τε*, where the figure changes.

1317. **μάλ' αὖθις,** *again and again.*

1318. **κέντρων** : the *points* formed on the brooches by the projection where the point of the pin was secured. Each brooch in this case was an arc in shape, its pin being the chord. See Dict. Antiq., FIBULA. — **τῶνδε** : he raises them as if to look at them. See on 1297.

1319. *Yes, and it is no wonder,* etc.

1321-1324. *O friend, thou art still my faithful attendant. For thou submittest still to care for me, the blind. Woe, woe!*

1327. **τοιαῦτα** : adverbially.

1329. See 377.

1332. **νίν** : *ὄψεις* in 1328.

1334, 1335. **ὁρᾶν** and **ὁρῶντι,** *to have sight,* but **ἰδεῖν,** *to see* (G. 202, 1; H. 716, a).

1337-1339. *What object of sight then is there yet for me to see with satisfaction, or what can I love, or what is there that may address me that I can still hear with pleasure, O friends?* — The full order would be : *τί βλεπτὸν δῆτά (ἐστι ἔτι) ἐμοὶ (βλέπειν ἁδονᾷ), ἢ (τί) στερκτὸν (ἐστι ἔτι στέργειν), ἢ (τί) προσήγορον ἔτ' ἔστ' ἀκούειν ἁδονᾷ, φίλοι;* The three infinitives limit their respective nouns, *βλεπτόν, στερκτόν,* and *προσήγορον* (G. 261, 2, N.; H. 767), though it is possible to construe these as the objects of the infinitives, which then in turn became the subjects of *ἐστί*. It is further possible (so Wolff) to make *βλεπτόν* and *στερκτόν* at once subjects of *ἐστί* (understood), *what have I yet worth seeing or loving?*

1343. **μέγα** : adverbially.

1347. **τοῦ νοῦ,** *thy penetration,* i. e. *thy perception* of thy misery (G. 173, 3; H. 592, a).

1348. The ordinary interpretation is, *how I should have wished that I had never recognized thee* (i. e. *if it would have been of avail*), where **ἄν** belongs to **ἠθέλησα** (G. 222 and 226, 2; H. 746 and 752), and the aorist infinitive denotes action prior to the action of that verb. But it is a fatal objection to this interpretation that, after a verb of *wishing,* the dependent infinitive never refers to time prior to that of the verb on which it depends. With this interpretation reference is generally made to 1217. Restoring to **ἀναγνῶναι** its proper time-force the meaning will be, *how I should have wished* (i. e. *had it been possible*) *not to recognize thee.* Better still, **σέ** can be made the subject of *ἀναγνῶναι,* when the meaning is, *how I should have wished* (i. e. *if it had been in my power*) *thee not to recognize thyself.* But this was prevented by the *penetration* of Œdipus. Cf. *τοῦ νοῦ*, preceding line. The supply of *σαυτόν* here is somewhat harsh.

1349. *May he perish, whoever he was, who took me in the wild from the fierce fetter on my feet,* etc. Here, in his passion, Œdipus throws the brooches, which he has so far held in his hands, upon the stage.

1359. **ὧν**: antecedent to be supplied. So in 1362.

1362. **ὁμογενής**, *consort,* used actively.

1364-1366. *But if there still be an evil heavier than his fellow, this fate allots to Œdipus.*

1368. *For thou wert better no longer be than live blind.* For *κρεῖσσον* (ἂν) *ἦν μηκέτ' εἶναί σε, κ. τ. λ.* Cf. —

> *Thou wert better* gall the devil, Salisbury:
> If thou but frown on me, or stir thy foot,
> I 'll strike thee dead.
> King John, Act IV., Scene 3.

1369-1415. The passion of the speaker rises in regular gradations till it culminates in the wonderful outburst of 1391-1408. Then, in great contrast, his language subsides into a tone so pitiful and pathetic that it greatly moves the compassion of the hearer.

1371 sqq. Cf. the sentiment here with that in 999. See also on 1274. Cf. further—

> *With what eyes could* we
> Stand in his presence humble?
> Paradise Lost, II., 239, 240.

1373. **οἷν** (G. 165, n. 3). — **ἐμοί**: as in 768.

1374. **κρείσσον' ἀγχόνης**, *for which hanging would be an insufficient punishment.* Cf. the common expression, *hanging is too good for him.* Or, as Camp. translates, *which I would rather have died by strangling than do.*

1376. **βλαστοῦσα** and **ἔβλαστε**, to be taken with **τέκνων**, are attracted into an agreement with **ὄψις.**

1379. **τῶν** (G. 140, n. 4; H. 243, D).

1380. **κάλλιστ' ἀνὴρ εἷς τραφείς,** *who had been reared better than any other one man.*

1381. **ἀπεστέρησα** (G. 164, n. 2; H. 580, a). — **ἐννέπων**: cf. 241-243.

1383. **καὶ γένους τοῦ Λαΐου**: sc. *ὕστερον φανέντα,* since the oracle did not declare that Œdipus was the murderer, but only led the way to the discovery of this fact. But the speaker had, of course, no such ellipsis in mind. It is quite in keeping with his present agitation, and highly dramatic, that he should thus confuse the utterance of the oracle with the development to which it led.

1385. **ὀρθοῖς ὄμμασιν**, *with steady, unflinching eye*, as one conscious of no wrong. Cf. 528. — **τούτους**: he indicates the Chorus by a gesture. It will be noted he is speaking to the choragus.

1386. **ἥκιστά γε**, *nay, not so.*

1388. **μὴ ἀποκλῇσαι**: "It is to be observed that where this construction occurs [the one explained in G. 283, 6 and 7; H. 847, a], the circumstances of the negation are generally actual and present. In a purely hypothetical case [as here], or one actual but remote in time, *μή* alone is used." CAMP.

1389. **ἦν** (G. 216, 3; H. 742).

1391 – 1408. He recounts in wild passion the four prominent times in his life: 1391 – 1393, his exposure in babyhood; 1394 – 1397, his home at Corinth; 1398 – 1402, his fatal parricide; 1403 – 1408, his still more fatal marriage with his mother.

1392. **ἔδειξα**: as *ἦν* in 1389.

1395, 1396. **οἷον κάλλος κακῶν ὕπουλον**, *what a fair outside but festering underneath with ills.* *οὐλή* was the cicatrized wound. Cf. —

> It will but skin and film the ulcerous place;
> Whiles rank corruption, mining all within,
> Infects unseen.
>
> HAMLET, Act III., Scene 4.

1399. **δρυμός** repeats **νάπη**, and **ὁδοῖς**, **κέλευθοι**.

1400. **τοὐμὸν αἷμα πατρός**, *mine own blood from a father's veins.* Not merely *my father's blood*, but, as indicated in the translation, a double meaning in *τοὐμόν*, *my father's blood which was also my own.*

1406. **πατέρας**: Œdipus; **παῖδας**: his children; **ἀδελφούς**: both, since they were the offspring of the same woman. — **αἷμ' ἐμφύλιον** may be either *one kindred blood*, and sustain the relation of predicate to the three preceding accusatives (G. 166; H. 556), or may mean *murder of kin*, and be parallel to them in syntax.

1407. Wolff, throwing out the commas, translates **νύμφας γυναῖκας μητέρας** as a compound noun, calling Jocasta the *bride-wife-mother* of Œdipus.

1409. **ἀλλά**: he checks himself.

1411. **θαλάσσιον**: an adjective for an adverbial phrase, equalling *εἰς θάλασσαν*. Cf. *πετραῖος*, 478, and *ἐκτόπιον*, 1340.

1416. **ὧν**: i. e. *περὶ τούτων ἅ*, to be taken with *βουλεύειν*. — **ἐς δέον**, *to meet thy need*. See here G. 139, N., the ordinary prose expression being *εἰς τὸ δέον*. For this use of *εἰς* to express the *end*, see lexx., V., 2: A, III. — **ὅδε**: as *τήνδε* in 632.

1417. **τὸ πράσσειν καὶ τὸ βουλεύειν**, *to act and to counsel*, in apposition with *δέον*. The infinitive used to express purpose is *without* the article. See G. 265.

1420. *What argument* (**πίστις**, see lexx., II., 2) *that I advance will appear just to him?* Œdipus believes Creon completely estranged, and that he will regard with coldness any requests he may make of him.

1423. **κακῶν**, *wrong deeds*.

1424. He turns abruptly to the attendants and addresses them with some harshness.

1425, 1426. **αἰδεῖσθε** has a double construction following it, the accusative **τὴν φλόγα** and the epexegetic infinitive **δεικνύναι**: *reverence at least the all-feeding flame of the royal Sun, and be ashamed to exhibit thus openly such a pollution*. — **Ἡλίου**: cf. Ἅλιον in 661.

1427 sqq. **τὸ μήτε γῆ, κ. τ. λ.**, *a pollution which neither earth nor the sacred element of water nor the light of day will endure;* namely, from fear of pollution. — **τό**: as in 1379. — **μήτε**: the use of *μή* shows that the statement in the relative clause has a conditional as well as causal force (M. 65, 4, rem.), *if neither earth nor, etc., is about to endure it* (G. 221, N.).

1430. **τοῖς ἐν γένει**: cf. 1016. — **μάλιστα**: to be taken with **εὐσεβῶς**.

1432. **ἐλπίδος**: the word has here the same meaning that it has in 771.

1433. Cf. the use of *ἦλθον* in 1358.

1434. **πρός**: see lexx., A, III., 2.

1435. **τοῦ χρείας τυχεῖν**, *to obtain what desire?*

1437. **φανοῦμαι προσήγορος** = *προσαγορεύσομαι*, passively. Cf. 790. — **μηδενός** (G. 176, 2; H. 582, a).

1438. The oracle certainly had been explicit enough. See 100, 101. But since it has developed that *Œdipus, the King*, is the guilty one, Creon will not venture to inflict punishment until the shrine at Delphi has again been consulted and has confirmed its former utterance. This, of course, would take time.

1439. **εἰ ἔχρῃζον**, *if I did not desire*.

1440 sq. *Yes, but the oracle clearly was all for destroying*, etc. — **πᾶσα**: predicate to **ἐδηλώθη**.

1441. **μέ**: cf. note on 1383. — **ἀπολλύναι**: in a broad sense so as to cover either alternative, banishment or death. So *μίασμα ἐλαύνειν* in 97, 98. In syntax it is an object infinitive, as if we had *ἐκεῖνος σαφῶς ἐκέλευσεν*.

1442. **ἵν' ἕσταμεν χρείας**: Schol. Min., *ἐνταῦθα τῆς χρείας ὅπου ἐσμέν, ἤγουν ἐν ταύτῃ τῇ χρείᾳ ἐν ᾗ ἐσμεν.*

1445. **τἄν**: i. e. *τοὶ ἄν.*—**πίστιν φέροις** = *πιστεύοις.*

1447. **τῆς κατ' οἴκους**: Jocasta.

1450. **ζῶντος**: my bones may be laid to rest here after death, but let not the city be corrupted by my *living* person. —**οἰκητοῦ**: not from *οἰκέτης.* — **τυχεῖν**: see lexx., A, II., 2.

1451. **ἔνθα κλῄζεται, κ. τ. λ.**: *ἔνθα* (*ἐστὶ ὁ*) *Κιθαιρὼν οὗτος,* (*ὃς*) *οὑμὸς κλῄζεται.*

1453. **ἐθέσθην**: note the voice and number.

1454. *That I may die in accordance with their wishes who were seeking to destroy me.*

1457. **μή**: sc. *σωζόμενος.* The phrase is equivalent to *εἰ μὴ ἐσωζόμην.*

1459 sq. *But* (*as to the fate of my children*) *of my boys indeed I would not have thee, Creon, add to thyself the care.*—**παίδων τῶν ἀρσένων**: limit of *μέριμναν.*

1461. **ἔνθ' ἂν ὦσι**: cf. *ἔνθ' ἂν ᾖ* in 672.

1462. **παρθένοιν**: the case is suggested by the construction above (*παίδων προσθῇ μέριμναν*), but after the long descriptive sentence (1463-1465), the expression changes, and the thought is resumed under a new form in **αἷν μοι μέλεσθαι.**

1463. **χωρίς**, *apart*, explained by **ἄνευ τοῦδ' ἀνδρός** in the next line. The father and daughters always ate at the same table.

1464. After **ἀλλά** supply *αἷ* as subject of *μετειχέτην* (G. 156, N.).

1466. **αἷν, κ. τ. λ.,** *for whom care thou for my sake.*—**μέλεσθαι**: for *μέλου*, as *φάσκειν* in 462. — **καὶ μάλιστα, κ. τ. λ.**: Creon here motions to an attendant to go within and fetch Antigone and Ismene, which he departs in haste to do.

1467. **ἀποκλαύσασθαι**: note here the force of the middle voice, *to bewail our woes.*

1469. **τἄν**: as in 1445.

1471. He stops in his address to Creon and listens eagerly, and as he listens, hears the sobbing of his daughters as they are conducted across the court, before they emerge from the palace. —**φημί**: the enclitic anomalously retains its accent. The words are emphatic and stand *extra metrum.*

1472. **τοῖν φίλοιν**: masculine form for the feminine (G. 138, N. 5; H. 521).

1475. **λέγω τι**, *am I right?*

1477. **παροῦσαν**, *still existing, yet strong.*

1478. **τῆσδε τῆς ὁδοῦ**, *in reward for this their coming.* A causal genitive.

1479. **φρουρήσας** (G. 279, 2, and 204, N. 2; H. 801). See also lexx., *τυγχάνω*, B, II., 1.

1480. The two girls who have been led in by the attendant come up close to their father's side. Œdipus is still standing.

1482. **ὑμῖν**, *to your grief.* Dativus incommodi.—The subject of **ὁρᾶν** is **ὄμματα** in the next line.

1490, 1491. **κεκλαυμέναι ἀντὶ τῆς θεωρίας**, *bathed in tears instead of pleased with the spectacle.*

1498. **ὅθεν ἐσπάρη**: a contracted expression for *οὗ ἐσπάρη καὶ ὅθεν ἐγένετο.*

1503. In the order of the thought **ἀλλά** precedes the vocative.

1506. **πτωχὰς ἀνάνδρους**: predicates to *ἀλωμένας.*—**ἐγγενεῖς**, *being thy kinswomen.* To be taken attributively with *σφέ.*—**ἀλωμένας** (G. 279, 3; H. 799).

1515. **ἅλις, κ. τ. λ.**: literally, *sufficient* (*is the point*) *where thou art come out* (i. e. *which thou hast reached*) *weeping*, i. e. jam satis lachrymasti. That **δακρύων** is the participle is shown by the quantity of the second syllable.

1516. **καιρῷ** is a poetic dative of time.

1517. **ἐφ' οἷς**, *on what conditions.*

1518. **ὅπως** (G. 217, N. 4; H. 756, a).

1519, 1520. **τοιγαροῦν, κ. τ. λ.**: Creon means that there is very little doubt that when the oracle is again consulted it will command his exile. But Œdipus mistakes the force of his answer and asks, *do you then promise me this? No*, says Creon, *for I am not fond of saying what I do not mean*, referring to his statement in 1442, 1443, that in this exigency they must again consult the god. See on 1438. Œdipus is obliged to rest content with this.—**ἃ μή, κ. τ. λ.**: cf. the expression in 569.

1522. **πάντα κρατεῖν**, *to have your own way in everything.*

1523. **ἀκράτησας**: see *ἀγώ* in 6.—**τῷ βίῳ**, *during thy life.*—**ξυνέσπετο**: *συνήνεγκε, συμφέροντα ἦν.* Schol. Min.—Œdipus enters the palace through the central door, conducted by Creon, and followed by his daughters and the attendants. The leader of the Chorus addresses his fellow choreutæ.

1524. **Οἰδίπους**: subject of *ἐλήλυθεν* below in 1527.

1526. *Who was not eying with envy the enviable fortunes of his citizens.* **ζήλῳ καὶ τύχαις** by hendiadys for *ζηλωταῖς τύχαις.* This verse is probably corrupt.

1528 sqq. The order is, *ὥστε* (*τινά*), *ἐπισκοποῦντα ἐκείνην τὴν τελευταίαν ἡμέραν ἰδεῖν, ὀλβίζειν μηδένα ὄντα θνητόν, πρὶν ἂν παθὼν μηδὲν ἀλγεινὸν περάσῃ τέρμα τοῦ βίου.*—**ἰδεῖν**, *to see it* (G. 265; H. 765).

Ultima semper
Expectanda dies homini; *dicique beatus*
Ante obitum nemo supremaque funera debet.

OVID.

DEVIATIONS FROM THE TEXT OF CAMPBELL'S EDITION OF 1871.

The reading before the colon is that of the present edition; that following it is the reading of Campbell, which it has replaced.

18. οἱ δ' ἐπ' : οἵδε τ'.
194. ἄπουρον : ἔπουρον.
200. ὦ τᾶν πυρφόρων : ὦ πυρφόρων.
206. προσταχθέντα : προσταθέντα.
208. ὅρη : ὅρεα.
214. σύμμαχον : ⏓ ⏑ —.
221. αὐτός, οὐκ : αὐτό, μὴ οὐκ.
258. γ' : τ'.
492, 493. πρὸς ὅτου χρησάμενος : ⏑ ⏑ — — πρὸς ὅτου.
657. λόγῳ σ' ἄτιμον : λόγῳ ἄτιμον.
666. φθινὰς : φθίνουσα.
667. ψυχάν, τάδ' : ψυχάν, καὶ τάδ'.
682. δάκνει : δάπτει.
689. ἄναξ : ὦναξ.
695. πόνοις : *πόνοισιν. — σαλεύουσαν : ἀλύουσαν.
697. γένοιο : δύναιο*.
866. οὐρανίᾳ αἰθέρι : οὐρανίαν δι' αἰθέρα.
870. μή : μάν. — κατακοιμάσῃ : κατακοιμάσει.
877. ὤρουσεν : [*ἐξ]ώρουσεν.
893. θυμῶν : †θυμῷ. — εὔξεται : †ἔρξεται.
906. Πυθόχρηστα Λαΐου : Λαΐου [⏓ — ⏑ — ?].
1062. ἐὰν : ἂν *εἰ.
1099. τᾶν μακραιώνων κορᾶν : τῶν μακραιώνων ἄρα.
1100 – 1102. πατρὸς πελασθεῖσ', ἢ σέ γ' εὐνάτειρά τις : [*που] προσπελασθεῖσ', ἢ σέ γέ τις †θυγάτηρ.
1195. οὐδὲν : οὐδένα.

1197. ἐκράτησας : *ἐκράτησε.
1200. ἀνέστας : ἀνέστα.
1205. τίς ἄταις ἐν ἀγρίαις, τίς ἐν πόνοις : †τίς ἐν πόνοις, τίς ἄταις ἀγρίαις.
1212. ἐδυνάσθησαν : ἐδυνάθησαν.
1216. ὦ : [—].
1219. ἰακχίων : ἰαχέων.
1303. φεῦ φεῦ, δύσταν' : φεῦ δύστανος.
1304. σε, θέλων : σ', ἐθέλων.
1310. δι' ἅλας πέταται : διαπέταται.
1343. τὸν μέγ' ὀλέθριον : τὸν *ὄλεθρον μέγαν.
1348. ποτ' ἂν : ποτε.
1350. νομάδ' : νομάδος.
1389. ἦν : ἦ.
1393. ἦν : ἦ.

RHYTHMICAL SCHEME OF THE LYRICAL PARTS OF THIS DRAMA.

I.

Parodos, verses 151–215.

Str. α'.

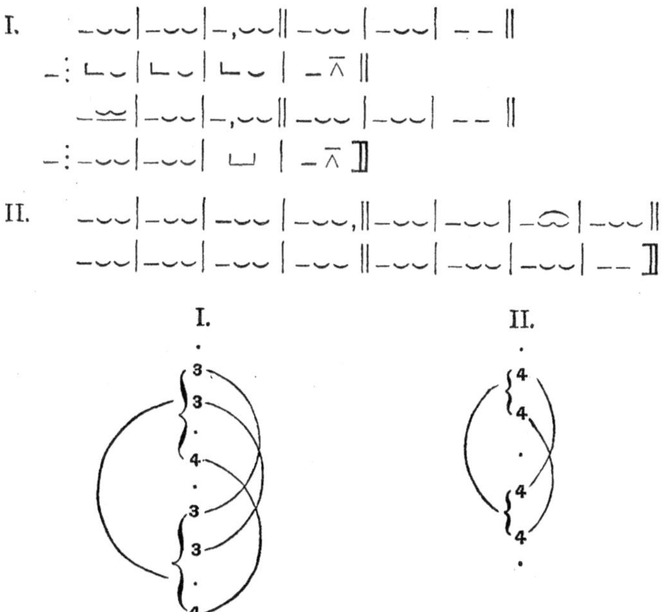

Str. β′.

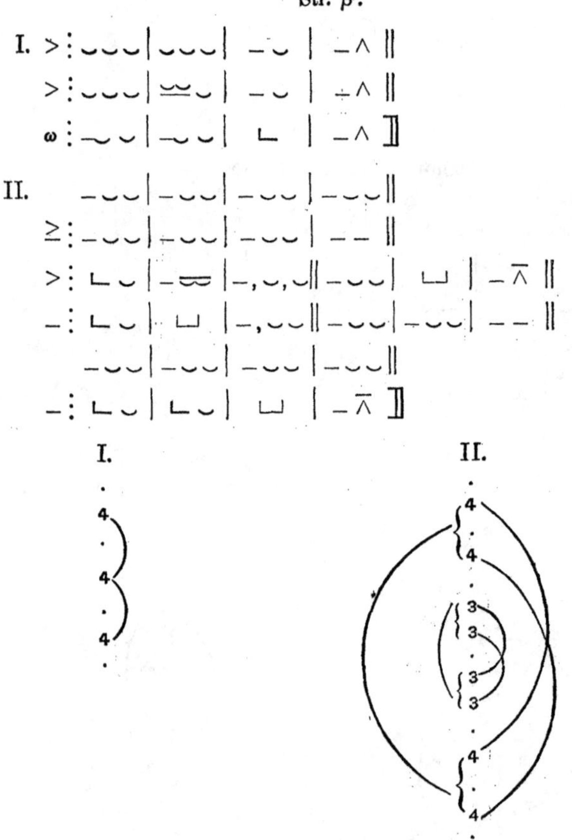

Str. γ'.

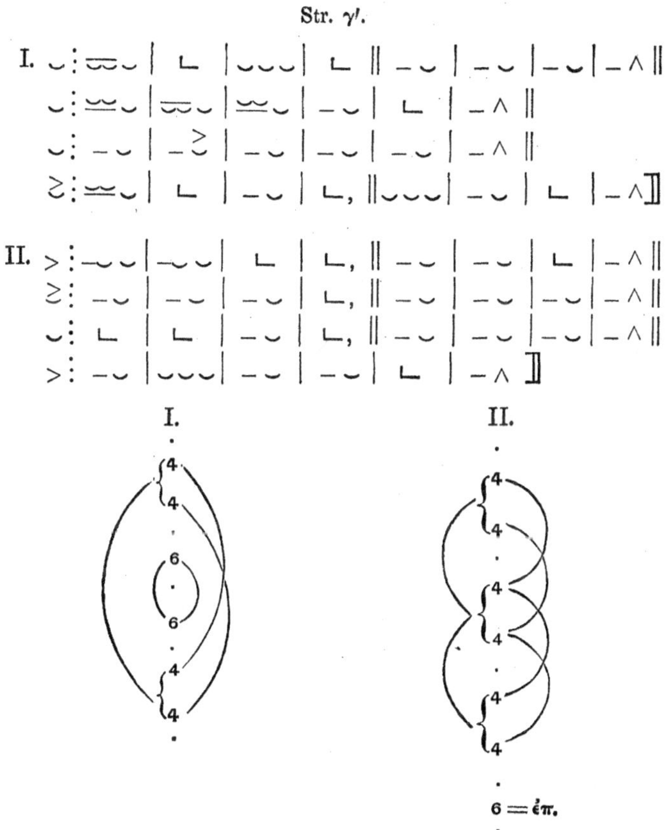

II.

First Stasimon, verses 463–512.

Str. α′.

I. ⏑ ⁝ – ⏑ | ⌞ | –⏑⏑ | – ⏑, || – ⏑ | – ⏑ | ⌞ | – ∧ ||
– > | – > | –⏑⏑ | – ⏑, || – ⏑ | – ⏑ | ⌞ | – ∧]]

II. > ⁝ –⏑⏑ | – ⏑ | – ∧ ||
> ⁝ –⏑⏑ | – ⏑ | – ∧ ||
⏑ ⁝ –⏑⏑ | ⌞ | – ∧]]

III. ω ⁝ –⏑⏑ | –⏑⏑ | – > | – ∧ ||
ω ⁝ –⏑⏑ | –⏑⏑ | – ω̆ | – ∧ ||
> ⁝ –⏑⏑ | – > | – ⏑ | ⏑⏑⏑ | ⌞ | – ∧]]

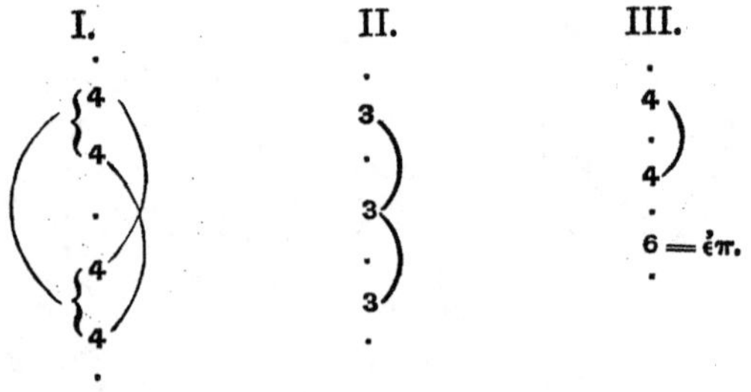

I.	II.	III.
.	.	.
4	3	4
4	.	.
.	3	4
4	.	.
4	3	6 = ἐπ.
.	.	.

Str. β′.

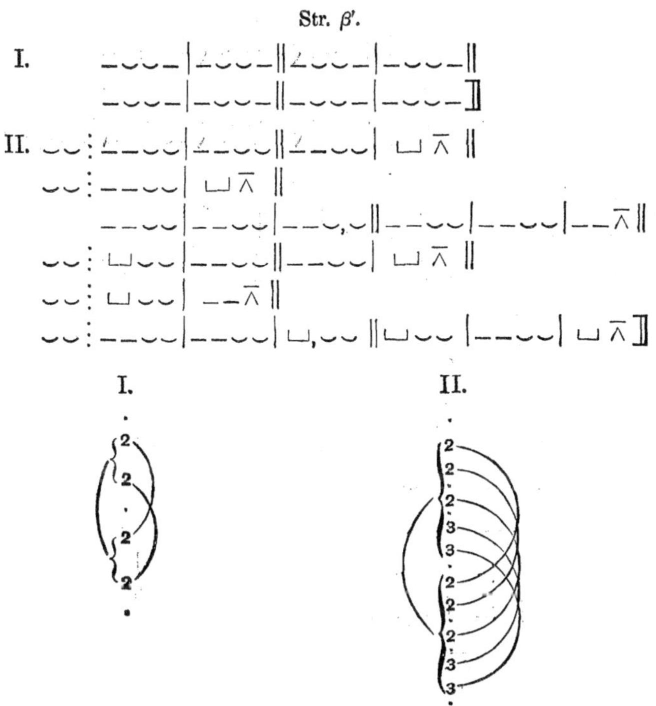

III.

First Kommos, verses 649–668 : 678–697.

I. ⏑ ⁝ – ⏑ | ⊔ | – ⏑ | ⊔ ‖ – ⏑ | ⊔ | – ⏑ | – ∧]]

Dimeter.

II. ⏑ ⁝ – ⏑ | ⊔ | – ⏑ | ⊔ ‖ – ⏑ | ⊔ ‖ – ⏑ | – ⏑ | – ⏑ | – ∧]]

Trimeter.

III. ⏑ ⁝ ⏑ ⏑ – ⏑ | –, > ‖ ⏑ ⏑ – ⏑ | – ∧ ‖
≥ ⁝ ⏑ ⏑ – ⏑ | – ⏑ ‖ – – ⏑ | – ∧]]

Trimeter.

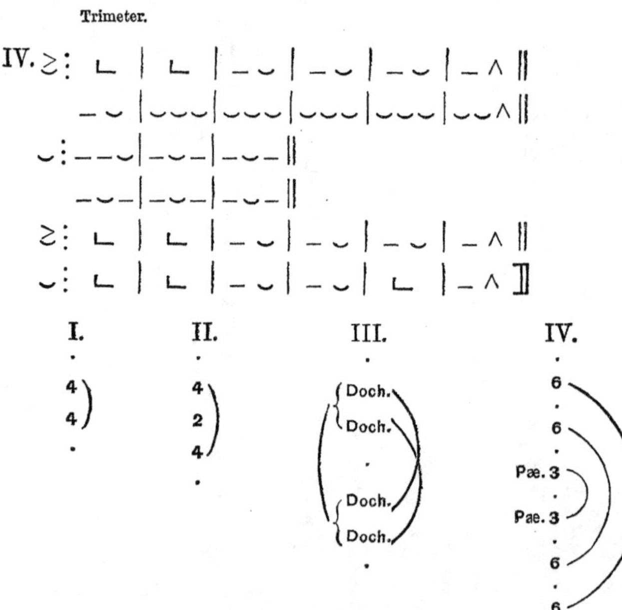

IV.

SECOND STASIMON, VERSES 863–910.

Str. α′.

I. > ⁝ – ⏑ | ∟ | – ⏑ | – ⏑, ‖ – ⏑ | – > ‖ – ⏑ | – > | – ⏑ | – ∧]]

II. ≥ ⁝ – ⏑ | – ≥ | – ⏑ | – ⏑ | ∟ | – ∧ ‖
≥ ⁝ ⏑⏑⏑ | –⏑⏑ | – ∧ ‖
> ⁝ ⏑⏑⏑ | ∟ | – ⏑ | – ⏑ | ∟ | – ∧]]

III. ≥ ⁝ –⏑⏑ | – ⏑ | – > | –⏑⏑ | – ⏑ | – ∧ ‖
⏑ ⁝ – ⏑ | – ⏑ | –⏑⏑ | ∟ ‖ –⏑⏑ | ∟ | ∟ | – ∧ ‖
ω ⁝ – > | –⏑⏑ | – ⏑ | ∟ | ∟ | – ∧]]

I.	II.	III.
.	.	.
4	6	6
2	.	.
4	3	4
.	.	4
	6	.
	.	6
		.

Str. β'.

I. – ⏑ | ⏑⏑⏑ | – ⏑ | – ⏑ ||
– ⏑ | – ⏑ | – ⏑ | – ∧ ||
≥ ⋮ –⏑⏑ | – ⏑ | ∟ | – ∧ ||
– ⏑ | – ⏑ | – ⏑ | – ∧ ||
≥ ⋮ –⏑⏑ | – ⏑ | ∟ | – ∧ ||
– ⏑ | – ⏑ | – ⏑ | – ∧]]

II. > ⋮ – ⏑ | – > | – ⏑ | – ⏑ | ∟ | – ∧ ||
> ⋮ – ⏑ | – > | – ⏑ | – ∧ ||
≥ ⋮ – ⏑ | – > | ⏖⏑ | – ⏑ | ∟ | – ∧]]

III. ⏑ ⋮ ⏖⏑ | ∟ | – ⏑ | – ⏑ | – ⏑ | – ∧ ||
– ⏑ | – > | – ⏑ | – ⏑ ||
– ⏑ | – > | – ⏑ | – ≥ | – ⏑ | – ∧ ||
≥ ⋮ –⏑⏑ | – ⏑]]

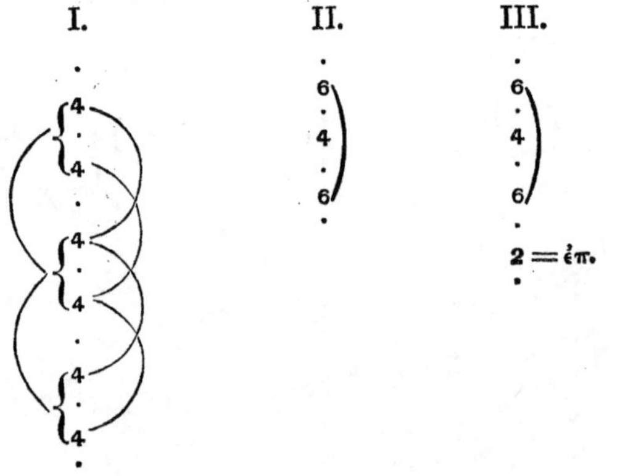

I.	II.	III.
. 4 . 4 . 4 . 4 . 4 . 4 .	. 6 . 4 . 6 .	. 6 . 4 . 6 . 2 = ἐπ. .

V.

Hyporchema, verses 1086–1109

I. –⏑⏑ | ⌞ | –⏑ | –⏑, ‖ –⏑ | –> | –⏑ | –∧ ‖
–⏑⏑ | –⏑⏑ | –≥ | –⏑ | ⌞ | –∧ ‖
–⏑ | –> | –⏑ | ⌞, ‖ –⏑ | –> | –⏑ | –∧]]

II. –⏑⏑ | –> | –⏑ | –∧ ‖
–⏑ | –> | –⏑ | –⏑ ‖
–⏑ | –> | –⏑ | –> ‖ –⏑⏑ | –⏑⏑ | –≥ ‖ –⏑ | –⏑ | ⌞ | –∧ ‖
> ⋮ –⏑⏑ | –⏑ | ⌞ | –∧ ‖
–⏑ | ⌞ | ⌞ | –∧]]

I.

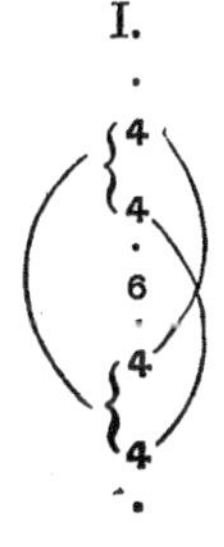

II.

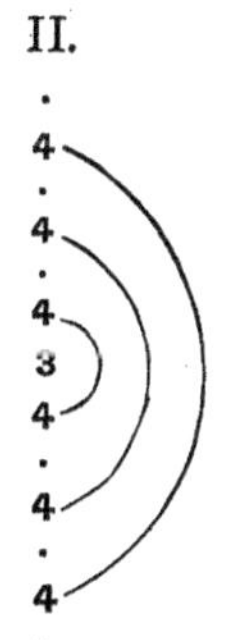

VI.

Third Stasimon, verses 1186–1222.

Str. *α′*.

	Scheme	Verse
	⌞ | —⏑⏑ | —⏑ | —∧ ‖	1.
	—> | —⏑⏑ | —≥ | ⌞ ‖ —> | —⏑⏑ | ⌞ | —∧ ‖	2–3.
	⌞ | —⏑⏑ | —⏑ | —∧ ‖	4.
	—> | —⏑⏑ | —⏑ | —∧ ‖	5.
	—≥ | —⏑⏑ | —⏑ | —∧ ‖	6.
	—> | —⏑⏑ | ⌞ | —∧ ‖	7.
≥ ⋮	⌞ | —⏑⏑ | —⏑ | —∧ ‖	8.
≥ ⋮	⌞ | —⏑⏑ | —⏑ | ⌞ ‖ —≥ | —⏑⏑ | —⏑ | —∧ ‖	9–10.
	⌞ | —⏑⏑ | ⌞ | —∧]]	11.

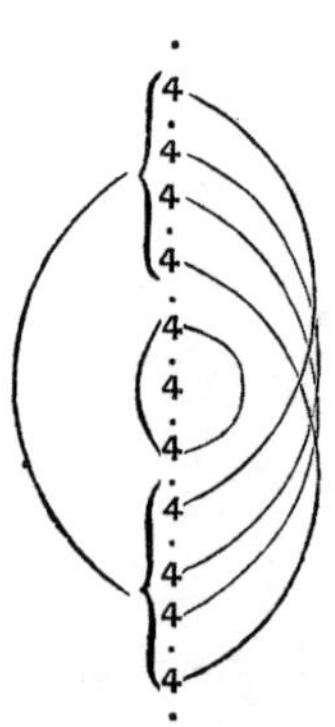

Str. β'.

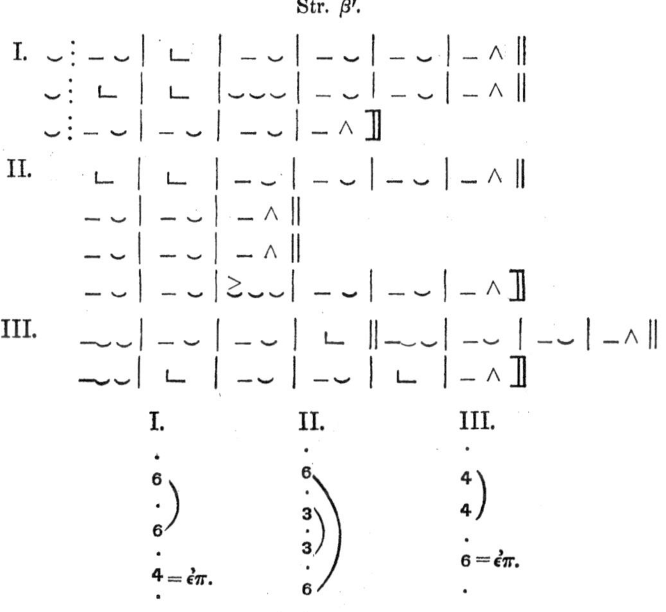

VII.

Second Kommos, verses 1313 – 1368.

Str. α′.

◡ ⋮ ⊔ ◡ | – ∧ ||

◡ ⋮ ◡ ◡ ◡ ◡ ◡ | ◡ ◡, ◡ || ◡ ◡ ◡ ◡ ◡ | ◡ ◡ ∧ ||

◡ ⋮ ◡ ◡ – ◡ | –, ◡ || – – ≥ | – ∧]]

– –

Trimeter.

Trimeter.

Trimeter.

Trimeter.

Doch. = πρ.

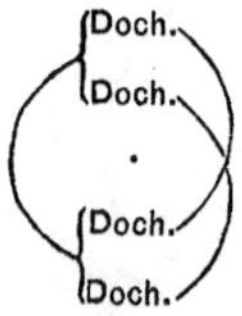

Doch.
Doch.

Doch.
Doch.

Str. β′.

I. ⏑ ⁝ – – ⏑ | –, ⏑ || – – ⏑ | – ∧ ||
⏑ ⁝ ⏑⏑ ⏑⏑ ⏑ | –, ⏑ || ⏑⏑ ⏑⏑ ⏑ | ⏑⏑∧]]

II. ⏑ ⁝ – ⏑ | – ⏑ | – ⏑ | – ⏑, || – ⏑ | ⌞ | ⌞ | – ∧]]

III. ⏑ ⁝ ⏑⏑ – ⏑ | – ∧ ||
≥ ⁝ – ⏑ | – ⏑ | – ⏑ | – ⏑ | – ⏑ | – ∧ ||
≥ ⁝ – ⏑ | – > | – ⏑ | – ∧ ||
⏑ ⁝ – ⏑ | ⌞ | – ⏑ | ⌞, || – ⏑ | – ⏑ | – ⏑ | – ∧ ||
⏑ ⁝ – ⏑ | ⌞ | ⌞ | – ⏑ | – ⏑ | – ∧]]

IV. ≥ ⁝ ⏑⏑ – ⏑ | ⏓, ⏑ || ⏑⏑ – ⏑ | – ∧ ||
⏑ ⁝ ⏑⏑ – ⏑ | –, > || ⏑⏑ – ⏑ | – ∧ ||
⏑ ⁝ ⏑⏑ – ⏑ | ⏑⏑, ⏑ || ⏑⏑ – ⏑ | – ∧ ||
> ⁝ ⏑⏑ – ⏑ | – ∧]]

Trimeter.

Trimeter.

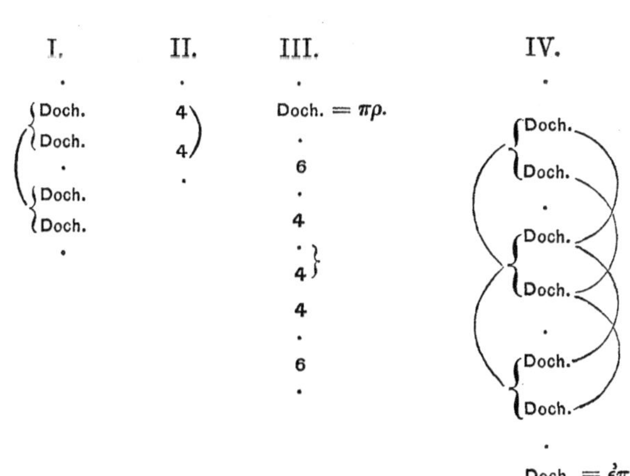

TECHNICAL DIVISIONS OF THE ŒDIPUS TYRANNUS, WITH THE NUMBER OF VERSES IN EACH, AND THEIR RHYTHMS.

πρόλογος............... 1 - 150............Iambic Trimeter.

πάροδος................151 - 215............Dactylic, Logaoedic, and Choreic.

ἐπεισόδιον α'..........216 - 462............Iambic Trimeter.

στάσιμον α'..........463 - 512.. ....Logaoedic, Choriambic, and Ionic.

ἐπεισόδιον β'.........513 - 862............Iambic Trimeter.

(Includes a **κομμός**, 649 - 668 : 678 - 697, Choreic, Dochmiac, and Choreic-Paeonic.)

στάσιμον β'..........863 - 910 ....Logaoedic.

ἐπεισόδιον γ'..........911 - 1085............Iambic Trimeter.

ὑπόρχημα ....1086 - 1109............Logaoedic.

ἐπεισόδιον δ'.........1110 - 1185............Iambic Trimeter.

στάσιμον γ'..........1186 - 1222............Logaoedic and Choreic.

ἔξοδος.. ....1223 - 1530............Iamic Trimeter, Anapaestic, and Trochaic Tetrameter.

(Includes a **κομμός**, 1313 - 1368, Dochmiac and Choreic.)

COMMENTARY.

The references are to the "*Introduction to the Study of the Rhythmic and Metric of the Classical Languages.*"

PROLOGOS, verses 1-150.

On πρόλογος see the lexx. The rhythm employed is the *iambic trimeter* (so called. See § 10, VII.). This is the verse in which most of the dialogue of the Attic drama is composed. The following scheme shows its constitution in Sophocles:—

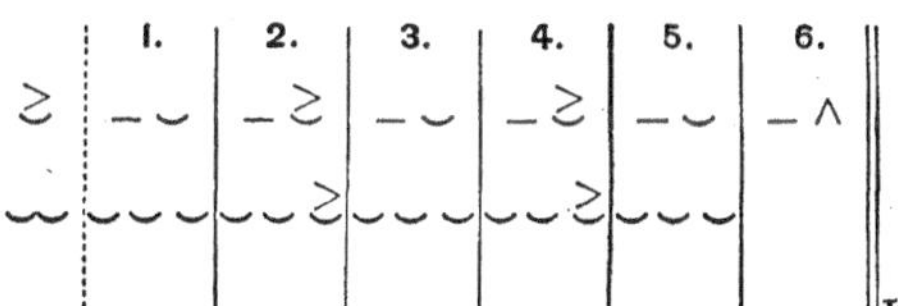

The fundamental measure is the *choree,* § 8, 2, V. See further § 16, 1 and 2. On *anacrusis,* § 7, 5. On *diaeresis, caesura,* and *break* in this verse and its *composition from two tripodies,* § 26, 3, III. With the last half of § 26, 3, III. compare § 21, 2, and particularly under this 2) and I. On *syllaba anceps,* § 19, 2, I., 3). On *catalexis,* § 9. In verse 13 μὴ οὐ are pronounced as one syllable, a case of synizesis. Elision at the end of the verse, as in verse 29, is infrequent. See § 19, 2, I., 1).

(In his *Griechische Metrik,* § 25, 5-8, Dr. Schmidt has shown with customary acuteness the congruence of the matter and form of the choruses of this drama. The inquiring student is especially referred to this.)

PARODOS, verses 151-215, Rhythmical Scheme, I.

On πάροδος, § 33, 4, A, I. On *strophe* and *antistrophe,* § 32 and § 33, and particularly § 32, 7, and § 33, 1, II. On the *period,* § 24. On the different *final pauses* that may occur, § 9, 1.

στρ. α′, PERIOD I. The rhythm is *dactylic.* See § 8, 2, I.; § 10, I.; § 22, 1. See further § 21, 2, and note that in accordance with the law there announced the first and third verses cannot be classified as single sentences, but must be regarded as composed of two sentences (κῶλα) each, § 18. The beginning of a rhythmical sentence within a verse is marked *in the text* by a black letter. On the *caesura* of these verses, § 19, 2, III. On the *Doric measures* in the second verse, § 12, 1. See here Appendix, II. On the general subject of *metrical responsion*, § 17, and on the particular case in verse third, § 17, 2, I. On the *contraction* (*syncope*) in verse four, § 11, 3, and § 11, 6, III. The period is *palinodic*, § 34, 3, and § 36, 1 and 5. Period II. *Dactylic* as before. Also, as before, *palinodic*. The second sentence of verse five seems to contradict the law (Schmidt, *Compositionslehre*, § 17) that *the pure uncontracted dactyl* (— ⏑ ⏑) *cannot close a sentence unless at least the preceding measure be also an uncontracted dactyl.* But it is easy to see that the first syllable of ὥραις in the strophe and ἄτας in the antistrophe had two notes, ♫. The same occurred in the case of Θήβας above in the third verse of the strophe, as its responsion to Ἄρτεμιν in the antistrophe clearly shows.

στρ. β', I. Logaoedic, § 13. The metrical sign ω = ⏕ = ♬, and the syllables it here represents constitute the anacrusis. On the subject of *sixteenth notes*, § 15. On the *cyclic dactyls* in the third verse, § 13, 3. A *repeated stichic* period, § 34, 2, and § 36, 4. II. *Dactylic.* On the *responsion* of the long and short syllables in the anacrusis of verse five, § 17, 2, II., B. A *palinodic-antithetic* period, § 34, 7, and § 36, 9.

στρ. γ', I. *Choreic*, § 8, 2, V.; § 10, IV.; § 22, 5. A *palinodic-antithetic* period. II. *Choreic.* A *repeated palinodic* period, § 34, 4, and § 36, 6. With ἐπῳδικόν (*postlude*), § 32, 4, and § 32, 7, VI.; § 35; § 36, 11.

First Epeisodion, verses 216 – 462.

On ἐπεισόδιον see the lexx. The rhythm as in the prologue.

First Stasimon, verses 463 – 512, Rhythmical Scheme, II.

On στάσιμον, § 33, 4, A, II.

στρ. α', I. *Logaoedic* and *palinodic.* II. *Logaoedic*, and *repeated stichic.* III. *Logaoedic.* On the third measure of the seventh verse in the strophe, § 15, 1. Corresponding to this there occurs in the antistrophe an irrational choree. A *stichic* period, § 34, 1, and § 36, 3, with *postlude.*

στρ. β', I. *Choriambic*, § 8, VII.; § 10, VI.; § 21, 2, IV.; § 22, 7. *Palinodic.* II. *Ionic*, § 8, VI.; § 10, V.; § 21, 2, IV.; § 22, 6. On the *protraction* in the third verse and following, § 11, 7, 1). *Palinodic.*

Second Epeisodion, verses 513 – 862.

With the exception of the included κομμός, *Iambic Trimeter.* θεῶν in v. 536, πόλεως in v. 630, and δυοῖν in v. 640 are cases of synizesis, the last being unusual.

First Kommos, 649 – 668 ; 678 – 697, Rhythmical Scheme, III.

On κομμός, § 33, 4, A, V.

στρ., I. *Choreic* and *stichic.* II. *Choreic* and *mesodic,* § 32, 4 ; § 34, 6 ; § 36, 10. III. *Dochmiac,* § 23, 4. *Palinodic.* IV. *Choreic-paeonic.* On the *paeon,* § 8, VIII. ; § 10, VIII. ; § 21, 2, III. : and on the admission of the *bacchius* (§ 8, IX. ; § 10, IX.) as the first measure in verse eleven, § 23, 3. An *antithetic* period, § 34, 5 ; § 36, 8, B.

Second Stasimon, verses 863 – 910, Rhythmical Scheme, IV.

στρ. α'. I. *Logaoedic* (probably, see, however, Appendix, I.) and *mesodic.* II. Idem. III. *Logaoedic* and *antithetic.*

στρ. β', I. *Logaoedic* and *repeated palinodic.* II. *Logaoedic* and *mesodic.* III. Idem with *postlude.*

Third Epeisodion, verses 911 – 1085.

Iambic trimeter.

Hyporchema, verses 1086 – 1109, Rhythmical Scheme, V.

On ὑπόρχημα § 33, 4, A, IV.

στρ., I. *Logaoedic* and *palinodic-mesodic,* § 34, 8 ; § 36, 10, ad fin. II. *Logaoedic* and *mesodic.*

Fourth Epeisodion, verses 1110 – 1185.

Iambic trimeter.

Third Stasimon, verses 1186 – 1222, Rhythmical Scheme, VI.

στρ. α'. *Logaoedic* and *palinodic-mesodic.*

στρ. β', I. *Choreic* and *stichic,* with *postlude.* II. *Choreic* and *antithetic.* On the third measure of the seventh verse, § 17, 2, D. III. As period I.

Exodos, verses 1223 – 1530.

On ἔξοδος see the lexx. With the exception of the κομμός the rhythms are as follows : 1223 – 1296, 1312, and 1369 – 1514, *iambic trimeter,* except 1468, 1471, and 1475, which stand *extra metrum.* 1297 – 1311, *anapaestic,* § 8, 2, II. ; § 10, II. ; § 11, 6, II. ; § 21, 2, II. 1515 – 1530, *trochaic tetrameter,* § 26, 3, II.

Second Kommos, verses 1313–1368, Rhythmical Scheme, VII.

This κομμός could be classified as a *monody* (ἀπὸ σκηνῆς), § 33, 4, A, VI., since, with the single exception of verse six in the second strophe and antistrophe, the chorus replies only in trimeters and that at the end of the strophe and antistrophe in each case.

στρ. α'. *Dochmiac* and *palinodic.* On the *protraction* in the *prelude,* § 11, 7, 2).

στρ. β', I. *Dochmiac* and *palinodic.* II. *Choreic* and *stichic.* III. *Choreic,* with a dochmius as *prelude.* A *mesodic* period. Note particularly § 36, 10. IV. *Dochmiac* and *repeated palinodic,* with *postlude.*

APPENDIX.

I. — Concerning the Differentiation of Choreic and Logaoedic Rhythms.

The logaoedic rhythm, as well as the choreic, answers to the modern $\frac{3}{8}$ measure, or more properly, since the ancients delivered slowly and solemnly, to our $\frac{3}{4}$ measure. Specimens of *pure* choreic strophes are especially common in Aeschylus, e. g. in the *Agamemnon*, the *Choephori*, and *Eumenides;* but these too in single places have a somewhat more lively character, i. e. they admit single measures like —◡ ◡.

If a song in logaoedic rhythm is examined, as Prom. I., it is found that it also does not necessarily remain constant; and accordingly Prom. I., str. β′, is choreic, but returns at its close to the more lively logaoedic rhythm.

If the contents are regarded, the greater animation and excitement will be perceived in logaoedic composition, much more repose in choreic.

But how can an exact boundary line be preserved here? If chorees are intoned more vivaciously, they will sound quite like logaoedics even in music; a few series like – ⩾ | –◡◡ | – ◡ | – ∧ ‖ will then make them quite analogous to logaoedics.

Let us consider modern melodies in $\frac{3}{4}$ measure, however little these may be suited to the comparison, since the forms of their measures are so little constant. How much is here left in *single cases* (of course not in all) to the judgment of the executing musician. One employs livelier ictuses, and so approaches the ancient logaoedics; another gives the same notes with more repose, and so approaches the ancient chorees.

The ancient trimeters, however, are the best and at the same time a perfectly certain proof. From the pure ground form ⩾ | – ◡ | – ⩾ | – ◡ | – ⩾ | – ◡ | – ∧ ‖ to ◡◡ | –◡◡ | –◡◡ | –◡◡ | –◡◡ | –◡◡ | – ∧ ‖ there exist the most imperceptible transitions; and yet no one will be able to doubt, that in every case one and the same verse, one and the same metre, occurs.

Cf. Schmidt, *Griechische Metrik*, § 19, 3.

In this way the question concerning the intonation also is answered. Even in pure logaoedic strophes one did not always necessarily intone ⁝— ⁝◡, but also, where more repose was intended, ⁝— ◡. This too can be proved. For first there are many very lively logaoedic strophes that have come down to us, with springing series like —◡◡ | └— | —◡◡ | └— ||, while on the contrary there are others more quiet and measured with series predominating with forms like —◡ | —◡◡ | —◡ | —◡ | └— | — ∧ ||, etc. Again, we frequently meet in long compositions only series like —◡ | —◡◡ | —◡ | —, ◡ || —◡◡ | —◡ | └— | — ∧ ||, etc. in both strophe and antistrophe, while on the other hand elsewhere almost solely series like — > | —◡◡ | —◡ | — ∧ ||, in strophe as well as antistrophe. And finally, in most cases, forms like —◡ | —◡◡ | —◡ | — ∧ || and — > | —◡◡ | —◡ | — ∧ || constantly interchange in the same strophe, or in strophe and antistrophe correspond — ≳ | —◡◡ | —◡ | — ∧ || or even —◡◡ | — ≳ | — ≳ | — ∧ ||, etc. It is clear that the poet-composer did not rigorously prescribe how the composition should be performed. For how otherwise could he have given :

Str. —◡ | —◡◡ | —◡ | — ∧ || Str. — > | — > | —◡◡ | — ∧ ||
Ant. — > | —◡◡ | —◡ | — ∧ || Ant. —◡ | —◡ | —◡◡ | — ∧ ||

The feeling of the performer, then, and the contents of the poem should vary its delivery; here it should be livelier, there more measured, and attention should be paid to the development of the entire composition.

II. — On the Differentiation of Dactylic and Doric Rhythms.

The case here is exactly parallel to that of the chorees and logaoedics, that is, the measures agree in the main, in this instance, as follows: —

Dactylic Rhythm.	*Doric Rhythm.*
$\frac{4}{8}$ measure,	$\frac{4}{8}$ measure,
solemn and measured and therefore uniformly consisting of the forms —◡◡ | and — — |, less often ⊔ |.	somewhat more lively, powerful, tense, and energetic; therefore the common series └—◡ | — — |, etc.

We must name therefore according to the general character, allow transitions, and in particular remember that the pathetic productions of dramatic poetry could not be rigorously confined to a simple type. But that nevertheless the two sorts of measure can be accurately distinguished is shown on the one hand by the rigidly dactylic hexameter, in which measures like └—◡| cannot occur at all, and on the other by the rigidly Doric strophes of Pindar.

In Œd. Rex. I., str. α′, therefore, both periods are dactylic, in accordance with the solemn temper of the chorus ; but nevertheless both contain at the same time so much of excitement that the greater measuredness of the dactyls is very appropriately given a livelier color by means of series of Doric character (yet always a $\frac{3}{8}$ measure, like the dactyls). And the more individual unrest at the beginning of str. β′, how fittingly expressed in series of logaoedic rhythm. Cf. here Schmidt, *Griechische Metrik*, § 25, especially § 25, 2.

THE END.

Cambridge : Electrotyped and Printed by Welch, Bigelow, & Co.

GREEK.

Wholesale. Retail.

GOODWIN'S GREEK GRAMMAR. By William W. Goodwin, Ph. D., Eliot Professor of Greek Literature in Harvard University. Half morocco $1.25 $1.56

The object of this Grammar is to state *general principles* clearly and distinctly, with special regard to those who are preparing for college. In the sections on the Moods are stated, for the first time in an elementary form, the principles which are elaborated in detail in the author's "Syntax of the Greek Moods and Tenses."

GREEK MOODS AND TENSES. The Fonrth Edition. By William W. Goodwin, Eliot Professor of Greek Literature in Harvard University. 1 vol. 12mo. Cloth. pp. 264 . . . . 1.40 1.75

This work was first published in 1860, and it appeared in a new form — much enlarged and in great part rewritten — in 1865. In the present edition the whole has been again revised; some sections and notes have been rewritten, and a few notes have been added. The object of the work is to give a plain statement of the principles which govern the construction of the Greek Moods and Tenses, — the most important and the most difficult part of Greek Syntax.

GOODWIN'S GREEK READER. Consisting of Extracts from Xenophon, Plato, Herodotus, and Thucydides; being a full equivalent for the seven books of the Anabasis, now required for admission at Harvard. With Maps, Notes, References to GOODWIN'S GREEK GRAMMAR, and parallel References to CROSBY'S and HADLEY'S GRAMMARS. Edited by Professor W. W. Goodwin, of Harvard College, and J. H. Allen, Cambridge. Half morocco 1.60 2.00

This book contains the third and fourth books of the Anabasis (entire), the greater part of the second book of the Hellenica, and the first chapter of the Memorabilia, of Xenophon; the last part of the Apology, and the beginning and end of the Phaedo, of Plato; selections from the sixth, seventh, and eighth books of Herodotus, and from the fourth book of Thucydides.

LEIGHTON'S GREEK LESSONS. Prepared to accompany Goodwin's Greek Grammar. By R. F. Leighton, Master of Melrose High School. Half morocco 1.25 1.56

This work contains about one hundred lessons, with a progressive series of exercises (both Greek and English), mainly selected from the first book of Xenophon's Anabasis. The exercises on the Moods are sufficient, it is believed, to develop the general principles as stated in the Grammar. The text of four chapters of the Anabasis is given entire, with notes and references. Full vocabularies accompany the book.

LIDDELL & SCOTT'S GREEK-ENGLISH LEXICON. Abridged from the new Oxford Edition. New Edition. With Appendix of Proper and Geographical Names, by J. M. Whiton.

Morocco back 2.40 3.00
Sheep binding 2.80 3.50

LIDDELL & SCOTT'S GREEK-ENGLISH LEXICON. The sixth Oxford Edition unabridged. 4to. Morocco back . . . 9.60 12.00
Sheep binding . 10.40 13.00

We have made arrangements with Messrs. Macmillan & Co. to publish in this country their new edition of Liddell & Scott's Greek Lexicons, and are ready to supply the trade.

The English editions of Liddell & Scott are *not stereotyped;* but each has been thoroughly revised, enlarged, and printed anew. The sixth edition, just published, is larger by one eighth than the fifth, and contains 1865 pages. It is an *entirely different work* from the first edition, the whole department of etymology having been rewritten in the light of modern investigations, and the forms of the irregular verbs being given in greater detail by the aid of Veitch's Catalogue. No student of Greek can afford to dispense with this invaluable Lexicon, the price of which is now for the first time brought within the means of the great body of American scholars.

LATIN.

Wholesale. Retail.

ALLEN & GREENOUGH'S LATIN GRAMMAR. Founded on Comparative Grammar. By J. H. ALLEN and J. B. GREENOUGH. pp. 268 . . . . $1.25 $1.56

" A complete Latin Grammar, to be used from the beginning of the study of Latin till the end of the college course." The forms of the language and the constructions of Syntax are fully illustrated by classical examples and by comparison with parallel forms of kindred languages.

ALLEN & GREENOUGH'S LATIN METHOD. A Method of Instruction in Latin, being a Companion and Guide in the study of Latin Grammar, with Elementary Instruction in Reading at Sight, Exercises in Translation and Writing, Notes and Vocabulary. pp. 108. With Supplement and Syntax. 1875 . . . . .80 1.00

ALLEN & GREENOUGH'S CÆSAR (Gallic War, Four Books). With very full Notes, Copperplate Map, and References to their Grammar as well as Gildersleeve's 1.20 1.50

Do. without Vocabulary 1.00 1.25

ALLEN & GREENOUGH'S SELECT ORATIONS OF CICERO. Chronologically arranged, covering the entire period of his Public Life. Edited by J. H. & W. F. ALLEN and J. B. GREENOUGH, with References to Allen & Greenough's Latin Grammar. Containing the Defence of Roscius (abridged), Verres I., Manilian Law, Catiline, Archias, Sestius (abridged), Milo, Marcellus, Ligarius, and the Fourteenth Philippic. With Life, Introductions, Notes, and Index 1.40 1.75

ALLEN & GREENOUGH'S VIRGIL. Six Books of the Æneid and the Bucolics. With Introduction, Notes, and Grammatical References to Allen & Greenough's and Gildersleeve's Latin Grammars. The text is founded on that of Ribbeck, variations from that and from Heyne being given in the margin 1.40 1.75

ALLEN & GREENOUGH'S SALLUST. The Conspiracy of Catiline, as related by Sallust. pp. 82. Cloth 80 1.00

ALLEN & GREENOUGH'S CICERO DE SENECTUTE (*CATO MAJOR*), in uniform style with Allen & Greenough's Cicero. pp. 57. Cloth . . . . .60 .75

ALLEN & GREENOUGH'S OVID. Selections from the Poems of Ovid, chiefly from the Metamorphoses. With Index of Proper Names. pp. 282 . . . . 1.20 1.50

The attempt has been made to give in a reading book, suitable for students beginning Latin poetry, something like a complete picture of the Greek mythology, at least of the great narratives which have entered more or less into modern literature. About a thousand lines of the Elegiac verse are added, taken from most of the poet's other works.

ALLEN & GREENOUGH'S SHORTER COURSE OF LATIN PROSE: Consisting chiefly of the Prose Selections of Allen's Latin Reader (to p. 134), the Notes being wholly rewritten, enlarged, and adapted to Allen & Greenough's Grammar; accompanied by Six Orations of Cicero, — the Manilian, the four Catilines, and Archias. With Vocabulary 2.00 2.50

ALLEN'S LATIN READER. 12mo. 518 pages. Consisting of Selections from Cæsar, Curtius, Nepos, Sallust, Ovid, Virgil, Plautus, Terence, Cicero, Pliny, and Tacitus, with Notes, and a general Vocabulary of Latin of more than 16,000 words 2.00 2.50

ALLEN'S LATIN SELECTIONS. Containing the same as Allen's Latin Reader, without Vocabulary 1.25 1.56

ALLEN'S LATIN LEXICON. 12mo. 205 pages. (Being the Vocabulary to the Reader.) Cloth 1.00 1.25

ALLEN'S LATIN PRIMER. A First Book of Latin for Boys and Girls. By J. H ALLEN. 155 pages. Cloth 1.00 1.25

This is designed for the use of scholars of a younger class, and consists of thirty lessons, carefully arranged (an adaptation of the Robertsonian method). so as to give a full outline of the Grammar, accompanied by Tables of Inflection, with Dialogues (Latin and English), and Selections for reading.

ALLEN'S LATIN COMPOSITION. Adapted to Allen & Greenough's Latin Grammar. By W F. ALLEN. 107 pages. Cloth . 1.00 1.25

This book includes a careful review of the Principles of Syntax, as contained in the Grammar, with practice in various styles of composition (from classical models), Vocabulary, and Parallel References to other Grammars.

ALLEN'S MANUAL LATIN GRAMMAR. Prepared by W. F. and J. H. ALLEN. 12mo. 148 pages, with Index. Cloth . . 1.00 1.25

Approved by Harvard College as indicating the amount required for admission.

ALLEN'S LATIN LESSONS. 12mo. 134 pages . . 1.00 1.25

LEIGHTON'S LATIN LESSONS. Prepared to accompany Allen & Greenough's Latin Grammar. By R. F. LEIGHTON, Melrose High School.

This work presents a progressive series of exercises (both Latin and English), illustrating the grammatical forms and simpler principles of syntax Synonymes and rules of quantity are introduced from the first. The text consists of about a dozen of Æsop's Fables, translated from the Greek for these Lessons; extracts from L'Homond's Viri Romæ (Romulus and Remus); Horatii and Curatii; Lives of Cato, Pompey, Cæsar, Cicero, Brutus, and Augustus; the Helvetian War, from Woodford's Epitome of Cæsar. All fully illustrated with Notes, References, and Maps. Full Vocabularies accompany the book, with questions for Examination and Review of the Grammar . . . . . , ... 1.25 1.56

MADVIG'S LATIN GRAMMAR. Carefully revised by THOMAS A. THACHER, Yale College. Half morocco 2.40 3.00

The most complete and valuable Treatise on the language yet published, and admirably adapted to the wants of Teachers and College Classes.

THE LATIN VERB. Illustrated by the Sanskrit. By C. H. PARKHURST. Cloth . . . . .40 .50

WHITE'S JUNIOR STUDENT'S COMPLETE LATIN-ENGLISH LEXICON. Morocco back 2 40 3.00
Sheep 2.80 3.50

WHITE'S JUNIOR STUDENT'S COMPLETE LATIN-ENGLISH AND ENGLISH-LATIN LEXICON. By the REV. J. T. WHITE, D. D., of C. C. C. Oxford, Rector of St. Martin, Ludgate, London. Revised Edition. Square 12mo. pp. 1058. Sheep 3.60 4.50

"The present work aims at furnishing in both its parts a sufficiently extensive vocabulary for all practical purposes. The Latin words and phrases are in all cases followed by the name of some standard Latin writer, as a guaranty of their authority; and as the work is of a strictly elementary character, the conjugations of the verbs and the genders and genitive cases of the substantives are uniformly added. In the preparation of this portion of the book, DR. WHITE has had the assistance of some of the best scholars both of Oxford and Cambridge." — *Guardian.*

WHITE'S JUNIOR STUDENT'S COMPLETE ENGLISH-LATIN LEXICON. Sheep 2.00 2.50

We have contracted with Messrs. Longmans, Green, & Co., of London, for the sole agency in this country for the above Latin Lexicons, and shall endeavor to meet the demands of the trade.

www.ingramcontent.com/pod-product-compliance
Lightning Source LLC
LaVergne TN
LVHW050531100826
845148LV00002B/515

* 9 7 8 1 4 2 5 5 1 9 2 3 0 *